Managing eZ Publish Web Content Management Projects

Strategies, best practices, and techniques for implementing eZ publish open-source CMS projects to delight your clients

Martin Bauer

PUBLISHING

BIRMINGHAM - MUMBAI

Managing eZ Publish Web Content Management Projects

Strategies, best practices, and techniques for implementing eZ publish open-source CMS projects to delight your clients

First published: October 2007

Production Reference: 1231007

Published by Packt Publishing Ltd.
32 Lincoln Road
Olton
Birmingham, B27 6PA, UK.

ISBN 978-1-847191-72-4

www.packtpub.com

Cover Image by Vinayak Chittar (vinayak.chittar@gmail.com)

Credits

Author

Martin Bauer

Reviewers

Jennifer Zickerman

Łukasz Serwatka

Senior Acquisition Editor

Douglas Paterson

Development Editor

Mithil Kulkarni

Technical Editor

Ajay.S

Editorial Manager

Dipali Chittar

Project Manager

Patricia Weir

Project Coordinator

Abhijeet Deobhakta

Indexer

Monica Ajmera

Proofreader

Chris Smith

Production Coordinator

Shantanu Zagade

Cover Designer

Shantanu Zagade

About the Author

Martin Bauer is the Managing Director of designIT, an Australian-based content management specialist practice. Martin has ten years experience in web development and web-based content management. He is the world's first certified Feature-Driven Development Project Manager. Prior to his role as Managing Director, Martin held a variety of roles across a range of industries. This experience includes careers in law, advertising, and IT. Martin's breadth of expertise has culminated in a focus upon the delivery of effective content management solutions.

There are two people who have played a significant role in this book.

The first is Jeff Deluca who has taught me most of what I know about project management and has been a guide and inspiration in many areas.

The second is Bruce Morrison who taught me everything I know about eZ Publish and was instrumental in the delivery of every eZ Publish project I've worked on as well as many of the practices in this book, in particular, the structure of an eZ publish specification.

Both Jeff and Bruce are far more knowledgeable than me in project management and eZ publish respectively, and I hope that I've been able to distill what I've learnt from both of them into this book.

There are two other people who I have to thank for their help: Karl Latiss who provided the backing, support, and belief in taking the direction to focus on effective content management solutions with eZ Publish; and Antony Svasek who was invaluable in helping me to run designIT while I worked on delivering projects and writing this book.

About the Reviewers

Jennifer Zickerman is a writer, editor, and publisher who has worked extensively in the field of open-source software development. She is currently Manager of Knowledge Products at eZ Systems.

eZ Systems is the creator of the eZ Publish Open Source Enterprise Content Management System.

As head of the eZ Press, Jennifer Zickerman is the publisher responsible for the books *eZ Publish Basics* (a developer and administrator's introduction to eZ Publish, written by Balasz Halasy) and *eZ Publish Content Management Basics* (an introduction to publishing content using eZ Publish, written by Bergfrid Marie Skaara).

Łukasz Serwatka holds a computer science, engineering degree and currently works as a Software Engineer at eZ Systems. His main focus is the development of eZ Publish-based solutions.

He has written many extensions and applications to build on top of the eZ Publish framework, and is an active member of the eZ Publish Community. Łukasz is also co-creator and eZ Publish administrator of the biggest PHP website in Poland—php.pl. His personal website and blog about eZ Publish development is at `http://serwatka.net`.

Table of Contents

Preface

Why write yet another book on project management? The simple reason is that we still need to improve when it comes to web development and especially content management. The majority of the issues that I've experienced when it comes to delivering solutions with eZ publish, or any other web technology for that matter, have been issue of management. Rarely, has the technology been the issue. With eZ publish, the technology aspect is well covered; this puts an even greater emphasis on the importance of management and knowing how to successfully deliver projects on time, on budget with agreed function.

This book doesn't attempt to state the best way to manage projects; for each project, there are different challenges to be overcome and there's no one perfect way. What this book contains is a series of practices that have over time proved to be effective in delivering eZ publish-based projects on time and on budget. Not every part of the book is relevant to every project, and it is not always necessary to do things in exactly the order and in exactly the way described here. It is a series of techniques and practices that you can use to help you manage your projects.

The main reason I wrote the book was to share the lessons learned from the numerous projects that I was involved in and found what worked and what didn't when it came to eZ publish-based projects, and by doing so, to help others to improve their ability to successful deliver projects.

What This Book Covers

Chapter 1 examines the differences between traditional software development and content management and how that affects the way we approach content management as a discipline. We cover some of the myths that exist when it comes to web development and content management as well as the types of solutions implemented using content management systems. Finally, we look at the different types of websites and web applications to gain an understanding of the common types of websites and applications that have emerged over the past ten years.

Chapter 2 provides an overview of information architecture and design in relation to content management systems.

Chapter 3 gives you an overview of how eZ publish is structured and the key elements that are used in most projects.

Chapter 4 first helps you understand the requirements of an eZ project and then shows you how to plan your project through a project brief and planning workshop. It also covers how to deal with estimations and the issues that arise at this point of the project.

Chapter 5 covers how to specify the functionality of a website that is to be implemented in eZ Publish. The chapter covers the overall content model that identifies the key classes and their relationships to each other.

Chapter 6 explains the importance and purpose of a content model in eZ publish projects.

Chapter 7 helps you with planning a project (standard and staged approach) and teaches you the approach for pricing your project.

Chapter 8 covers in detail what's involved in risk management and how to apply it to eZ publish projects.

Chapter 9 provides a series of management techniques that are straightforward to apply and will go a long way to keeping your eZ project on track.

Chapter 10 helps you set up and configure your environments for eZ projects. It provides you with information on content population (automated and manual).

Chapter 11 helps you understand the different types of testing that are required for eZ publish projects.

Chapter 12 provides guidance on how to train users of the end solution including how to draft training manuals and run training sessions.

Chapter 13 outlines the most common areas of maintenance and support for an eZ project.

Appendix A provides a full sample specification of a project that brings together the elements outlined in Chapter 5.

Who is This Book For?

This book is for people responsible for the implementation and management of eZ publish projects, and is ideal for people building sites for medium to large clients. If you're a project manager running an eZ publish web content management project and you want to learn how to run your projects more efficiently, or you want a better understanding of all the elements involved in eZ publish web content management projects this book is for you.

This is not an implementation guide or a book to learn eZ publish from — you will not be able to build a site by following this book. It is for people who have experienced eZ publish projects, or are considering them. Web developers new to eZ publish should read *Learning eZ publish 3: Building Content Management Solutions* first.

Conventions

In this book, you will find a number of styles of text that distinguish between different kinds of information. Here are some examples of these styles, and an explanation of their meaning.

New terms and **important words** are introduced in a bold-type font. Words that you see on the screen, in menus or dialog boxes for example, appear in our text like this: "clicking the **Next** button moves you to the next screen".

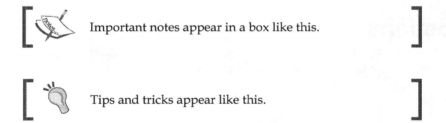

Important notes appear in a box like this.

Tips and tricks appear like this.

Reader Feedback

Feedback from our readers is always welcome. Let us know what you think about this book, what you liked or may have disliked. Reader feedback is important for us to develop titles that you really get the most out of.

To send us general feedback, simply drop an email to feedback@packtpub.com, making sure to mention the book title in the subject of your message.

If there is a book that you need and would like to see us publish, please send us a note in the **SUGGEST A TITLE** form on www.packtpub.com or email suggest@packtpub.com.

If there is a topic that you have expertise in and you are interested in either writing or contributing to a book, see our author guide on www.packtpub.com/authors.

Customer Support

Now that you are the proud owner of a Packt book, we have a number of things to help you to get the most from your purchase.

Errata

Although we have taken every care to ensure the accuracy of our contents, mistakes do happen. If you find a mistake in one of our books—maybe a mistake in text or code—we would be grateful if you would report this to us. By doing this you can save other readers from frustration, and help to improve subsequent versions of this book. If you find any errata, report them by visiting http://www.packtpub.com/support, selecting your book, clicking on the **Submit Errata** link, and entering the details of your errata. Once your errata are verified, your submission will be accepted and the errata added to the list of existing errata. The existing errata can be viewed by selecting your title from http://www.packtpub.com/support.

Questions

You can contact us at questions@packtpub.com if you are having a problem with some aspect of the book, and we will do our best to address it.

1
Understanding Web Content Management

In order to manage something, it's important to understand it. Without understanding, there is no context for decision making. Rather than launching into using eZ Publish, it's important to understand why we use content management systems and how they differ from other types of projects. Content management is unique; I've heard some Content Management professionals go so far as to say content management is not an IT project. That debate doesn't really matter, what matters is understanding what makes content management different from other development projects, in order to be able to manage them effectively.

This book is primarily aimed at managers and business analysts who are given the task of implementing a content management system using eZ Publish, although it is also useful for developers and designers who will be involved in the project. It aims to provide an overall framework for defining and implementing an eZ publish-based project.

This chapter examines the differences between traditional software development and content management, and how that affects the way we approach content management as a discipline. To begin with, we look at content management projects as opposed to software development projects and identify the key differences between them. Then, we look at some of the myths that exist when it comes to web development and content management as well as the types of solutions implemented using content management systems. Finally, we look at the different types of websites and web applications, to gain an understanding of the common types of websites and applications that have emerged over the past 10 years.

Why Use a Content Management System?

There are a number of reasons why content management systems have become a specific type of solution, and have business advantages to be gained from their use. Initially, websites were simply static HTML pages that linked to each other. Maintaining these sites required an understanding of HTML and the ability to create web graphics. This meant that anyone wanting to keep their website up-to-date would either have to learn HTML or pay someone who understood HTML to make the changes for them. Given that keeping a website current is an important factor in its success, the ability to manage the content on the website becomes increasingly important. Over time, custom-built applications emerged that allowed people to update content without needing technical skills; also, clients wanted to save costs by having content managed in-house rather than having to outsource it to web professionals.

The end result is that a market emerged for web-based applications that allowed clients to control the content on their websites without having to be technically proficient in HTML: i.e., content management systems. There were other advantages as well: the separation of presentation from content, the ability for the client to enter the content and be sure that it would be presented using the correct look and feel, the ability to easily re-use content, the ability to have all content searchable, the ability to schedule the release and removal of content on the site, the ability to dynamically create related content to keep the reader interested, the ability to have multiple content creators working on the system at the same time, etc.

The key to content management is allowing non-technical people to keep websites up to date. It means that the people who create content can focus on what they do best, create content. The system provides them with a way to easily present that content on the Web, and that's why content management systems have become so popular. But what has emerged is that there is a lot more to content management than simply cutting and pasting content into the system; there is a range of other factors to consider.

A content management system is only a tool that helps achieve a business goal. It's a web publishing system and, like any printed publication, there are numerous decisions to be made: e.g., the purpose of the publication, the audience, the nature, source and structure of the content, the way content is to be presented, etc. The additional dimension that content management systems bring into play is that they are dynamic. The content can be re-shaped and represented in many different ways; it can also change depending on who is viewing it, e.g., members of a site might see more than the general public. A CMS can also contain interactivity that requires business logic and rules.

In summary, a content management system is far more than just software that allows people to easily update websites; it's a publishing and communication system that allows people to communicate and interact via the Web.

Content Management versus Development

Software development, as an industry, has been around for over 40 years. Web development has been around for a little over 10 years, content management has really only emerged in the last 5 years as an industry in its own right. The question is, how does that affect the way we manage CM projects? The best way to understand this is to look at the differences between traditional development and content management. Through the differences, we will be able to see how best to approach content management projects as a discipline in their own right.

In traditional development, there are many established methods to choose from. There are dozens of books that you can read and courses you can attend to learn how to manage projects. In the early days of web development, the prevailing mindset was that the rules of traditional development didn't apply; it was a new world and needed a new way of doing things. This was akin to throwing the baby out with the bath water. Sure, web development was different from traditional development, but not so much that the rule book needed to be re written. It did need to be adapted to the new environment but not totally ignored. The result was that many people in web development simply made it up as they went along. Now that content management has emerged, there's a chance that a similar mindset could emerge and the lessons still being learned in web development and long since learned in traditional development will be once again be ignored. This would be a big mistake. That's not to say you can copy an approach from traditional or web development to content management, but there is much that can be adapted.

So, what makes content management different? Why can't we simply pick a known and documented process for software development and use that? The main reason is that there are elements to a content management project that aren't covered in existing processes. Therefore, we need to be aware of the differences, so that when we select a process, we know what it covers and what we have to adjust for a content management project.

To start with, let's look at example of a traditional project versus a content management project. To do this, I'm going to use cricket as an example. For those of you not familiar with cricket, you can substitute football or any sport you like.

Test Cricket

A game of test cricket is played over a period of five days on an oval. Each team gets two opportunities to score as many runs as they can. A team is made up of 11 players, each with their speciality. Most players are either a batter or bowler. One player is the wicket keeper (for football fans, substitute strikers, defenders, and goalie). The positions each player takes on the ground and the role they play is well established. There are traditional game plans. The rules are well known (and debated at times) with official adjudication by professional referees (who still manage to make bad decisions!).

Test cricket is a well known, accepted, and understood game. The rules and strategies have been established over time and although they have evolved, the basics are the same.

20–20 Cricket

20–20 cricket is a new version of cricket. It's played on the same ground, but each team only gets 20 overs each to score as many runs as they can. The game takes less than half a day and has a far quicker and more intensive pace than test cricket. The strategies for 20–20 are different from test cricket even though it's based on the same game. Similarly, we are used to traditional software projects lasting years but content management projects are expected to be completed in as little as a month (depending on the scale of the project).

So, what we have here are sports based on the same game. But each has its elements that are unique and require a specific approach. The same goes with traditional projects and content management projects. Both are projects and the basic principles apply, but the approach taken will differ depending on the type of project. Test cricketers won't necessarily make good 20–20 cricket players and vice versa. Assuming a project manager used to traditional development will be suitable for content management is being short sighted. What is important is to understand the role being played and having the right person to play that role.

Key Differences

If we look into the key differences between traditional projects and content management projects, it's easier to see why we need to be careful about how we approach content management projects.

Methodologies

As mentioned previously, the approach to implementing a content management system is not the same as a traditional software development process. Unfortunately, there are no defined methodologies for content management, because the industry is still taking form. In essence, we are working it out along the way through trial and error. The reason that no methodologies exist is that content management brings together a range of disciplines that have never been combined before. Therefore, we have to look at existing methodologies for each discipline and adapt them to content management project, and where there are no existing practices, form new ones.

So, we can't rely on a tried and trusted approach because there simply aren't any. Part of what this book is trying to achieve is to define a set of practices that will help Project Managers to deal with content management projects until the industry matures enough and methodologies emerge.

Stakeholders

One of the major challenges in content management projects is the wide range of stakeholders that are involved. For a traditional application, you would expect the business owner/manager to be the key stakeholder, as well as including other people or departments that are to use the application or will be affected by it. The application may never need to involve marketing, public relations, communications departments, etc. In content management projects that are public facing, the number of stakeholders can be far greater as the end result will affect many departments in a company.

For example, a car parts manufacturer might build an application that allows its suppliers to look up information on the parts that it sells. This could be a simple database that is provided to the suppliers on a CD-ROM. Chances are that the marketing department and public relations would have little involvement as this is a business-to-business style solution and is a tool to help the supplier. The public would be unlikely to get access to such an application. However, if the same functionality was to be supplied via a website, it's highly likely that the look and feel of the information would have to fall within corporate style guides. If the information was highly technical, it could require restricted access so that only suppliers would be able to access that information. This would require the establishment of user accounts and management of those accounts that would not be required for the CD-ROM distributed once every 12 months. There would also be considerations regarding the upkeep of the information, which would impact on who manages that content internally. Suddenly, what was a straightforward task of supplying product information via CD-ROM becomes a more complex process when done via a content management system as more stakeholders are involved in websites than traditional applications, especially when the information is public facing.

Experience Levels

This is a major problem when it comes to content management projects. It's not hard to find people who have been working on software or web projects for 10 or more years. When it comes to content management, it's hard to find someone with more than a few years experience. When it comes to eZ publish, it's only been around since 1999, so the most experienced people are likely to have a maximum of seven years working with it. The reality is, finding experienced eZ publish developers is difficult and most will need to be trained. Becoming proficient in eZ publish takes at least three months of development work after having been trained. Doing sophisticated work with extensions and integration is something that should be left to developers with over a year's experience.

In terms of the other roles played on eZ publish projects, experience with the technology is less important, but experience with content management is very important. Once again, these people are hard to find. Because of this, the people that end up working on content management projects rarely have the right experience. It's not a question of ability, it's simply one of training. There are no established training courses or methodologies for content management. We are making things up as we go along.

The people that are drawn to content management tend to have varied backgrounds. Some with experience in web development, some with information management, some with writing and documentation; but very few have an understanding of all elements. There are very few courses dedicated to content management. It's a new field and we are finding our way in what works and what doesn't. It's going to take time for the industry to become better established and the necessary skills better understood. Until that point, all we can do is cut our teeth on projects, learn from our mistakes, and hopefully, make fewer mistakes on the next project.

The other difference between content management and traditional projects is the breadth of skills required. Content itself is something that web developers have had to deal with, but not to the same level as required in content management. It works in a different way. It also combines workflow, business processes, and data manipulation. These elements are well understood in traditional development, so getting people with that sort of experience can help. But chances are, they won't be used to the limitations of a web browser as the client interface.

No matter how you look at it, staffing content management projects will continue to be a challenge until the industry has matured enough to have established practices and people, able to study what's involved before working on their first project. In the meanwhile, projects will continue to suffer from inexperienced or inappropriate staff.

Project Scales

Web projects can be quite small, lasting a week or two. Content management projects tend to be larger but still can vary in size quite significantly. A simple installation of eZ publish with minimal customization can be done in under a week. Larger jobs can take over a year from start to finish. It stands to reason, then, that the approach taken for smaller jobs would be different from larger jobs. As a rule of thumb, the bigger the project, the more rigour and discipline required. Basically, there is no one-size-fits all approach. For each project, the approach needs to be tailored to fit the particular needs of that project.

Project Experience and Understanding

Having a client that understands what they are truly asking for is a blessing. It's also extremely rare. But we can't simply blame the client. As professionals, it's our job to explain things to the client, so that they do have an understanding. In the early days of the Web, it felt like half of the time was spent explaining to clients how a website worked. Nowadays, most people get the basics. Not so with content management, however. There is still a poor understanding of how these systems work and how best to implement them to achieve business objectives.

Another problem is that the use of the Web as a business tool is also changing at a rapid rate. The way we interact with websites is changing, the expectations of the users are increasing, and how things will pan out, no one knows — although if you are willing to part with significant amounts of cash, I'm sure there are plenty of research companies out there that are willing to take a guess at what will happen!

But mostly, it comes down to the client knowing what they want. I can't tell you how many times I'm asked, "Tell me what it can do and I'll tell you what I want". My standard response is "Tell me what you hope to achieve and I'll tell you how we can make it happen". It's too easy to focus on the features and ignore the business objectives. If a project doesn't have clear objectives, how can we tell if the solution implemented has succeeded?

Interfaces

In eZ publish projects, we are mostly dealing with web browsers. But one of the key benefits of eZ publish is its separation of presentation from content so that you can output to other formats and devices, e.g. XML, RSS, RFT, wireless devices, etc. Not only that, there are new devices emerging and we don't know what the future will hold.

Myths

As any industry develops, statements are made that become well known and accepted. The problem is they are not always true. Picking the facts from fiction can be difficult. This is particularly true in web development and now, content management development. Most of these myths are based on ignorance; that's why it's important to understand the nature of what we are dealing with so we can see through the lies.

Myth no. 1

Content management can ignore the rules of traditional project management.

This was the mistake that the cowboys of the early web era made, and it was a costly mistake paid for by clients who didn't know any better, many of whom paid ridiculous amounts of money for very little. Unfortunately, the same has happened in content management for similar reasons. The basic principles of understanding the project objective, properly capturing requirements, scoping the project, and establishing clear roles and responsibilities were too easily forgotten simply because it wasn't a normal project. Regardless of the fact that content management projects have a number of differences, the basics still apply. The question is how to apply them appropriately.

Myth no. 2

Content managed sites are just like a static website.

I have to admit, I only discovered this myth by believing it myself and then learning the hard way. There is a linear mindset in most websites; a page is a page, that's it. It might be linked to and from different pages, but a website is made up of a series of pages and functions. Content managed sites are different; pages are constructed dynamically from content elements, which can appear on many parts of the sites in different ways. It's a different mindset altogether that takes time to appreciate and understand. A content managed site is not just another website; it's a web publishing system, an application in its own right.

Myth no. 3

It's easy, it's only a website, it can't be THAT expensive!

This is the hardest myth of all to convince people is wrong. Websites appear simple, a site created using a content management system should appear simple to the user, but that doesn't mean that it's simple to achieve. The best designs are often simple, but making them that simple takes great skill. That's what many people fail to appreciate when it comes to content management, it looks and sounds easy. Just install the software and away we go. That's like saying, just install Word and you can write a book. The system is just the tool, a means to an end.

In the case of content management systems, the end can be the automation of a business process that used to be handled manually. A static website just presented information; a content management system can be a business tool that allows a business to interact with its customers in a more effective and efficient manner. Whenever business processes are involved, great care and attention needs to be taken in defining exactly how that business process will be automated via a website. Getting this wrong can mean the business could end up loosing revenue and customers rather than increasing revenue and gaining more customers.

It takes a lot of thought and planning to deliver a solution that works well and looks simple.

Myth no. 4

Software developers are great at implementing content management systems.

It's a bit like asking a fighter pilot to fly a helicopter, sure, he might know how to fly but a helicopter isn't quite the same as a jet fighter. It also doesn't mean that a fighter pilot couldn't learn and adapt to flying helicopters but it would require training and understanding as to how helicopters work as opposed to jet fighters. The point is making sure the right people are playing the right roles on the project. Just because a content management system is a piece of software, it doesn't mean it isn't specialized and therefore needs a specialized approach.

Types of Websites and Web Applications

Content management systems combine content-focused and task-focused websites into one solution. It's important to understand the different natures of content-versus task-focused solutions so that we can be sure to cover the different needs of each solution. The following definitions are based on Jesse James Garrett's work on user-centered design in his book The Elements of User Experience. Later, we'll examine common types of solutions that combine hypertext and web applications.

Static Websites

A static website is actually a "hypertext system", i.e. a series of hypertext files connected to each other with links. Hypertext systems are content-focused and are about providing access to that information in an efficient manner via a web browser. If you break down a hypertext system into its different layers, you can see what's required to create one.

Objectives

These will be derived from business needs to present information to meet specific objectives. Commonly, the objectives are marketing or communication goals. A good example is to promote a business through a corporate website.

Content Requirements

This defines the content elements required to build the hypertext system in order to meet the business objectives. For example, a corporate site may wish to present case studies to illustrate what the company is capable of. The content requirements would outline the structure of the case studies and what information will be needed.

Information Architecture

This defines how the site will be structured at a high level. How the content is to be organized in a logical fashion so that the users of the system will understand. It provides a context for the content elements.

Information and Navigation Design

This defines how the content is to be presented on each page and how users will navigate throughout the system. It's often missed or mixed in with the information architecture and visual design, but should be considered in its own right.

Visual Design

The visual design defines the visual treatment of the content, e.g., the text, graphics, and navigation. It's hard to separate information design from visual design and there is, in fact, some overlap between these elements of a hypertext system. Ideally, the visual design is the last element defined; but far too often, a design mock-up is done that actually mixes the information architecture, information and navigation design with the visual design and it's hard to then make changes without affecting all of these elements. It can be very confusing if there is not a clear understanding of the different elements and the role they play in a hypertext system.

Web Applications

There are only two things you can do with a website; communicate or interact. Web applications are about interacting with users, e.g., making a booking or submitting a request. A web application is no different to a traditional application except that it uses a web browser as the interface and the Internet for connectivity.

Objectives

The objectives for a web application can be quite diverse, ranging from providing a simple feedback form through to automating business processes such as bank loan applications. The nature of the application will depend on the business needs but will either be focused on generating revenue e.g. online sales, or improving efficiency e.g. online business processes.

Functional Specification

A functional specification defines the features that the application will deliver. The features may be grouped into feature sets. The specification will define how the application will deliver these features to the user. It will contain details of how business processes will be implemented. It is not a technical document as such—it doesn't contain database schemas and object models. It describes the functionality that the application will deliver.

Interaction Design

The interaction design will most likely be captured in the functional specification but should be considered an element in its own right. Interaction design shows how the user will interact with the application, the flow of screens, and the options at each stage of the application.

Information and Interface Design

Applications have interactions that follow a series of defined steps. Navigation is limited to the tasks the user can perform and is mostly defined by the interaction design. Basically, you don't want people to be jumping around a web application when they are in the middle of a task such as filling out a loan application. What is important is how the screen is laid out, how the buttons and form elements are arranged, what parts of the screen are dynamic, what changes when an action is performed. All of this is captured in the information and interface design.

Visual Design

As with hypertext systems, the visual design defines the appearance of text, graphics, and navigation. It is clearer with web applications to understand the role of the visual design. It is applied to the interface design to make it attractive and useable. By starting with the visual design, it's obvious that you are making decisions about the interface and interaction design, which may or may not be appropriate. Although the visual design is what we first notice, and is important, it should be the last element to be addressed in a web application.

Static Websites versus Web Applications

If we compare the elements in hypertext systems and web applications, we can see there are some elements in common but the core elements differ.

Static Websites	Web Applications
Visual Design	Visual Design
Information & Navigation Design	Information & Interface Design
Information Architecture	Interaction Design
Content Requirements	Functional Specification
Objectives	Objectives

Given that the elements differ, it's obvious that, when building a web application, we need to take a different approach to building a hypertext system. The challenge with content management systems is that they are almost always a combination of the two, which means all the elements have to be considered. For some parts of the given solution, you'll be drafting interaction designs; for other parts you'll need navigation design. And then you'll have to work out what to do with navigation when the user is the middle of an interaction. This is why content management solutions have a greater level of complexity than a static website. There are more elements to consider and also how those elements interact in one solution.

Web Solution Categories

Over time, a number of well defined categories of web solutions have emerged that combine hypertext systems and web applications into particular categories of solutions. Knowing there are patterns for these solutions can help make decisions for solutions that you may be asked to implement. It's about not re-inventing the wheel. If the website you are working on falls into one of the categories defined below, you can leverage an existing approach and reduce the risk in your project.

The categories below are based on a presentation from G. Kappel, "Web Engineering: Old Wine New Bottles" ICWE, 2004, Munich.

Interactive

This is good example of a content-focused web application. The content of a website is dynamically generated in response to a user request. Form-based input, e.g. Search forms, is the primary mechanism for communication between client and server.

Examples:

- Product databases
- Public transport schedules
- Search engines

Transactional

A transactional solution contains complex user interactions with many levels. Interactions often result in database queries and transactions. Well defined business logic is required and implemented strictly.

Examples:

- Online banking
- e-Shopping
- Reservation systems

Workflow-Based

Workflow-based solutions are similar to transaction sites but are based on existing business processes and provide a more complex service to the user. They can be internal, business to business, or business to consumer. A prerequisite for a workflow system is an established business process.

Examples:

- e-Government
- Patient workflows in health care systems
- Multi-level approval systems

Collaborative

These are solutions that unstructured and adaptive. Their focus is to support communication, e.g. groupware. They support shared information and workspaces. They assist people to work together through sharing information.

Examples:

- Wiki
- Forums & chatrooms
- e-Learning platforms

Knowledge-Based

This is access to information via the Web or web-based systems. It is similar to a hypertext system but is more dynamic in that information can be presented in different ways on different pages. These solutions support knowledge management and derivation of new knowledge via re-use.

Examples:

- Enterprise portals
- Intranets
- Extranets

What does All This Mean for eZ Publish Projects?

We are in a young industry with inexperienced people and clients that often lack an understanding of what they want. There are no established processes and procedures. And expectations from users are increasing as the Internet is used more and more as a business tool.

According to Alistair Cockburn (an internationally renowned project manager and IT strategist), developing solutions is actually making ideas concrete in an economic context. With website solutions, we are crossing even more boundaries than software development. eZ publish solutions bring marketing, communication, interaction, information, and business processes together.

If we fail to improve the way we manage projects, we will keep making the same mistakes. The reason for this book is to help provide a framework for eZ publish projects that deals with the most important aspects and will hopefully lead to better results.

In short, the better we understand the situation, the better we can deal with it. This book is not about a silver bullet; there is no such thing. There is no single approach to make all projects work. What this book does is define a framework that helps us deal with a complex and changing environment. From this, we are better placed to create quality solutions.

Summary

Content management as a discipline combines the practices of building a static website with building a web application. Because of this, we need to be aware of the requirements of content-focused and task-focused solutions. Given that there are no methodologies in place that cover both aspects of content management systems we need to adapt existing approaches.

Underlying this is the importance of understanding the specific needs of each part of the solution and taking the appropriate approach so that the end solution works together. This means having a clear understanding of the roles required and having the right people on the team to fill those roles.

2

Information Architecture and Design

The purpose of this chapter is to provide an overview of information architecture and design in relation to content management systems. Decisions made on how the site is structured have an impact on how the content management system will be implemented. Understanding the impact of these design decisions will help to ensure the content management system is implemented in an effective manner, both during the development and in the ongoing use of the system.

Information Architecture

The term information architecture has been around for many years and is now a term that many people use with ease; however, I'm sure that if you asked ten people their definition of information architecture, you'd get ten different answers. Not wanting to add an eleventh definition, this is simply an overview of what information architecture is about. For a detailed explanation, read the polar bear book — *Information Architecture* by Rosenfeld and Morville.

In its simplest terms, information architecture is how a site is structured. It is most commonly represented by a site map. There are two main approaches that can be taken in structuring a site — content oriented or task oriented. Although it's not always that simple, more often than not, sites end up a combination of the two.

Task Oriented

A task-oriented site is focused on making it clear and simple for a user to perform a task on the site, for example, book tickets, search, buy a product, submit an application, etc. The following screenshot shows the homepage of an airline. The main purpose of this site is to allow people to book a ticket; therefore the main part of the screen is made up of a form that lets users find out when flights are leaving for a particular origin and destination. Note that the main navigation is used for the content-oriented part of the site.

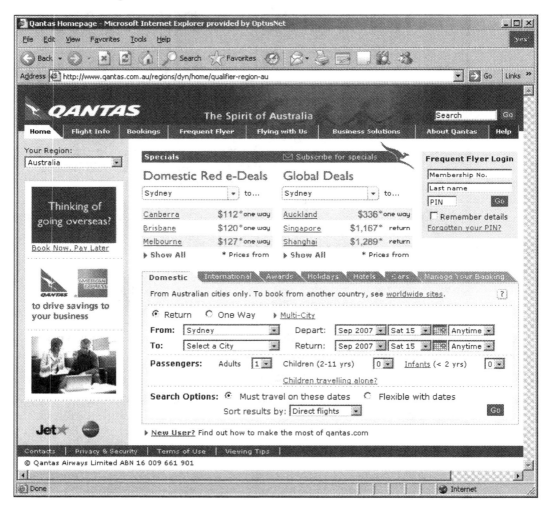

Content Oriented

In the early days of the Web, sites were mainly content orientated. Many still are, and the art of structuring content in a meaningful way is still a challenge where many sites go wrong. The most common mistake is to structure content the way the business sees it as apposed to the way the user sees it. Structures should be organized by subject or topic from the user's perspective. For example, a business that manages waste removal may structure its departments according to the type of equipment that is used, ranging from hand held through to industrial sized. From the user's perspective, they are more interested in the type of waste they have to deal with — not the type of equipment involved. In this case, it would make more sense to present the services offered in terms of the type of waste, such as paper, chemical, liquid, etc. rather than organize the site according to the different equipment used. It often happens that the internal departments of a business don't mean anything to the public, they care about the product or service that they are interested in.

The following screenshot is of The Age newspaper website. It is a content-rich site with the major stories noted by headlines and links to more details. Other stories are accessible by the main navigation, which is topic based.

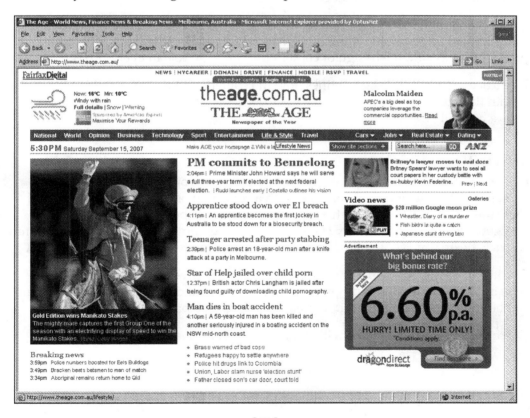

Five Facets of Design

In content management projects, design doesn't just refer to the look and feel of the site but goes much deeper into the entire design of the site from the content through to the presentation. Understanding that design goes much deeper than the surface and how to bring the different elements of design together will have a significant impact on the success of the end product.

Content Modeling

Rarely do people think about the design of content. Database designs are common, information design is becoming better understood, visual design is well known; but content design is almost unheard of.

Information design relates to how the content is to be presented on the web page. Content design refers to the structure of the content itself and is not related to how the content is to be presented. It involves the naming of each type of content, the definition of each attribute, and the type of data that it will contain, as well as how the content type relates to other content types.

Given the number of projects delivered using eZ publish, let alone other content management systems, it seems to be a massive oversight. Especially with the eZ publish framework, the design of content plays a huge role in every project.

In particular, content design defines how the content will be structured and stored within the site. It's a cross between a database table and object class, and is referred to as a content class.

Content Class

One of the most important parts of every eZ publish project is to gather all the content, analyze it, and then come up with a collection of content classes that will meet the needs of the end solution. This is often where people new to eZ publish will get stuck — using too many classes creates development overhead, using too few restricts flexibility. Knowing what's "just right" is a matter of skill and experience.

The key to deciding when a content class is required is when the content has a repeatable structure that is different from other content on the site. A lot of content can be presented with a generic content class, e.g. web page.

There are two clear cases that will dictate if a content class is required.

The first case is when the content has an existing, repeatable structure, e.g. a product has a number of fields that contain product information. These collections of fields are unique to that type of content, just like a database table has a number of fields of a particular type.

The following table is an example of a product content class. You'll see that it has a set of fields and also the type of data that is to be stored.

Attribute	Datatype
Product Name	Text
Product Category	Rich text
Description	Rich Text
Image	File
Cost	Numeric

The second case where a content class is required is when the display of that content is specified in a set and repeated manner. For instance, a news article is to be displayed in a particular way: As a list of news items and then each individual news item.

The list of news items is to show the title, author, publication, and date only. In this case, the system needs to be able extract those fields only. If the author, date, and publication were all stored in a single field, it would be difficult for the system to extract ONLY those fields to be presented on the page. Also, unless the date was an individual field, it would be difficult to extract news items based on date or sort and filter on that field. In this situation, a content class would be created that had each of these elements as individual fields. It provides clarity for the content creator, consistency in display, and makes it easy for the system to deal with.

Attribute	Datatype
Title	Text
Author	Text
Date	Date
Publication	Text
Description	Rich text

However, it should be noted that having too many different content classes can be as bad as having too few content classes. The number of content classes required is dependent entirely on the nature of the content itself. This will dictate when you need to create a content class. This is covered in more depth in the chapter on content modeling.

Information and Navigation Design

Navigation design deals with how people move around a site; information design is how the information is presented on a particular page. They work hand in hand as the navigation design may depend on the nature of the information being presented.

Information Design

Information design is structuring information to facilitate understanding.

Although not as much as content design, information design is often forgotten or left to the last minute in which someone has to come up with a quick solution. Rarely is all the content considered upfront and therefore information design can't be done fully. A good example of information design taken seriously is any major newspaper website. There is always an abundance of content and it needs to be balanced and structured right so that it is easy for the user to see what the major news of the day is (of course, that doesn't mean all newspapers get it right!).

Normally, we represent information design with the use of wireframes (see the following diagram). A wireframe is like the skeleton of a page. It represents all the elements on a page but without the graphic design.

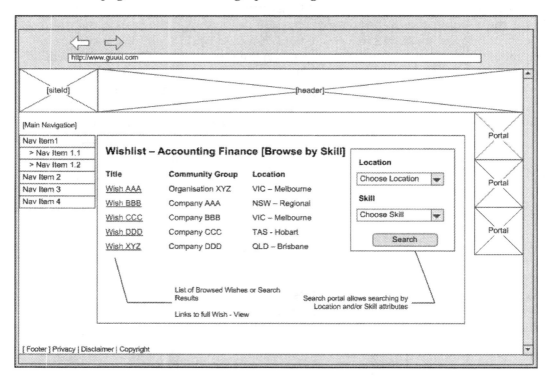

In this wireframe, we are showing the results of a search for wishes. A wish is a request from a community group for help, e.g., someone to help with bookkeeping. The wireframe shows the matching wishes as a list. Each wish is a link to the full details of that wish. Also shown is how the navigation is to be displayed. In this case, navigation is down the left-hand side of the page with sub-navigation appearing indented underneath the selected nav item.

Through a series of wireframes, we can cover all the content that is to be represented on the site and how it is to be structured. Naturally, the final look and feel will have an impact on the way the elements are ultimately represented, but at least there is a good indication of what information is to be displayed and how it is to be structured.

Navigation Design

Navigation design is about how the interface elements are organized to help the user move through the site.

Simply put, it's how people get around a website.

We can break down navigation into number of different types:

1. Primary: This covers links to the main parts of the site and is persistent throughout the site.
2. Secondary: This refers to links to content within a particular section of the site.
3. Tertiary / Quaternary: Depending on the depth of a site, there may be links to content within sub-sections or sub-sub-sections of a site.
4. Supplementary: This covers links to additional information or content related to the particular page being viewed.
5. Contextual: This refers to links within the content, embedded within the page.

6. Utility: This refers to links that are not used on a regular basis but may be needed at any point throughout the site, e.g. Contact us, Search, Privacy, Terms & Conditions, etc.

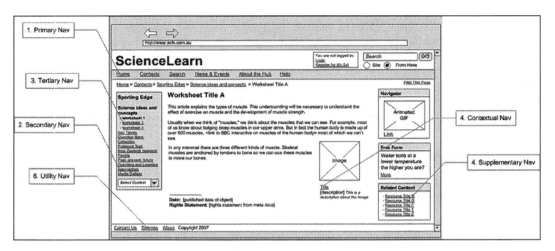

Interaction Design

Interaction design is how functionality is designed to facilitate user tasks, i.e. how the user interacts with the site. It can be as simple as a search form and results display, or cover a more complex workflow such as a multi-page survey with conditional questions. It's mostly represented by a flowchart.

The purpose of interaction design is to map the flow of actions and interactions between the user and the system. The following flowchart is a simple example of a user signing up to be a member of a website. The steps are:

a) Member enters details.

b) Details are checked to ensure they are valid (e.g. required fields entered, email address is valid, postcode is valid, etc.).

c) Confirmation link is sent via email to member.

d) Member confirms by clicking on email.

e) Account is activated.

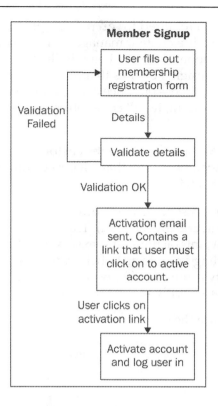

Interaction design captures the business logic of a site and is extremely important to get right. It will impact on how the site is built and how people will interact with it; if done poorly or without enough thought, it can make the site difficult to use or fail to achieve the goals it was designed to achieve. Therefore, it's important to take great care in designing interactions for your site.

Jesse James Garrett has come up with an entire visual vocabulary for documenting interaction design: `http://www.jjg.net/ia/visvocab`. If you're not used to doing interaction design, it's a great way to get started.

Technical Design

This encompasses what we call design in traditional software development, i.e.:

- Application architecture
- Solution architecture
- Object model
- Class and sequence diagrams
- Database schema

The level of technical design required for eZ publish projects can vary quite dramatically. As eZ publish is a content management framework, much of the technical design has been done. If the site being built is content-oriented, there is no need for any technical design. For sites that have interactivity, i.e. extensions, technical design will be required—but once again, it depends on the level of complexity. At its greatest extent, it will cover object models, class diagrams, and database schemas.

As a minimum, all projects should capture the custom classes. For a large complex project, there should be documentation that covers custom classes, interaction, object model, class diagram, and database schema.

The following diagrams represent technical design details for the Good Company project (http://www.goodcompany.com.au). This was a project that included custom content, workflow, interactions, and extensions. The Good Company website was centered around finding volunteers to help community groups. The core was a "wish" that a community group would post on the website, and then volunteers would search for wishes and apply for one that they could help with.

The first step was to capture the overall model.

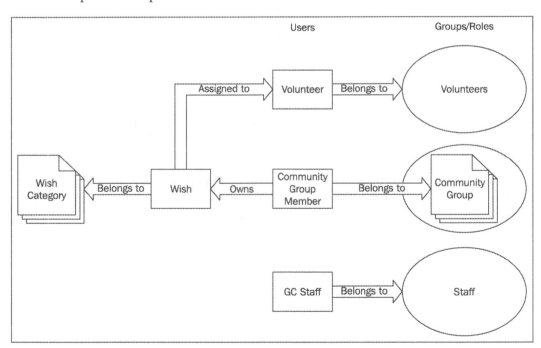

In this diagram, we can see that the wish is central to the model. A wish is provided by the community group and then is assigned to a volunteer who is a member of the volunteers group. We also show the Good Company staff (GC Staff) as a member of the staff group. So, what we have captured here is a high-level overview of the main objects in the system and how they relate to each other, as well as, the core users and groups that need to be set up for appropriate permissions to be applied.

Following on from the overall model, there are interactions required for volunteers and community groups to sign up. The following diagram shows the flow for a community group to sign up.

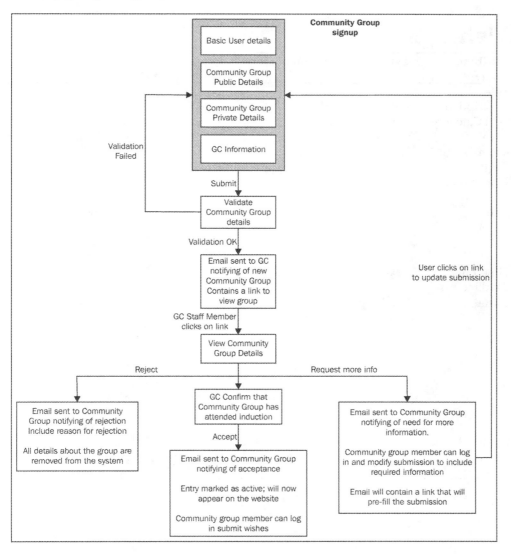

What we can see in this diagram is that there are a number of steps that are required for a community group to be accepted on the site. Not only do they have to enter their details, they also need to be approved by a Good Company staff member, as well as confirming that they have completed an induction. This is capturing business logic and is important to get right as it can be costly to change at a later date — not to mention the impact on the business.

The next diagram defines the wish content class: all the attributes that are required, whether they are mandatory, the type of attributes, whether it's available to the public, etc.

Wish

Attribute Name	Type	Mandatory	Public Information	Notes
Title	Text	Y	Y	
Description	Rich Text	Y	Y	
Skill Category	Single option ?	Y	Y	Require list of options.
Level of Expertise Required	Single option	Y	Y	Require list of options.
Time required	Text	Y	Y	
Location	Single option	Y	Y	Require list of options.
Size	Single option	Y	N	Options as: • Individual • Team • Larger group
Timeframe/ deadline	Text	Y	Y	
Status	Single option	Y	N	Internal attribute. Options are: • Submitted • Open • Reserved • In Progress • Resolved • Reporting • Complete
Contact Name	CG User	Y	?	Implied as the contact person will also be a system user.

Finally, at the end of all of this, there's an underlying database schema that indicates how the information is to be stored as additional tables within eZ Publish.

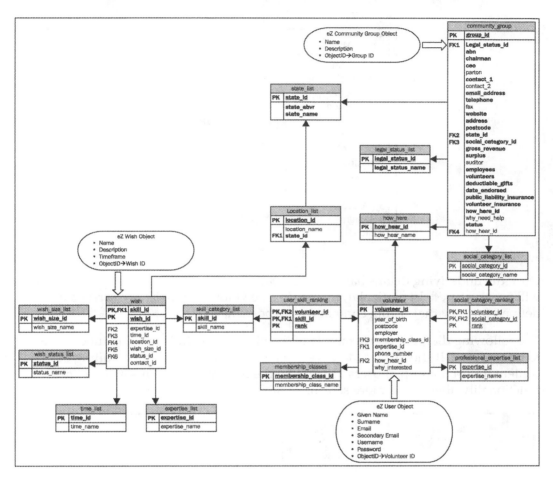

Along with the database diagram, a class diagram would be created of each class that was to be programmed within the system. Note that in this case we are referring to classes in their traditional sense, not content classes.

The following diagram shows the definition of the wish class. The full class diagram would show ALL classes and how they relate to each other.

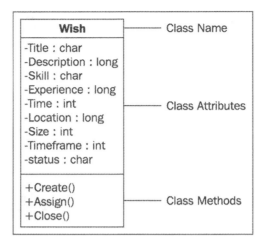

Once the underlying details have been captured we can look at the way the interfaces will be structured. In particular, there was a need for administration screens to be defined for how the custom content was to be managed.

The following diagram is an example of the high-level administration functionality to be captured. It shows that there were screens for the viewing and editing of content for each group of users. Given that the community groups had the most functionality, there were more screens required.

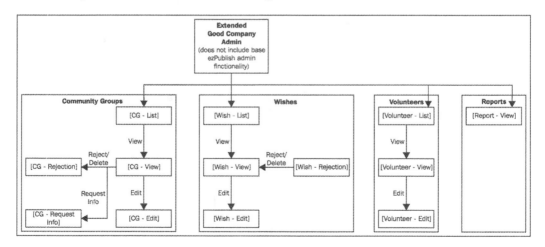

From the overview, the details of each screen were captured in a wireframe. The following wireframe shows what would be on the screen when a community group was editing the details of a wish.

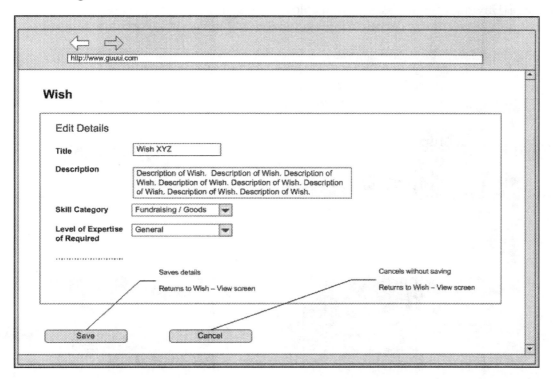

Visual Design

Last but not least, there's visual design. It's the one design element that everyone knows, i.e. how the site looks. Visual design covers the visual treatment of text, graphics, page elements, and navigation. Most web-design firms will represent a visual design through a series of screenshots, the goal of which is to define contrast and uniformity.

Contrast

The concept of contrast is simple, what is it that you notice first? What stands out most on the page? It is through contrast that we bring information architecture to life. If a wireframe lacks color and depth, through visual design, we can alter the way the information is perceived.

A small heading in white with a bright red background will get more attention than the same heading in black on white. For example, in the screenshot below, the elements that stand out the most are the two blocks at the bottom of the page. Having different background colors draws the eye, very quickly. This site communicates that it's about bringing together volunteers and community groups.

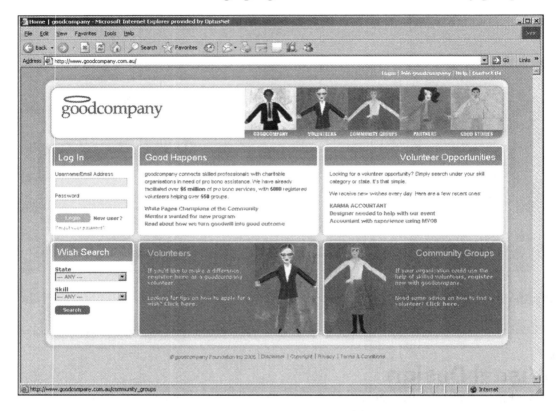

The idea of contrast is to ensure the elements of the page that you want the user to see stand out the most. Contrast is created through three elements:

- Size
- Position
- Color

By altering these three elements, we can create a hierarchy of importance for elements of the page that, if done well, will intuitively communicate the level of importance of each part of the page, if done poorly will leave the user confused.

Uniformity

While contrast is used to create a sense of visual hierarchy, uniformity is used to create a consistency in approach. Uniformity is about a visual language that is used throughout the site that is easy for the user to understand. For example, the main page heading is always a set color and font size, images are always left-aligned, links are always indicated with an arrow, etc.

In the world of graphic design, we are used to comprehensive style guides for corporate branding. The same mindset needs to be applied to websites but is often forgotten.

A Common Mistake

The most common mistake made in visual design is doing a visual design BEFORE having completed the content and information design. Doing the visual design first will force the designer to make a series of assumptions regarding content, navigation, site requirements, and information design. Once a client sees a visual design, they will expect the end result to be the same. It is a huge mistake that can cause untold problems later down the track when the interaction design fails to match the visual design and either changes have to be made to the visual design, which have to be explained to the client, or the interaction design is compromised. If at all possible, visual design should be done later.

However, in commercial reality, we are often asked to present a visual design as a part of a bid to win a project. Saying no (even though it's the right thing to do), can jeopardize chances of winning the project. In this case, all you can do is state as clearly as possible that the design is representative of a style only and is subject to change. Chances are the client will not remember this small but significant point, but at least you will have it as something to fall back on when the inevitable changes to the visual design surface.

Visual Design Issues

There are a myriad of issues when it comes to visual design, many more than for any of the other elements of designs mentioned so far. There is a single reason for this. When it comes to visual design, everyone thinks they are an expert! For the other elements of design, most people are happy to leave it to true experts, but when it comes to visual design, everyone has an opinion. The most heated debates in conference rooms regarding websites will almost always be about visual design.

There are a number of common approaches to visual design, each with its own strengths and weaknesses. Although you may not be able to change the approach taken, at least by understanding it you can help to shape the outcome rather than being a part of the problem.

Design by Default

Every site has a design. It might not be very good, but it will exist. When design fails to be considered as an element in its own right, a default approach is taken. What this means is that the design will follow an existing approach.

Design by Fiat

It's a hard to pick the worst offender of visual design issues but design by fiat has to be close to the top of the list. Design by fiat is when one person dictates the visual design based on their personal preferences. If the person dictating the visual design is an expert, then it can work, if not, the results can be disastrous. On a recent project, after the visual design had been approved and implemented, the CEO demanded that drop-down menus be added. When asked why, the answer that came back was "because he likes them". It didn't matter if usability studies had shown drop-down menus can cause frustration in older users; this site was going to have them. None of this mattered because the CEO was employing design by fiat.

When this happens, user needs aren't considered and best practice is ignored. It can also cause problems with the existing design creating rework. It's impractical to think we can prevent design by fiat, all we can do is hope to educate our clients enough to trust us to do what we do best.

Design by Committee

This is along the same lines as design by fiat with the blame shared across a group of people rather than a single individual. The end result is often a compromise that tries to keep everyone happy except for the most important person, the user. The reason the results are often poor is that expert views are not considered and the project objectives can be obscured by committee members arguing over personal preferences. At times it can combine design by default, and by fiat all in one!

All I can say about design by committee is to quote this well known saying…

"In all the parks in all the cities you'll never see a statue of a committee."

The Average User

As a part of dogmatic debates, the concept of the "average" user can be used to justify a particular argument. E.g. "users prefer drop downs". This is a flawed argument because, and I'm sorry to upset anyone new to web design, there is no such thing as the average user. Such a creature is no more real than the abominable snowman or Santa Claus. Sure, I'd be happy to sustain the myth of the average user if it meant we could have another public holiday in celebration but it's of no use when it comes to visual design. Web users are unique and idiosyncratic; we all have our own likes and dislikes, expectations, and assumptions.

Rather than thinking in terms of the average user, we need to appreciate the particular audience for the website we are building; know their individual intentions, experience, cultural backgrounds, and age; to realize that it's not about the average user but appreciating the complexity of people. This means that not everyone will like the design created; what matters is that as many as possible of the right people do, i.e., the people that the site has been created for.

The Right Questions

Like most things, visual design comes down to asking the right questions and avoiding design by default or fiat.

For example:

- Will using drop-down menus with these items and this wording in this context create a good experience for our target market?
- Will using drop-downs better help us achieve the project objectives?

If All Else Fails

If you can't avoid any of the design issues outlined, then the only answer is to put it to the test. Hopefully, that's in a controlled environment with expert testers and a formal report, if not, as happens too often, the visual design is tested by putting the site live and seeing how people respond. Both tests work but the latter is more expensive and potentially embarrassing.

Summary

The key is to understand the role that information architecture and design play in the end solution. Knowing what is good or bad design in this case is a role for the experts, not the person managing the project. What matters is that as a manager, you are able to appreciate the difference between information design and interaction design, so that you can ensure that it is dealt with properly as a part of the project. There are many books that deal with each of the elements of design outlined in this chapter, if you want to know more; but really, it's the design experts that should know these books intimately. As a manager, you simply need to appreciate that all elements of design need to be considered to ensure a successful outcome.

3

eZ Publish Overview

What is eZ Publish?

eZ publish is a content management framework. A base set of features and functions that make up the core of a content management system. It can be used as a system straight out of the box with its standard functionality which provides the majority of the features clients are likely to need. However, often clients require parts of the system to be customized to their needs. This is where the approach taken in the eZ publish framework comes into its strength.

Separation of Layers

One of the greatest strengths of eZ publish is the way it cleanly separates layers.

In traditional software architecture, there are four layers:

- User Interface
- Business Logic
- System Interface
- Data Access and Storage

The theory is that each layer should be independent from the other layers so that changes can be made within a layer without affecting the rest of the system. This is also, known as the "black box" concept, that is, the inner workings of one layer is like a black box to the other layers. The benefit of this is that each layer can be updated, modified, or replaced without having to change any of the other layers. E.g. a particular solution might use Postgres as a part of the data access layer, but the client has decided that they want to move to Oracle. If the business logic layer has been cleanly separated from the data layer, it means that only the data layer has to be modified to work with Oracle instead of Postgres.

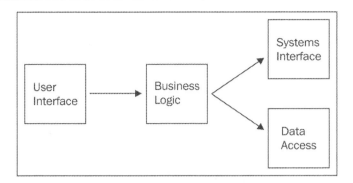

Unfortunately, in many web applications, the presentation, business logic, and data access layers become intermingled making it difficult to update and modify without running into trouble. eZ publish solves this by ensuring the layers are cleanly separated. This means you can change one layer without impacting the other layers. A common example is that you can change the entire look and feel of a site quickly and easily without affecting the rest of the system.

The way in which eZ publish achieves this is through the use of designs, templates, content classes, and extensions.

- The user interface is created through a combination of design and templates.
- Business logic is created through sections, access control, and extensions.
- Data access is built into the framework.
- System interface is provided by extensions.

Initially, it's not obvious as to why this idea of separation of layers is so powerful. When initially building a system, allowing the layers to be mixed might lead to a quicker result; it's not until working on larger systems with many developers or once the system requires updates and maintenance that the layered approach proves to be far superior. The benefit of the eZ publish framework is that the layered approach is built in.

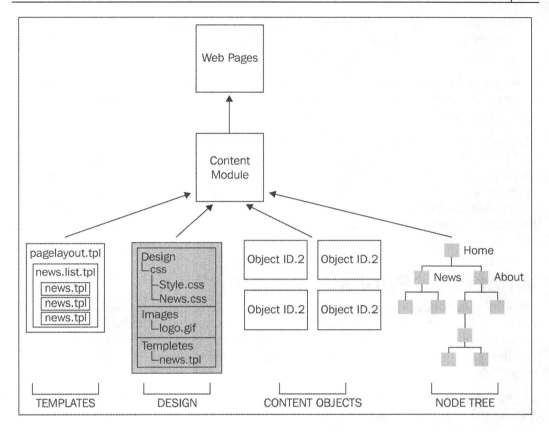

Managing Content

There is no one ideal way of managing content. eZ publish doesn't pretend to be all things to all people, no one solution can be. What eZ publish does offer is a well thought-out and constructed administration interface that is logical and easy to learn.

On the users' side, most people can grasp the basics in an hour. People using eZ publish over time soon learn the advanced features that can make managing content quicker and easier.

On the administrator and developer side, the core features are in place and can easily be extended to allow for customized content and site structures as well as modifying the presentation layer to meet your client's needs.

However, eZ publish isn't the be all and end all; what it does it does very well and compares favorably with other systems. Whether it's the right system for your needs will depend on the nature of your project.

There are some systems that focus only on e-commerce (e.g. OSCommerce), which will have more in built shopping features that eZ publish, but for a standard shop, eZ publish is more than suitable. Where eZ publish wins over the more specific systems is in its ability to be modified and extended to meet specific needs. In reality, eZ publish can be used for a wide variety of projects; whether it's the right tool for a particular project will depend on how much modification is required in comparison to more specialized tools.

What is eZ Publish Good For?

What eZ publish does well is provide a solid, reliable framework that will meet the needs of the majority of content management needs. In particular, it is ideal for standards based sites that require strict adherence to XHTML/CSS standards. As clients only deal with the content, it is easy to ensure that the site remains standards compliant.

The fact that it is backed by eZ Systems means that as an offering, it's likely to be around for a long time. Since it was first released, eZ publish has grown significantly in functionality, and now has a strong community and user base providing a stability that provides confidence for both the user and developer alike.

There are thousands of examples of eZ publish worldwide and a growing partner network, so anyone thinking of using eZ publish isn't on their own. Unlike other open-source solutions where you often have to rely on your own abilities to work things out, there are plenty of resources to provide support and assistance should you need it. Naturally, such support isn't free but the fact that the system is licence-free helps to offset the costs associated with support.

Where eZ publish really shines is in its clean separation of layers, meaning that as a developer, you can focus on only customizing the areas that are unique for your project rather than having to start from scratch. The idea of managing exceptions, the areas that need to be different, means energy is put into the areas of greatest value; the core work has already been done. Put simply, you don't have to re-invent the wheel.

Internal Structure and Configuration

eZ publish is broken into three parts, modules, kernel, and libraries.

Modules contain the standard features provided by eZ publish. By default, the modules are:

- Content
- Media Library
- Shop
- Search

You can add your own modules, should you need them while creating extensions.

The kernel contains the core code of the system.

The libraries provide a range of functions for the core code.

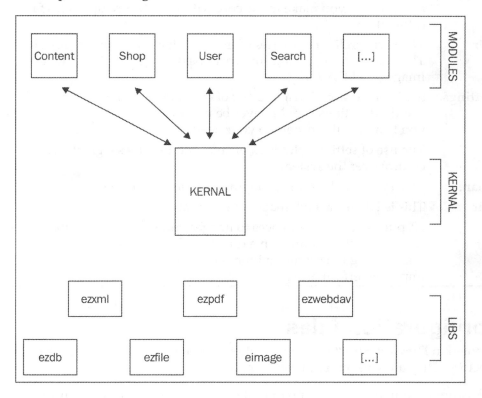

Directory Structure

/bin	Contains a range of scripts that can be run from the command line to perform tasks that can't be done via the administration interface or are quicker via the command line. E.g. clearing the cache, verifying files, subtree move / copy, creating a static cache, checking templates, etc.
/design	All files to do with the look and feel of the site are stored in the design directory. These include: • Stand and custom template files • Stylesheets • Images
/doc	Contains documentation such as change logs, explanation of features and functions, standards, etc.
/kernel	This is the core eZ publish code — you should avoid touching this as any changes you make to the core will make future upgrades far more difficult.
/lib	The kernel relies on a series of libraries that are stored in this directory. The libaries cover a range of functions dealing with the database, images, webDAV, XML, etc.
/settings	Settings are stored in a number of configuration files (ini files). The standard settings should never be modified; the use of overrides allows you to adjust the system to your needs. The use of settings files is extensive, and provides a great deal of control over the system.
/share	This is where the static configuration files are stored.
/var	This is where cached images and files are stored. eZ publish stores references to images and files in the database and stores the actual content in a directory. Doing this rather than storing binary files within the database helps to improve performance.

Configuration Files

As noted in *Directory Structure*, configuration files are located in the /settings directory. They all have an .ini extension.

Each configuration file controls a part of the system, e.g. image.ini controls the formats allowed and the standard sizes (small, medium, large). The default configuration files contain all directives and provide good comments to explain what each of these does.

The most important of all configuration files is `site.ini`. This contains important information such as database name, password, design, content, site access, file, and email settings.

Configuration files are divided into blocks, each with a collection of relevant settings. E.g.:

```
# Place comment here
[DatabaseSettings]
DatabaseImplementation=ezmysql
Server=sql.internal.dbserver.site.com
Database=aipex
User=aipex
Password=PaII95q!
Charset=iso-8859-1
Socket=disabled
# Make sure to confirm default email address with client
[MailSettings]
AdminEmail=admin@site.com
EmailSender=admin@site.com
```

The Lego Approach

eZ publish is a bit like Lego. It provides a clean base and a series of "blocks" that you can use to create your solution. How you combine these blocks will determine how the system works. Most of what you'll need is already provided in the framework but if you need to, you can add your own custom blocks to achieve what you need.

So, what do I mean by blocks?

There are three types of blocks:

- Content blocks
- Display blocks
- Functional blocks

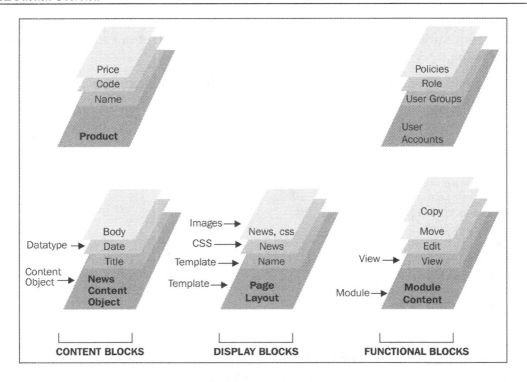

Content Blocks

The content blocks are formed by data types that combine to form content types. These are the basis of the system. eZ publish being a content management system, content is the core of all solutions.

The data types already exist within eZ publish; you simply select a number of them together to create a content class. The content class is like a table in a database. This defines the structure of the content that the system will store.

Display Blocks

The display blocks are templates that combine to form a page. A template is a combination of HTML and eZ publish code.

A template gets the content from content classes and organizes it to produce HTML output.

A template will often contain other templates to create the final HTML output. E.g. a template that shows a listing of news items will use a loop that contains another template that shows a single news item to produce a list of news items.

Functional Blocks

eZ publish contains a number of built-in modules that provide blocks of common functionality required in a content management system. A good example is the "search" module. This allows you to search all content in the database by keyword and return a list of results. There's no need to build your own search.

Other modules include user management, login, view, edit, etc.

You can create your own modules if there's a custom functionality that your solution requires.

It's through the configuration of the content, display, and functional blocks in eZ publish that you have the incredible flexibility to produce solutions. And if there's anything missing, the system can be extended to meet your exact needs without having to touch the core code, thus making upgrades much easier.

Data Types, Content Classes, and Objects

All content is stored in datatypes that are then combined to form content classes; the actual content is called an object.

Datatype

A datatype is the smallest unit of storage. It's similar to a field in a database table.

eZ publish comes with a standard set of datatypes that provide the majority of content storage needs, e.g. text line, text block, date, image, file, email. The following table shows the most commonly used datatypes.

Text line	A single line of unformatted text
Text block	Multiple lines of unformatted text
XML block	Multiple lines of formatted text
Integer	Handles an integer number
Float	Handles a decimal number

You can, however, create your own custom datatype if your needs aren't covered by what eZ publish provides by default.

Content Class

A content class is made up of a collection of datatypes. It is similar to a table in a database. The class itself doesn't store any data, it simply defines the structure of the data to be stored.

eZ publish has a selection of inbuilt content classes that will cater for the majority of users' needed. As with datatypes, you can create your own.

The following table is an example of a custom news item Content Class:

Attribute	Datatype
Headline	Text line
Author	Text Line
Publication	Text Line
Photo	Image
Date	Date
Body	XML block

Object

An object is an instance of a content class, i.e. it contains the actual content. There can be multiple objects of the same content class, each with its own object ID.

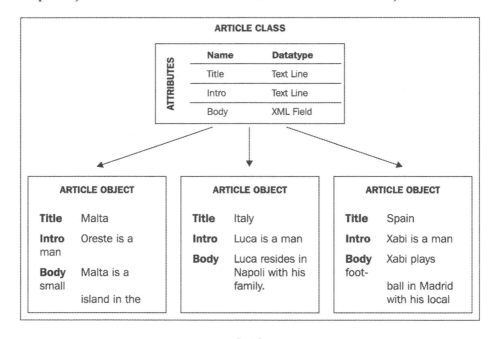

Attribute	Datatype	Object
Headline	Text line	Man Lands on the Moon
Author	Text Line	Lois Lane
Publication	Text Line	The Daily Planet
Photo	Image	
Date	Date	20th July, 1969
Body	XML block	American Neil Armstrong has become the first man to walk on the Moon. The astronaut stepped onto the Moon's surface, in the Sea of Tranquility, at 0256 GMT, nearly 20 minutes after first opening the hatch on the Eagle landing craft. Armstrong had earlier reported the lunar module's safe landing at 2017 GMT with the words: "Houston, Tranquility Base here. The Eagle has landed." As he put his left foot down first Armstrong declared: "That's one small step for man, one giant leap for mankind." He described the surface as being like powdered charcoal and the landing craft left a crater about a foot deep.

Versions

A commonly requested feature in content management systems is version control.

eZ publish provides this at the object level.

An individual object can have multiple versions. The current version of the object is called the "published" version. All other versions are called "drafts".

Each time the content of an object is modified, eZ publish creates a new version (draft) of the object. This means it's possible to see who made what changes to an object at any point in time.

Drafts can be created by different users. To access a previous version of an object, you make a copy of the old draft and publish it to make it the "published" version.

By default, eZ publish stores the previous 10 drafts of an object. If there are already 10 versions of an object, and a new one is created, the oldest draft is removed. You can increase the number of drafts stored via a configuration file.

Structuring Content

In eZ publish, content is structured using nodes and locations. Nodes are the tree structure that we normally would refer to as the site map. As there are times when we want to have a piece of content in more than one place in the site, an object can have multiple locations.

Nodes and Locations

The content structure in eZ publish is created by nodes. Each node represents a part of the site. A publish object is then associated with a node to be a part of the content structure.

E.g. Node ID 5 is associated with object ID 47.

This approach allows an object to be moved from one node to another without upsetting the site structure.

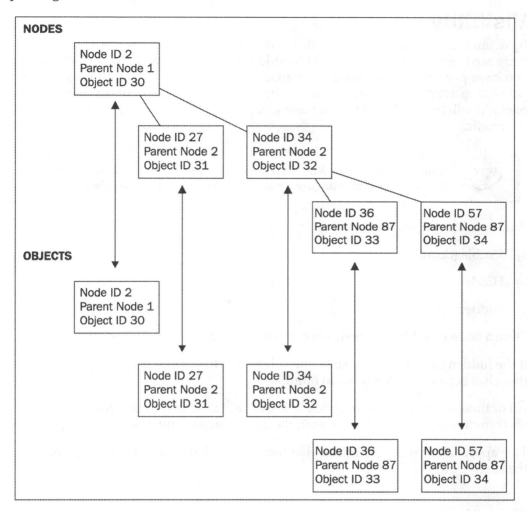

Locations

Objects can be associated with more than one node so that a particular object can appear in more than once place within the content structure. Each location is a combination of a node and an object.

For example, a particular object (in this case, a news item) can be found in the news section (presented by node ID 54) and in the press release section (represented by node ID 75).

The concept of locations provides a simple mechanism for content reuse.

Visibility

By default, an object associated with a node will be visible on the site. However, there are times that you might want to hide a node after it has been published, e.g. you have put up a press release but management have requested it be removed for political reasons. This is easily achieved by setting the node's status to "hidden". This means it will be visible in the administration section of the site but not visible to the public.

 Note: We are dealing with nodes, not the object. The node represents the site structure and changing what is visible or not is handled via the node.

A node has three visibility settings:

a) Visible (default)

b) Hidden

c) Hidden by superior

Once a node is hidden, all nodes beneath it in the tree are set as "hidden by superior".

If the hidden node is set to visible, then all its children become visible (unless one of them has been individually set to hidden).

All of these settings can be override in the `site.ini` configuration file. For instance, it's common to show hidden nodes in the administration interface.

This approach provides a high level of flexibility in hiding and displaying content on the site.

Sections

Nodes provide the tree structure of the site and define where an object is displayed. Sections provide the ability to then apply particular rules to a particular object regardless of where they appear in the node tree.

By assigning objects to sections, you can create groups of objects and apply individual rules to each group. E.g. you may choose to restrict access to all objects in a particular section unless the user has logged in or you may wish to apply a particular template to objects within a section so that they have a particular look and feel.

There are some rules:

- An object can only belong to one section.
- Section IDs can't be re-used or recycled.

A default eZ publish installation comes with the following sections:

- Standard (1)
- Users (2)
- Media (3)
- Setup (4)

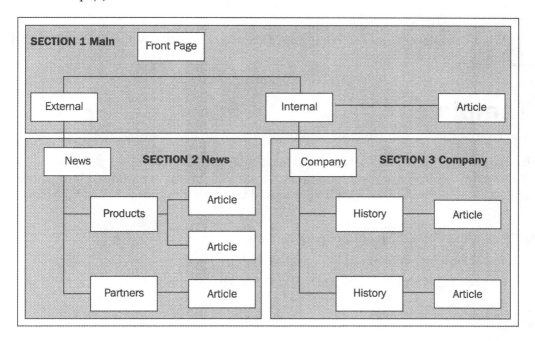

Assigning Sections

When a new object is created, its section ID will be the default section. When published, the object will inherit the section from its parent node and associated object.

In the case of objects that have multiple locations, (i.e. are associated with more than one node) the object will inherit the section ID of its parent node. This means if the section ID of the parent node is changed, then the child object section ID will also change.

Managing Sections

Even though sections are associated with objects, the administration interface allows you to manage sections at the node level. That means the object associated with the node inherits the section assigned to the node. This can be a little confusing when the relationship is with the actual object, but does make it easier to manage.

For instance, when the section of a node is changed, the section of the object that belongs to that node will be updated.

When the section of a node is changed, the section of all subsequent children of that node will also be changed.

 Note: As a section can apply rules for permissions and templates, removing a section can corrupt a site and should only be done with great care and consideration.

Templates

The template is the fundamental unit of site design in eZ publish.

It's basically a HTML file that contains logic to define how content is to be displayed. It's similar in concept to most template systems, e.g. Smarty templates. Or for those of you that use straight PHP coding, it would be a PHP file that contains HTML for display of content.

- All templates have the `.tpl` extention.
- A template contains HTML and eZ publish code.
- The HTML follows the XHTML 1.0 Transitional standard.

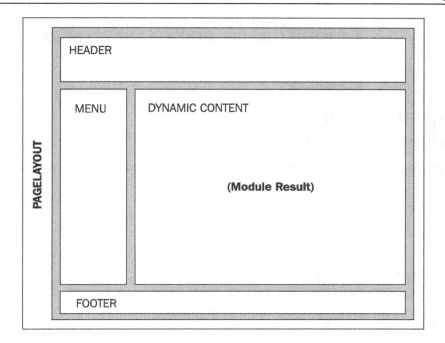

The eZ publish code follows their proprietary scripting language, which is quite similar to PHP in syntax. It's pretty much like most scripting languages and doesn't take much to learn.

eZ publish code makes it possible to get content from the database and perform logical functions, e.g. conditional statements (if/then) and looping (while/do).

Templates are combined to form the final HTML output. The main template is `pagelayout.tpl`, which contains the `html`, `head`, and `body` tags. It dictates the overall look of a site.

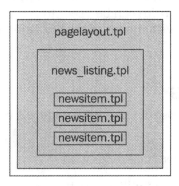

Each request to an eZ publish site will run the "view" of a module. In most cases, this will be the content module (more about modules later). The module will process the **pagelayout** template, which then in turn will process and include templates to then produce the final results, which will be returned to the user as flat HTML.

Template Code

All eZ publish code is contained in curly brackets {}.

The following is a simple example that will output a variable, in this case, the current time:

```
<h1>This is my title</h1>
<p>
    The current time is: {currentdate()|l10n( time )}
</p>
```

The resulting HTML would be:

```
<h1>This is my title</h1>
<p>
    The current time is: 12:14pm
</p>
```

View Templates

There are two main types of templates, node and system templates:

A node template is used when a node in the system is being viewed — i.e. a part of the site structure.

A system template is used when accessing functionality within the system.

The main differences between system and node templates are what variables you can access and what override rules can be used. In system templates, there will be specific variables associated with the functionality being used that you wouldn't access via a node template.

Node Templates

To access the content object associated with a node, eZ publish runs the "view" view of the "content" module.

E.g. `http://www.site.com/content/view/42`.

This is called a "system" URL and will access the content contained in the object associated with node no. 42.

If you are using virtual (friendly) URLs, then the system will automatically know which node.

E.g. `http://www.site.com/contact`

When a virtual URL is requested, the system will always return the full view mode.

Templates can be associated with the section or specific node; these are called override templates. The system will first look for an override template; if none exists for that particular section/node, then it will fall back to the default template.

When a node is requested and there are no matching template overrides, eZ publish will generate a page that is built up of the following elements:

Custom Node Templates

eZ publish has a default set of templates. Custom node templates are where you will commonly start to customize the display of content within the site. E.g. a node template can be applied to change the way news items are displayed on the site; this would most likely be called `news.tpl`.

A custom node is an override template and is triggered by the override system.

The override system can be configured to use particular templates depending on certain conditions, e.g. by node, by section, by content class.

$node

When the system uses a node template, the template has access to the `$node` variable.

`$node` is set by the system and contains an object that represents the requested node.

`$node` allows you to extract and display information about the specific node and content object associated with the node. This is how you access the actual information contained in the object.

Some common attributes of a node would be name, publication status, who created it, and who last modified it. E.g.:

`{$node.name|wash}`

This will get the name of the node and clean it (wash removes any characters that could affect the HTML).

You can also access all the attributes of the content object associated with the node.

E.g.:

```
{$node.object.data_map.address}
```

This command will return the content contained with the object attribute called "address".

System Templates

When eZ publish is not simply displaying content, it's performing some functionality and will use a system template.

There are default templates for all views of functionality provided by eZ publish. The default templates are located in the `templates` directory of the standard design.

A view typically uses a template that has the same name as the view. It will also be in a directory with the same name as that containing the module that the view belongs to.

E.g:

Name	Module/view (URL)	Template
Search interface	`/content/search`	`.../templates/content/search.tpl`
Login page	`/user/login`	`.../templates/user/login.tpl`
Shopping basket	`/shop/basket`	`.../templates/shop/basket.tpl`

Custom System Templates

As with custom node templates, you can create custom system templates to change what is displayed. E.g. the standard view of some search results contains the content class name as displayed in the following table:

Name	Type
Permission System	Article sub-page
OE 3.4: Fatal error	Bug
Wrapping in xmas paper	Bug
Wrapping event	Documentation page
Re: Image Duplicates	Forum message
Re: How do I contribute to documentation?	Forum message

You may wish to display more information and create a system template for a search that contains the creator and published date of the nodes returned. E.g.:

Name	Published	Author	Type
Permission System	13/03/2006 3:18 pm	Lukasz Serwatka	Article sub-page
OE 3.4: Fatal error	04/04/2005 4:17 pm	Björn Dieding@xrow.de	Bug
Wrapping in xmas paper	26/03/2003 10:04 pm	Terje D. Sætervik	Bug
Wrapping event	10/07/2003 10:15 am	Jo Henrik Endrerud	Documentation page
Re: Image Duplicates	12/04/2007 6:42 pm	Aristides Lamboglia	Forum message
Re: how to run script online without access to PHP	13/11/2006 11:54 pm	kracker	Forum message
Re: How do I contribute to documentation?	22/07/2006 8:03 am	kracker	Forum message

Usually, a custom system template will be a modified copy of the default template.

The automatic fallback system makes it possible to use a mixture of system templates (both custom and standard/default). This way you can create custom system templates only for the views that you need to modify and leave the rest as standard.

pagelayout.tpl

Pagelayout is the main template. It contains the html, head, and body tags and sets the overall looks of the site.

The following example is a basic pagelayout.tpl:

```
<!DOCTYPE html PUBLIC "-//W3C//DTD XHTML 1.0 Transitional//EN"
"http://www.w3.org/TR/xhtml1/DTD/xhtml1-transitional.dtd">
<html xmlns="http://www.w3.org/1999/xhtml" xml:lang="en" lang="en">
<head>
<style type="text/css">
    @import url({'stylesheets/common.css'|ezdesign});
</style>
{include uri='design:header.tpl'}
</head>
<body>
{$module_result.content}
</body></html>
```

Cascading Style Sheets

The pagelayout example makes use of a single stylesheet — `common.css`.

The command that imports the stylesheet refers to the correct design for the site and then accesses the file from the design directory. This makes sure you get the right stylesheet in case there is a stylesheet with the same name in the default design.

E.g. if the design name was `fedora` and the CSS file was `funky.css` the following output would be created:

```
@import url("/design/fedora/stylesheets/funky.css");
```

If the stylesheet specified doesn't exist, eZ publish will fall back to the stylesheets provided with the default design.

Module Result

In every request, eZ publish creates the array `module_result`. This is available only in the pagelayout template (i.e. not in any templates included within the pagelayout template).

It contains information about the module that was run, the view requests, and the output produced. The output is accessible in the content element of the array. E.g.:

```
{$module_result.content}
```

Template Override System

The beauty of the template system is that you only have to change the elements that you want to. If you're happy with the default templates, then all you need to do is create your own stylesheet to make it look how you want it to.

If you need to change the HTML produced, then you can create an override template that the system will use in place of the default template.

You can then decide under what conditions that template will be used. For example you could create an override template that is used for:

- All pages within a section
- A particular content class
- A particular node
- When a user has logged in

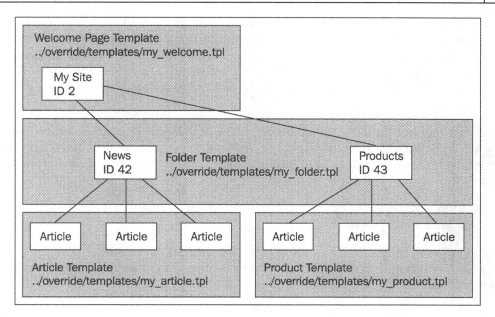

To get the system to use an override template, you create an `override.ini` configuration file and define the conditions for when that override template is to be used. E.g. if we want to use a particular template for all news items, we would include the following block in the `override.ini` file:

```
# Override for news items folders
[news]
Source=node/view/full.tpl
MatchFile=news.tpl
Subdir=templates
Match[class_identifier]=news
```

This override will then come into play every time a "news" content class is accessed. It will then use the `news.tpl` file in the override folder in the site design.

Designs

eZ publish comes with a standard design, just like it does with datatypes and templates. A design consists of templates, CSS files, non-content-related images, and font files. This dictates how your content will be presented.

At the simplest level, you can add your own CSS to change the way the site looks. If there are images you want to use in your CSS, then they go in the design directory. Finally, if the standard templates don't provide what you need, then you can add your own templates to override what eZ publish provides.

To create your own design, all you need to do is create a design directory and put in the templates, CSS, and images for your design and then update the siteaccess configuration file to include your design. The beauty of this approach is that you only have to add what you need to add and change. So, a unique design can consist of just a CSS file or you can go so far as to provide your own CSS, templates, and images.

Another benefit of the system is that you can have multiple designs and then define when the system uses which design. For instance, you might want to have two sites served from the one instance of eZ publish—then it's just a matter of setting the siteaccess to use the right design.

E.g. let's say you create a standard corporate site and also have an intranet that is accessed via a subdomain:

`http://www.site.com` will use the "corporate" design that exists in `/design/corporate`; `http://intranet.site.com`—will use the intranet design in `/design/intranet`.

Both sites can be managed via the one installation of eZ publish and can be managed via one administration interface.

Default Design

The default installation of eZ publish comes with two default designs, one for the front end and one for the administration interface. These are called:

- Admin
- Standard

The admin design contains all the CSS, templates, and images that make up the standard administration interface of eZ publish.

The standard design contains CSS and templates for a standard site display.

Like the default templates, these designs should never be changed, to make changes you create your own design directories and include whatever changes you want.

Design Structure

A typical design will contain the following subdirectories:

/fonts

This contains any font files that are used by the "texttoimage" template operator so that you can automatically generate images for navigation. As a rule of thumb, text-based navigation is a better way to design a site for numerous reasons: flexibility, speed of download, search engine friendliness, etc. But if your client insists on graphic-based navigation, the "texttoimage" template operator is very handy.

/images

This is for non-content images, i.e. images that make up the look and feel of the site but aren't a part of the content of the site and aren't entered via the administration interface. For example, a background image used across the top of the page would be stored in the images folder.

/overrides

This is where you store templates that are triggered by the override rules. E.g. if you wanted to have a news template that has an extra attribute such as "publication" you would create an override template called news.tpl and store it in the /overrides directory. Usually, you would copy the standard template used and then alter it rather than writing your own template from scratch.

/stylesheets

All stylesheets go in this folder; it's pretty straightforward. How exactly you structure your CSS is up to you but for some advice, check the *Implementation* chapter for one way to efficiently manage CSS files.

/templates

The main templates and custom templates go here. For many sites, you'll find a custom pagelayout.tpl in this folder.

siteaccess

The siteaccess is a directory that contains a number of configuration files (*.ini files). These ini files define which designs to use and in what order. This is where the override rules are placed in the override.ini file.

A siteaccess may use a number of designs for a single site.

When a page is rendered, the siteaccess defines which elements from which designs are to be combined to produce the end result. E.g. the default template is used in combination with a custom CSS and images to produce the page.

A siteaccess can use a combination of:

- One main design
- None or several additional designs
- One standard design

The `siteaccess` should have at least one main and one standard design. The standard design should always be set to the default design. When eZ publish looks for a specific design file, e.g. a CSS, but can't find it, it then will try to find it in any other designs that are defined in the siteaccess. The last port of call is the standard design, which is why it should always be in the `siteaccess`.

Access Control

eZ publish comes with a built-in permissions system that is similar to the users and groups systems that you find in a standard operating system. The flexibility and depth of the access control system means you have a great deal of control over who does what within the system, both on the front end e.g. for members accessing the site, and for providing different levels of administration, e.g. people that can add content to the entire site or just one section.

Like a normal user/group system, permissions are set and associated with a particular group; users are then assigned to a group and inherit those permissions. The control of permissions can be quite fine grained, but boils down to read, create, edit, and delete.

The access control system in eZ publish uses the following elements:

- Users
- User groups
- Policies
- Roles

A user is a valid user in the system.

A user group consists of users and can contain other user groups.

A policy is a rule that provides access to content or functionality.

A role is a collection of policies.

A role can be assigned directly to users or to user groups.

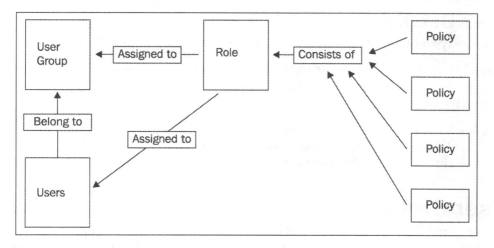

Users

A user is a special type of content object that contains information about the user and is associated with at least one group.

The default "User" class allows the storage of the following elements:

- First name
- Last name
- Email address
- Username
- Password

The last three elements are provided by the "User account" datatype.

User Account Datatype

The user account datatype is a special datatype that has special functionality within eZ publish. Any content classes that include the user account datatype will be considered valid users within the system.

When a user is created, it is enabled by default; however, you can disable the account via the administration interface. The account will still be in the system but the user won't be able to log in. This is particularly useful for editors who have worked on the site but have left the business—by disabling their account, all information regarding their activity is still in the system but that person no longer has access.

User Details

Like any content object, a user has a unique ID which is the same ID as the object.

This ID is used internally by eZ publish and other objects within the system. For instance, any content object created will contain the ID of the user who initially created the object.

This is why you shouldn't remove any users from the system, if you were to do so, then the details of the original user who created the object would be lost. It's much better to simply disable the account.

User Groups

A user group is also a content object that is associated with at least one node within the system. It can contain users and other user groups. E.g. you may have groups within groups. A good example is that you could have a user group called "Editors" then within that group you could have a number of groups that refer to different departments e.g. marketing, engineering, etc.

Editors

    Marketing

        Mary Pickford

        John Kotminas

    Engineering

        Dilbert Derbet

        Scott Young

This approach enables you to assign the same permissions to all editors and then provide different permissions for each department.

Policies

Policies are the rules that provide access to one or more functions of a module.

A policy consists of the following:

- Module name
- Function name
- Function limitation

For example if you want to provide access to an editor to view all content in the system, the policy would look like this:

Module	Function	Limitation
Content	All functions	No limitations

Or if you wanted editors to add files, but only in the media library, the policy would look like this:

Module	Function	Limitation
Content	Create	Class (file), Section (Media Library)

If you wanted to create a user who can access the membership area of a website, the policy would look like this:

Module	Function	Limitation
Content	Read	Section (Members)

Functions

Modules can have different functions; these functions are assigned to the module's views. A policy that provides access to a module's function can be restricted by one or more function limitations. e.g. the content module has the following functions—read / create / edit / delete / move.

This means you can have one group of users who are able to create and edit content but are not able to delete it.

Here are some further examples of function limitations:

Class

Limits the function to particular types of objects, e.g. file, image, news item.

Node

Limits the function to a particular part of the site.

Owner

Limits the function to the user who created the object.

Section

Limits the function to objects within a certain section (this is a common way to create a members-only area; you create a member user and then give them read access to this section).

Roles

So, we have a user that's made up of the user account datatype that belongs to a user group. Then, we define policies that we want to assign to a particular user or user group. These policies when combined are called a role. The role is assigned to the user group or specific user.

However, just to complicate matters, a role can have limitations of its own. For instance, a normal editor role would have the ability to read, create, and delete all content. But you might want to restrict some editors to one part of the system only. E.g. the marketing users are only allowed to add content to the marketing section. Rather than put that in the policy, you have a standard editor policy and then create another role to apply to the marketing group within editors that restricts them to the marketing section only.

 Note: You need to remember that role limitations will override the limitations of the role's policies. This means if the policy has no limitations (like the editor policies) then the role limitation will take precedence.

Typical role limitations are to a particular section or subtree.

Workflow

eZ publish contains a workflow system that allows you to create a process of functions with or without user intervention. E.g. you might want to make sure an article is approved before it is published, or you might want to confirm an order before making the financial transaction.

The way workflow works in eZ publish is built around events and triggers.

```
                    ┌──────────┐
                    │          │
                    │ Trigger  │
                    │          │
                    └──────────┘
                        │
                    ┌───────┐
                    │Starts │
                    └───────┘
                        ▼
                    ┌──────────┐
                    │          │
                    │ Workflow │
                    │          │
                    └──────────┘
                     ╱        ╲
            ┌────────────┐  ┌────────────┐
            │ Consists of│  │ Consists of│
            └────────────┘  └────────────┘
             ╱                          ╲
    ┌──────────┐                  ┌──────────┐
    │          │                  │          │
    │ Workflow │                  │ Workflow │
    │          │                  │          │
    └──────────┘                  └──────────┘
```

A combination of events then creates a workflow. A workflow can be stand-alone or belong to a group. Through this layering approach, you can create fairly complex workflows, but the more complex, the more problems can occur.

Firstly, the more complex a process, the more rigid it is and the less flexibility there is for work around. Unless the process is well-defined and understood, it can be perceived by users as a hindrance and barrier to getting their work done.

Secondly, the workflow system within eZ publish is not perfect; it has its bugs that have caused frustrations for a number of developers. That's not to say you should avoid it, but proceed with caution and check the forums for any information you can glean to help you avoid the frustrations others have already discovered (which goes for pretty much every part of eZ publish; but workflow seems to have proved to be the most troublesome).

Another note about workflows: in many projects, clients will request a workflow in the belief that it's necessary to achieve what they are after. This perception is not always true. There is quite a bit of debate over the use of workflows and how important they are. In fact, some prominent people in the content management industry have gone so far as to state that workflows are overrated and often not necessary.

"While workflow is a key component of content management systems (CMS), the unspoken truth is that workflow often fails (or is only moderately successful) in most organisations." James Roberston, Step Two (`http://www.steptwo.com.au/papers/cmb_noworkflow/index.html`).

From my experience in implementing over 30 eZ publish sites, workflow is rarely needed unless there is a specific business process that has to be flowed. Rarely is the business process well enough defined to be automated and attempts to do so can cause more problems that they can solve. That's not to say workflow doesn't have its place but before embarking on adding a workflow, you need to carefully examine if it's really needed and will add value to the system.

Events

An event is the smallest part of a workflow. It carries out a specific task.

eZ publish contains a range of events that can be used for everyday tasks. You can of course, create your own events for special needs — these have to be programmed directly in PHP. Some common events are:

- Wait until date
- Approve

A Workflow

A workflow is a collection of events that are executed in a set order when the workflow is running.

Workflows are contained within groups but the group has no special importance other than to provide a place for the workflows (a bit like a directory in a file system).

To start a workflow, you need a trigger. Then the events within the workflow are executed one by one. However, within the workflow there might be the need for another trigger to continue to the next event. These "internal" triggers are called a "multiplexer event.

Workflows are started by a trigger. There can be more than one trigger, for instance, a workflow can contain a trigger within it.

To summarize:

- A *workflow* is a collection of events — an ordered sequence of actions that will be executed when the workflow is running.
- Workflows can be placed in different groups. A *workflow group* is nothing more than a collection of workflows.
- A workflow is initiated by a *trigger*.
- The multiplexer event allows triggers within a workflow.
- A trigger is associated with a function of a module. It will start the specified workflow either before or after that the function has completed.

Standard Triggers

A trigger is associated with the function of a module — e.g. sending a piece of content for publishing. It starts the workflow either before the function starts or after it has been completed. Here's a list of standard triggers:

ID	Module	Function	Connection type
1	content	publish	before
2	content	publish	after
3	shop	confirmorder	before

The first trigger will cause an event to be performed before a piece of content is published, e.g. you would use this to implement an approval process before content is visible on the site.

Standard Events

As mentioned previously, there are a number of standard triggers in the system.

Approve

Allows you to have the contents of objects be approved by an editor.

Multiplexer

Starts other workflows from within a workflow.

Payment gateway

A generic solution for handling payment redirections to a payment gateway (note: there are a number of existing extensions for payment gateways that you can download from the eZ Systems website).

Simple shipping

Adds shipping costs to orders.

Wait until date

Will delay the publishing of content until a particular date for scheduled publishing.

Extensions

There is an incredible amount that you can do with the features contained within eZ publish but there are times when there's a specific feature that you require.

eZ publish allows you to create your own modules to extend the system to meet your specific needs. It does this through the extension system that allows you to program the functionality you need, and then incorporate it into the rest of the system.

Before you embark on creating an extension, you should see if someone has done the work for you; no need to reinvent the wheel! There are many extensions that have already been created and contributed to the community; chances are you can find something that will suit your needs or that you can use as a starting point, e.g. there are a number of payment gateways that have been built that you can install, others include import/export functions, workflows, datatype plugins, etc. The other thing to consider is whether the functionality you are after is on the road map for the next release.

eZ publish is constantly being extended and enhanced with new functionality. If you check what's due to be included in the next release, you might find the functionality you are after is being worked on and by waiting, you won't need to do the work yourself.

However, if you can't find what you need, then you'll have to create your own extension.

An extension is proprietary code that is stored in an extensions folder and accessed by the system as a module with views that you create.

To do this, you need to do the following steps:

1. Create the extension base directory.
2. Create the directories of extension.
3. Define the configuration file(s) of extension.
4. Initialize the extension in site.ini for every or single site access.
5. Develop the extension.
   - Create templates.
   - Create PHP files, etc.

There's quite a lot of detail that goes into creating an extension that is beyond the scope of this overview. To learn more, check the eZ Systems site for detailed documentation on creating extensions.

Creating an extension is not a trivial task; if you've never used eZ publish before, you'll want to take your time to understand how the system works in depth before attempting to create an extension. Typically, it takes a few months of working with eZ publish to get a good understanding of it, then you can start to look at creating extensions of your own.

Summary

In this chapter, we saw an overview of how Ez publish is structured and its key elements that are used in most projects.

Defining an eZ Publish Project

Planning an eZ publish project is more than just getting a set of requirements and working out timings for drafting the specification and implementation. There is a lot of information that is vitally important to the shaping of the project that isn't captured in requirements. What this chapter does is firstly explains requirements and then shows how to plan your project through a project brief and planning workshop. It also covers how to deal with estimations and the issues that arise at this point of the project.

Requirements

What are requirements? Put simply, they are a statement of what the client wants the project to deliver. However, they should be considered a wish list of what the client would like, as opposed to what the project is to deliver. The main mistakes made with requirements are assuming that they are complete and correct. Requirements are not always an accurate representation of what the client is after. That's not because the person who wrote them got it wrong but because the person providing the requirement hasn't communicated it accurately. Sometimes people think they know what they want but don't realize until they see the finished product that it doesn't work or make sense.

It's hard to manage a project without a clear idea of what the end result is supposed to be. That's what requirements are for, to define what the end result is supposed to be, and why. Requirements provide the basis on which subsequent decisions are made, so if there is a flaw in the requirements, it's highly likely the end result will be flawed. But making requirements flawless is a task fraught with difficulties on many levels. Getting it right and having that translate in to a successful result is so risky that Fred Brooks (Mythical Man Month) suggests we plan to throw the first result away, not something most clients want to hear. Maybe the answer isn't getting the requirements perfect, but reducing the potential for errors by understanding where the risks lie.

Capturing the Vision

First and foremost, requirements should capture the vision of what the client hopes to get out of the end result. Being able to capture and communicate any vision, let alone a complex project, is a difficult task and requires great skill.

In writing requirements, the author has to consider many aspects of the project. The expectations of what the project will deliver, the audience, business processes that the solution will have to work with (if they exist), any business or technical constraints—for example, the system must be able to support x number of transactions a day, it must be able to import data from an existing system, etc.—basically, everything and anything to do with the project. The author has to distil all of this into a single concise meaningful document—no mean feat.

Why Are We Doing This?

Capturing the overall vision gives us the high-level view of what we are trying to achieve. The next step is defining why we are doing this, what the objective of the project is.

When writing requirements, an author is generally faced with one of following three situations:

1. The client doesn't really know what they want or why.
2. The client can't agree on what they want.
3. The business hasn't yet established what is it they are after in detail, nor have they established a clear business case.

In the first situation, a project is envisioned but nobody has really thought through the details of why they are doing this. It seems absurd that a business would embark on a project without really knowing why they are doing it, but it happens all the time. It might seem like a good idea, born of internal political or market pressure but there is something fundamental missing. To work out if this is the case, all you need to do is ask a couple of simple questions like: "Why are we doing this" or "What exactly do you expect to achieve from this project?"

If you can't get a clear and concise answer, then it's probably a good idea to stop and get an answer. If you don't, down the track during the midst of the project, you're going to be faced with difficult questions that are hard to answer because it's not clear what the project is all about. For example, if the objective of your project is to get more people to fill out a survey, a requirement such as "let the user save results and complete at a later date" is pretty important as opposed to "provide an administration facility to produce reports on survey results". Both requirements are something the business would value, but both cost money and making a decision on which to include comes back to the objective of the project.

In the second case, the client has a good idea of what they want and why they want it. The problem is that in most cases, there is more than one person who has a say in the project's objective and they don't all agree, i.e. you don't have consensus.

For the project manager who is trying to achieve a meaningful result, not having consensus is a very dangerous and political situation. It may seem that you have a mandate to build the project but the reality is that within the business, some people don't agree and will either deliberately or subconsciously try to sabotage the project by not providing information when required, picking holes in the project, and generally being uncooperative. The risk here is that although the end result might actually fulfil the requirements, the client is not happy because people within the business have different expectations of what the project is supposed to achieve. It's a no-win situation. The key is to get that consensus upfront.

In the final case, the objective of the project changes during development. It's often the case that when a project starts, there is an objective in mind but down the track, when the client sees the result, they realize that their vision was flawed (see *Theory versus Reality*). It happens all the time and it's just a part of life. Sometimes we think it's going to work out a particular way and it just doesn't pan out. It's human nature and a part of software development; there's no such thing as perfect design. But when the client doesn't read and review requirements properly because they don't want to have to think about what it is they really want (and don't hold this against the business, knowing what you want is not easy) then you can pretty much guarantee that whatever you build will need rework as the client actually comes to terms with what they asked for. Once again, it's a part of human nature to procrastinate and not deal with things unless you have to. Thinking about what you want upfront is much harder than seeing the project come to life and realizing it's not quite right—it's easy to avoid thinking about requirements; it's much harder to avoid problems when you've got a launch date two weeks away!

In the ideal world, the business people know what they want, why they want it, and what they expect to achieve from it. In the real world, it's nowhere near that straightforward and even with the best of intentions, requirements can prove to be flawed. Getting perfect requirements is not the main priority, understanding how to manage imperfect requirements is far more useful. Realizing that we live in an imperfect world is important so that we don't fall into the trap of thinking that we have got everything right upfront. That's why we need to have measures in place to qualify requirements (which is covered later in the chapter) through techniques such as defining success and defining quality, which often will put the requirements in a more realistic light and bring a pragmatic approach to the project.

Theory versus Reality

Even with the very best intentions, a clear objective, full agreement, and rigorous testing and analysis of the requirements, sometimes things still go wrong. It's the dilemma of theory versus reality. We have a theory that a particular approach will achieve a particular result, we think it through, define the approach in a set of requirements and go ahead and build it. Then we test it on the audience and find out it doesn't quite work out as we expect. It happens all the time in many industries, e.g. TV shows, films, marketing, product development. How many times has a huge Hollywood blockbuster been hyped up and still ends up flopping at the box office? No doubt, a lot of thought and effort was put into creating the movie and it was probably even put through test viewings and rework — but still it flops even with all that work.

Software development is no different; we are producing something new and even with the best requirements, functional and usability testing, it can still turn out not achieve the original objective. It happens so often that Fred Brooks (Mythical Man Month) declared that we should plan to throw the first one away. It would be wonderful to be able to tell the business that "we've got the requirements and will build your project but when you get it, you'll have to throw it away and pay for us to build another one", but I can't see it going down too well. As, to quote Fred Brooks again, there is no silver bullet, all we can do is as much as we can to minimize the risk of things not working out as expected. The first step of which is to ensure the requirements are as realistic as possible.

Formats

Requirements come in all shapes and sizes: the written word, visual prototypes, or simply ideas in someone's head. In essence, a requirements document should contain a series of statements about what the end system has to achieve. Sometimes, this includes diagrams, flowcharts, uses cases, etc. but it's not mandatory. There is no perfect way to capture requirements.

There is no consensus in the industry on how best to capture requirements or even consensus within particular methods. Depending on the nature of the project and the nature of the client, one method might be more appropriate than another. The key is to make sure that it captures the vision as effectively as possible; in some cases the written word might be effective, in other cases, diagrams, pictures, flowcharts. etc. might be necessary to convey the vision. The key is to make sure everyone is on the same page and agrees on the content. How to go about it comes down to what works best for you and the client.

The Author

More often than not, writing requirements is the job of a single person. This is both a good and a bad thing. On the plus side, a single author promotes consistency, which is important. On the minus side, if the author is not good at capturing requirements you'll end up with consistently bad requirements. Then there is the question of whether the author is internal or external, i.e. is (s)he a part of the business or is (s)he a part of the software development team (e.g. a business analyst)? Once again, there are pros and cons associated with both situations. If the author is internal, they are likely to have a better understanding of the business so the requirements will be better informed from that perspective; however, the author might have a particular bias, which will be translated to the requirements. The key is not so much whether the author is one person, a team, internal, or external but whether the right person/ team is doing the job. Like almost everything in software development, it comes down to having the right person for the job.

Interpretation

In the study of law, one of the first things taught is statutory interpretation. This is a set of rules used to interpret legislation. The reason these rules exist is that the written language is not precise and can be interpreted in different ways. The "true" meaning of a piece of legislation, or a poem or even a painting is open to interpretation. The same applies to requirements. The client and author may have the same interpretation of a particular requirement and be in total agreement. Then, it is given to a developer who has their own interpretation and the end result turns out very different to what the client expected.

Get ten people in a row, give the first person a piece of paper with a sentence on it and get them to whisper it to the next person and so on down the line until the last person writes down what they were told. You can almost guarantee it will be different to what you started with. With requirements, there's the client who conveys what they want to the author, who interprets it into the requirements document, which is then interpreted by the project manager and the architect before being given to the developer who then converts the requirement to working code, which is then tested by a tester who interprets what the developer has produced against their reading of the requirements. Given the number of ways a requirement can be interpreted and how many people are involved, it's all too easy for things to go astray.

There are some simple techniques that can help to reduce the potential margin for error in interpretation. An effective technique is to create a glossary of definitions (you'll notice that the start of any contract or piece of legislation is a set of definitions). This helps to ensure everyone is talking about the same thing. You'd be surprised how often a word can mean different things to different people at different times! Another useful approach is to use consistent language — that of the client — use the words they use to describe something and make developers use the same terms, e.g. if the client calls customers passengers, use the term passengers, not customers!

Knowing How Much Detail to Capture

Avoid requirements at your own peril. You would not build a house without a set of plans; software is the same. However, there is a point where you can spend too much time defining things and never actually produce anything. The key to requirements is to define what the end result is supposed to be, and not work down everything to every last detail; that should be left for the specification. Remember requirements are about what the solution is to deliver, not how it is to be done.

The Last Word

Writing requirements is a daunting and dangerous task. Without them, a project is almost guaranteed to fail or end up taking far more time and money to produce than it needs to. With them, there's still the risk of the end result being wrong or flawed.

Project Brief

To start an eZ publish project means getting an understanding of what the client really wants. Basically, you need to draft a project brief. Although a project brief should be a straightforward document of only a few pages, it can be difficult to get it right.

A project brief contains the following elements:

- Organizational and Project Purpose
- Project Objectives
- Target Market

Organizational Purpose

The first thing to capture is what the purpose of the organization is. This is not for your benefit or the organization's but rather for the people working on the project that will be designing and developing the solution. The more they understand the organization, the better they will be able to design solutions.

The questions to ask are:

- What is the organization about?
- What do they do?
- What do they hope to achieve?

The final question here is very important; expectations are what can cause projects to fail. Unless they are stated and captured, they may only surface later in the project when management reviews the prototype and notices something is missing—by which point, it's going to be expensive and difficult to implement.

Project Purpose

There are many documents that can be pointed at when asking for the purpose of a project. These include documents such as a business case or requirements. However, often these documents are long and contain many details. What they lack is what a project purpose really is i.e.:

A clear, concise and measureable statement of the business outcomes the project is supposed to achieve.

This sounds simple but in reality is very difficult to write, and even more difficult to get everyone to agree to. It's more than what the organization hopes to get out of the project as it defines the specific outcomes to be achieved. Put simply, this tells you if you have succeeded or not. The expectations of what the organization hopes to achieve versus the concrete outcomes to be delivered.

A simple project purpose would be:

- Improve our ability to manage the annual survey
- Increase overall response rates for the survey
- Improve the quality of data gathered

This is a clear project purpose, we know what we need to deliver: an online survey. We also know what the organization expects from this survey: increased response rates.

This is where you want to start to manage expectations. In this case, creating an online version of the survey to improve management can be done with eZ publish and delivered successfully. That's straightforward. The second outcome is not so simple.

Just because the online survey works, doesn't mean it will increase response rates. That would require a campaign, to create awareness and make sure survey respondents know they can fill out the survey online. This is where you would want to argue that the second outcome is not within the scope of the development project and would be the responsibility of the organization itself. By managing expectations at this point, you can save a lot of time and grief.

In worst situations, the project may never get off the ground because there is no clear project purpose, and that's a good thing. Starting without a clear purpose will only make things harder, later down the track. You'll have nothing to refer back to when trying to prove the project was a success. It also comes into play during the design and specification phases. If a dogmatic debate arises over a particular aspect of the visual design, we can point to the project purpose and ask if it will help achieve the outcome. E.g., will it help improve the quality of data gathered or not; if the answer is yes, the design feature stays, if not, it goes.

Project Objectives

The project purpose contains the outcomes which are what the project will achieve for the organization. The way the outcome will be achieved is through delivering a number of objectives. Outcomes refer to the business benefits; objectives refer to how the project will achieve the outcomes. This will be covered further but the sequence is:

Objective   >   Output   >   Outcome

So, we have started with a purpose and outcomes; now we have to go back to the specific objectives for the project. E.g., for a standard e-commerce site, the objectives would be:

- To reliably capture orders and accept payments online
- To maximize the value of each transaction by on-selling and up-selling where appropriate
- To capture customer details for regular e-marketing and export purposes
- To appropriately communicate the brand personality/look and feel

This would lead to the business outcomes captured in the project purpose of increasing revenue.

Target Market

An important part of every project is understanding the audience. Ultimately, who will be using the site?

The questions we need to ask include:

- Who are we talking to?
- Primary, secondary, tertiary target markets:
    ◦ E.g. Graduate Careers Australia
    ◦ Primary Market—Students
    ◦ Secondary Market—Employers
    ◦ Tertiary Market—Careers Services

The reason we need to know this is so that during the design phase the specific needs of the audience are considered. For instance, an intranet has a very different audience to a corporate website. Knowing the target audience and that there may be more than one audience will help to shape the different elements of design appropriately.

Project Brief—The White Angel Foundation

This section summarizes our understanding of your business and your website goals and objectives.

The Organizational Purpose

"The Foundation is a community based charitable organization that supports eating disorder sufferers and their carers through direct financial relief, advocacy and lobbying, awareness campaigns, health promotion and early intervention work, and professional training in primary and secondary schools."

The Project Purpose

Three years after the launch of the original website, there is a need for the site to be reviewed and extended. The purpose of this project is to rebuild the White Angel Foundation website in order to:

- Refresh the design
- Improve the quality and structure of content
- Increase revenue through online shopping and donations

The core purpose of the website is to become the primary point of information for people interested in seeking information on eating disorders in Australia. The secondary purpose is to increase revenue through sales and donations.

The Project Objectives

The website should be a dynamic communication tool and achieve the following objectives:

- Promote positive body image
- Encourage hope and help seeking through stories and case studies
- Provide an information channel for sufferers of eating disorders
- Provide information to carers and families of sufferers
- Generate revenue through online sale of merchandise
- Generate revenue through an online donation facility
- Improve efficiency through selling tickets to events online

The Target Market

The target markets for the White Angel Foundation website are:

- Sufferers of eating disorders
- Community sector organizations and groups
- Media
- Donors and partners

Planning Workshop

The project brief gives us a high level-view of the project but doesn't give us the real information that we need to manage a project. There is a lot beneath the surface that needs to be exposed so that we truly understand what matters to the client. We do this by conducting a planning workshop. This planning workshop is based on the Rapid Planning Workshop created by Rob Thomsett (http://www.thomsett.com.au) and adjusted for content management projects.

The objectives of the planning workshop are as follows:

- Define success
- Determine Project Scope and Objectives
- Define objectives, outputs, and outcomes
- Define quality

Success

It may seem strange to define success. You'd think that delivering what the client wants on time and on budget would be considered success and it would, but there are other ways to achieve a successful outcome. Each client will have their own idea of success. One client may be willing to sacrifice features for a quicker delivery, another may be happy to extend the timeline to add in additional features. In both cases, the client gets what they want and the project is considered a success. In both cases, the project did not deliver on time, on budget with agreed functionality. This is where we need to start thinking outside the square.

The reality is that only 34% of projects are delivered on time and on budget (Standish Group Chaos Report, 2006); that's one in three! So the chances are your project is likely to run into problems of one type or another. That's just the way it is; even the best teams will run into trouble on projects, not because of their efforts but because of the clients changing their minds. Trying to fight this is foolish; the wise move is to establish upfront what success means to your client for their project. Once you understand that, you have something to work with, should issues arise during the project, or should I say when…

Success Factors

Working out what success means to your client for their project is a broad subject. Using the following success factors as a guide will make it easier for you to get a sense of what really matters to your client. It does become slightly more difficult when you have more than one client but I'll deal with that later.

The main success factors are listed below. They have been selected to deal with the obvious elements of the project, e.g. budget and timeline, as well as some of the less obvious factors such as quality and team satisfaction.

- Have satisfied stakeholders
- Meet the project's objectives/requirements
- Meet an agreed budget
- Deliver on time
- Add value
- Meet quality requirements
- Sense of professional satisfaction for the team

Stakeholder Satisfaction

In many projects, there are a number of people who have a vested interest. Chances are your client will represent another management that they have to report to. There may be several departments involved in the project. On a recent project, although I only had one direct contact, that contact had to report to eight different stakeholders which meant every decision had to be considered in light of the eight stakeholders' view points. Clearly, a time consuming task.

The important question is not what the stakeholders think but does it matter? Although there might be several stakeholders, do we need to take into account everyone's view?

Some stakeholders may be involved purely for political reasons and don't really matter when it comes to the project. So, the question here is do we have to make ALL of the stakeholders happy? That is, will the project still be considered a success if we make most, but not all of the stakeholders happy? If so, which stakeholders do we have to make sure we look after?

Another point to consider here is that it might not actually be possible to make all of the stakeholders happy; some may have opposing views. Some may simply be throwing their weight around because they can. If you are an external consultant then the internal politics aren't as important and you can focus on making the key stakeholders happy and not worrying about others. However, if you are managing an internal project, it might not be wise to upset stakeholders that you might need to deal with at a later date. The need for diplomacy is important, and the political landscape can have a large impact on how easy or difficult it will be to deliver the project.

These are the games that can be played in corporate situations that we want to avoid. It may be totally unrealistic to make all of the stakeholders happy. It may only matter to make one stakeholder happy, the one that is paying for the project; or perhaps it's the CEO. What matters is that you know who really matters.

These are difficult questions to ask, but they are very important and will make a difference to how you run the project and who's view point matters. In summary, the questions you want to ask are:

- Do all the stakeholders have to be happy?
- Is this actually possible?
- If not which ones?
- What are the risks of not making all the stakeholders happy?

Naturally, the answers to these questions and how you deal with them will differ depending on whether you are an external consultant or an internal project manager. For internal project managers, the long term impact of decisions made on this project need to be considered.

Meeting Project Objectives

Also stated in the Chaos Report quoted earlier was the staggering statistic that 45% of features built were never used and that only 20% of features were used often or always. That means that more than half of the work done on the project was for little benefit. It stands to reason then that for your project, there will be features that the client has requested that aren't going to be used. Of course, the difficult question to answer is which features they are. At this point, that's not the important question. At this point, the question that matters is whether everything in the requirements has to be delivered. If not, then you can use this later in the project to cut scope if you need to or trade a new feature for an original feature to keep the project on track. Many clients will ask for everything they can think of; that doesn't mean the project actually needs to deliver everything for the project to be considered a success. What's important here is for your client to appreciate that chances are, not everything they have asked for will be delivered. If you can achieve this, then you have a much greater chance of success.

In summary, the questions you want to ask are:

- Do we have to deliver everything in the requirements?
- If not which ones?
- What happens if we don't?
- What features *really* matter?

Although this is a very pragmatic view of which objectives are important, it's not always that easy for an internal project manager to be so clinical. The politics of internal organizations can color the decision-making process. In this case, the stakeholders are the clients and it's important to keep them happy. But, in reality, you can't always please everyone. Getting the stakeholders to make the decision can be a more effective political approach to shaping the project for success.

Meeting an Agreed Budget

From a sales perspective, the first thing you want to know is if the client has a budget and what the budget is. If you have a set budget, the goal is to work out what you can deliver for that budget and make the client happy that they got a good deal. However, there are times when the budget isn't large enough for the features required. If that's the case, then there are only two options:

1. Increase budget
2. Cut scope

Note, there really are only two options; getting people to work more hours is actually increasing the budget but hiding it in overtime. The question of budget is probably the most important. If you can't shift the budget, then you go back to the previous success factor—meeting project objectives and ask the client what they are willing to sacrifice to stay within budget. It can be quite confronting to ask such questions and could put both you and your and client in an awkward position. I make no apologies for this; effective project management is a difficult task. It's much better to deal with these issues upfront than later down the track when the client insists on all features within budget when it's not possible without you losing money on the job. In any project, there are three variables that can be adjusted: scope, timing, and budget. You need to know which of these are most important to the client and which ones you can move on.

In regards to budget, the questions you want to ask are:

- Is there a set budget?
- What happens if we go over budget?
- If we can't go over budget is there anything we can cut from the scope?

Delivering On Time

The last of the variables is time. Apparently, time heals all wounds; but it can cause havoc on a project if not managed appropriately. What you need to know is firstly, if there is a deadline, and by deadline I mean a hard deadline, not one that has arbitrarily been chosen by the client because they would like it by that time. If there is a deadline, the next question is whether the deadline is a soft or hard deadline. In reality, there is no such thing as a hard deadline; what you're looking for here is whether the deadline has dependencies that will cause issues if it's not met. E.g., the launch of the new website has already been announced to the media. That's sort of difficult to get around; not impossible but potentially embarrassing for your client.

So, first we need to establish if there is a deadline, second if it's fixed. If the deadline is fixed, you can then go back to the previous success factors to see if the client is willing to budge on what features are delivered or if they are willing to adjust the budget to get more resources onboard.

The idea here is to reinforce to the client that they might not be able to get everything on time and on budget and because of that they may need to make some compromises. What you are trying to work out is where your client is willing to compromise; what matters to them most, is it features, budget, or time? Having all the features is not an issue if the client is willing to increase the budget or timeline. Meeting a fixed deadline is fine if you can cut the number of features being delivered. The key here is understanding what matters most to the client.

 Note: If the client is not willing to compromise at all, the project risk will increase; the odds are that only 16% of projects will be delivered on time, on budget with agreed functionality. The question is whether you feel confident enough that your project will fall into that 16%.

In summary, the questions you want to ask are:

- Is there a deadline?
- Is the deadline fixed?
- If the deadline is fixed, is there anything in the scope we can cut?
- What happens if we don't meet the deadline?

Adding Value

So far, we have talked about the obvious elements of projects; adding value to the business isn't as obvious. We may not have even asked this question of the client and they may not have asked it of themselves. It may be the case that someone higher up has dictated that the project goes ahead, the reasons for which are not fully understood. And it may not matter; what you need to know is if that's the case. What this means is that you need to understand if the project actually has to add value to the business i.e. achieve a particular outcome for the business. If so, what happens if the outcome is not delivered? Will that cause a significant problem? E.g., loss of revenue? In the case of content management projects, the success of the project is dependent on the people that manage the content; if they aren't appropriately trained and capable of managing the content, it will affect the business outcomes. Perhaps it doesn't matter for this particular project as it's a political project or a trial project, but if it does matter, you need to know so that you can put appropriate measures in place—such as training, to make sure the project adds the value expected. It's a fundamental part of projects that is easily missed in the details of the project.

The key questions to ask are:

- Will the project deliver value to the business?
- Does this matter?
- If not, what is the reason for the project?

Meeting Quality Requirements

Quality can seem like an intangible aspect of a project; what's quality to one person is mediocre to another. That's fine; the goal is to understand what your client considers to be quality and how much it matters to them. For instance, you may be able to deliver the project on time but without ensuring cross-browser compatibility. This is something that I consider to be important; your client may not care if it works in the most popular browsers. Meeting minimum accessibility standards may be considered a mandatory feature, or not, depending on what matters to your client. That's what needs to be established; is there a standard that has to be reached and in a worse case scenario, what would happen if it wasn't reached? Would the client be open to legal action or potentially lose revenue? Knowing the quality requirements will help you to shape the features, budget, and timeline to ensure the project is a success.

The key questions to ask are:

- Is there a standard we have to reach?
- What is that standard?
- Does it matter if we don't reach it?

Team Satisfaction

The idea of team satisfaction is something that is rarely raised. Why would the client care if the team is satisfied? Isn't the goal to make sure the client is satisfied? Well, yes, but if the team is not happy, then it makes it much harder to deliver. A recent study rated "trust" as the most important factor in successful technical teams. If your team is not happy and don't trust each other, it's going to be a hell of a lot harder to deliver what the client wants. It's also important for the client to understand that they have a vested interest in keeping the team happy because it will mean better results for them. If they don't care about the team, then what happens after the project is delivered and there's a need for maintenance and support? How supportive are the team likely to be if they were pushed to work long hours to deliver in the first place and got no appreciation for that? Every time I've posed this question to a client, they have changed their viewpoint from not caring to making it one of the success factors of the project.

The questions to ask your client are:

- Do we care about the team?
- Do we mind if they have to work long hours?
- Do we mind if they aren't happy with the result?
- Will we need team members for ongoing support?

Success Sliders

Now that we know what all the success factors are, we need to get the client to rate them. It's an arbitrary rating system designed to establish the relative importance of each factor. What you need to do is: for each success factor find out how important it is on a scale of one to four. (Note: we use 1 to 4 so that we don't have a whole stack of features in the middle; if we used 1 to 5, it would be too easy for clients to pick the middle option, this way, they have to decide which side of the line the success factor sits.)

The following is an example outcome for success factors:

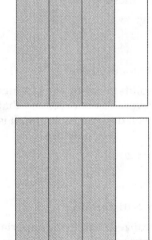

Have Satisfied Stakeholders

There are a number of stakeholders involved from the management team; the board in Sydney and Melbourne are major contributors. All up there are 4 key stakeholders to be considered. The Melbourne stakeholders have more sway than Sydney so should be considered first.

Rating: 3

Meet the Projects Objectives

There is a core level of functionality that is required to make the solution delivered worthwhile but there are some areas that might not be absolutely necessary from day one.

Rating: 3

Meet the Budget

Given the project has had to raise significant funding and withstand political pressure to make this a commercial project, there is no room to move on the budget.

Rating: 4

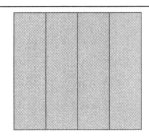

Deliver on Time

The initial deadline was March this year but due to funding issues, this was not possible. Now the deadline is flexible, the sooner the better, but if delivered in January 08 rather than Nov 07, it wouldn't be a major issue.

Rating: 1

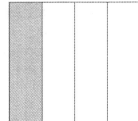

Add Value

The entire purpose of the project is to provide a higher level of business infrastructure, therefore it is very important that the solution adds significant value to the business.

Rating: 3

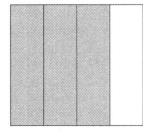

Meet Quality Level

The solution has to work, it must be functional. However, it's not necessary that it is the most elegant and well designed solution. It is more a business tool that a marketing device.

Rating: 2

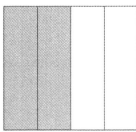

Team Satisfaction

We realized that it was important that the entire team was happy with the way things progressed as this will be a long term relationship that needs to last beyond the delivery of this project. However, there was a sense of realism that given the constraints of the project, there might be some need for compromise along the way.

Rating: 3

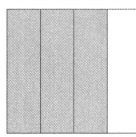

By using a visual sliding scale to represent the ratings given to each success factor, we can very quickly see what the client cares about the most. In the diagram below, it's easy to see the budget is by far the most important factor, and deadline is the least important. So, the project can be delivered late and with some movement in scope but it cannot go over budget. With team satisfaction, it was important for the client to acknowledge that after the project was completed, there would be an ongoing need for further development down the track so it was important that the team were happy with the outcomes so that they would be willing to work on future enhancements.

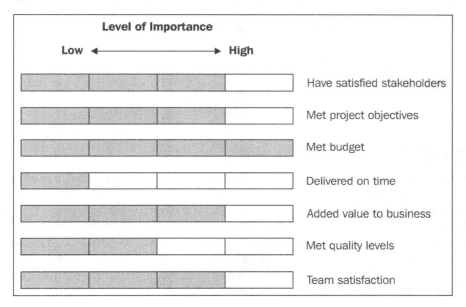

The goal of success factors is to understand what really matters to your client. It will change for every project and every client. You shouldn't assume that a second project for the same client will have the same success factors; it could have different drivers so you may need to manage it differently. The key is that both you and the client have a common understanding of what's really important. Of course, if you have a number of clients involved in the planning workshop, you may find yourself spending a lot of time helping them to come to a consensus. That's fine, better to do that upfront and get the arguments out of the way early. Sometimes, it's actually more important for the client to understand that success can be seen in different ways.

Project Scope and Objectives

In the project brief, we establish the project purpose and objectives. That's just the starting point; it doesn't necessarily mean the objectives are reasonable or achievable, but tackling that at the point of drafting the project brief is difficult. It's easier once you have established the success factors and then can reconsider the project objectives and establish what is in and out of scope for this project.

This part of the planning workshop is to achieve the following tasks:

- Take the project objectives to work out the project scope.
- State what's **in** scope.
- State what's **out** of scope.
- State what **might** be in scope.

The outcome is a clear statement of the boundaries of the project.

Project Scope

As with the success sliders, a visual representation is a great way to show what's in and out of scope. For each of the objectives, we decide if they are in or out of scope for this project. That doesn't mean they aren't done ever, just in this project. I often use "Stage 2" as a way of calming clients who get worried when they see features in the "out of scope" column. Another way to consider these features is that they are done by someone else. With the "to be decided" row at the bottom of the table, we can put objectives that the client would like to achieve but hasn't yet confirmed if they are absolutely necessary.

In Scope	Out of Scope
• Events Calendar • Product Catalogue • Distributed Authoring • 2-Level Authoring Workflow • Site Search	• Content Population (client to look after) • Real-time payments • Integration with ERP system
To be decided • Supplier extranet	

In the example above, we have a number of project objectives that are to be implemented and are considered in scope. The right column shows what is NOT in scope. In the case of content population, it's actually required for the project but will be outsourced so it's not in scope for our project team. It's important to explicitly state what's out of scope so that assumptions don't creep in later down the track. A typical example, I've learned the hard way, is you get to the point of data entry and the client says "I thought you were going to do that". At this point, unless you've stated clearly upfront that it's not in scope, you have a situation that you need to manage delicately.

When deciding what's in scope and out of scope, you can refer back to success factors to help with the decision-making process. If the client has already stated that budget is of primary importance, you can use this as leverage to move objectives to "might be" or "out of scope". Conversely, if budget is not an issue, you can have more objectives in scope and know that if more money is required, the client will be accepting of this.

Objectives, Outputs, and Outcomes

Understanding the difference between objectives, outputs, and outcomes takes time but when grasped, is a powerful way to cut through to what's behind a particular request or desire. Once you can break it down to the outcome, it can help you to come up with other ways to achieve the same result and give you more flexibility in solving a particular problem. Here's a brief explanation:

The objective is what we are aiming to achieve.

The output is what we actually deliver.

The outcome is what the business gains from our output.

For example, a particular objective might be to improve customer service, the output is a searchable products database, the outcome is a decrease in calls to the call centre. The following table shows how to represent this for the client so they can see what each element means in context:

Objective	Output	Outcome
Implement e-commerce	Online shopping facility	Increased revenue
Provide more information to customers online	Content management system	Increase efficiency
Improve customer service	Publish timetables online	Reduce costs for call center

In reality, there are only two outcomes that a business is after:

- Reduce cost by improving efficiency
- Increase revenue

If you boil everything down, an objective should lead to one of these outcomes, otherwise you need to question why you're doing it. For non-commercial organizations, e.g. government or not for profits—it can be different as they may truly have non-financial goals to achieve but for a business, it's either saving money or making money.

Quality

What is quality? Is it 99% uptime? Is it a high quality visual design? Is it quick response times? Is it ease of use? Is it security? Or all of the above.

We have already mentioned quality when looking at success factors but because of its importance, it's worth reviewing in its own right.

Quality is an intangible feature that, like visual design, can be very subjective and very different for each person. In fact, discussing quality tends to raise more debates for clients than most other success factors.

We all have our own internal measure of quality, but rarely do we state this explicitly, usually it's learned through trial and error. We show the client a result, they tell us it's not good enough and why. We fix that, re-present the solution and the client identifies another issue, and so on and so on. To save some of this grief, it's handy to have explicitly stated what the quality requirements for this project are.

When it comes to the individual quality factors, most of them are satisfied by eZ publish, so what we need to consider is the solution that we are creating on top of the eZ publish framework.

Quality Factors

- **Conformity**
  Does the solution have all the data, processes or functionality specified?

- **Useability**
  Is the solution easy to use and understand from the client's perspective?

- **Efficiency**
  Does the solution use the people, business process, hardware, software efficiently?

- **Maintainability**
  Is the solution easy to maintain and support?

- **Reliability**
  Does the solution perform reliably and is it free of errors?

- **Portability**
  Does the solution work properly in different environments (e.g. browsers, operating systems)?

- **Reusability**
  Does the solution require reuse or extension for a different purpose or application?

- **Security**
  Is the solution secure from unauthorized access and modification?

- **Auditability**
  Is it easily audited and is there sufficient reporting?

Measuring Quality

The key is what the client considers to be quality. We use the same rating system as we did for success factors, 1 to 4 (4 being the highest).

The initial reaction of clients is that everything should be of high quality. Then, when you look at each individual factor you'll find more reason surfacing. If you have a number of people representing your client, a good test is to get them to do individual ratings and compare to see the different views and work out a consensus. Normally, someone from IT will give maintainability high, someone from client service would put usability high. Both are important, but which is more?

If you get high ratings for everything, then you have a potentially unrealistic project with a high risk factor. Of course, everything is possible with enough time or money. What sometimes happens is a factor that hasn't surfaced to date emerges and affects the project significantly; it could be that security is of high importance, or reliability as the solution will be the main interface to clients and must be stable. All of this will influence how the solution is designed so it's good to have this clear upfront. It may already be stated in the requirements but going over it again and getting a rating will give you a better context as to the relative importance of that particular factor.

Remember, the client has already given you a rating for quality in the success factors so anything here needs to be considered in light of that rating. The goal here again is to understand what matters to the client and have it stated explicitly so everyone is on the same page.

The following table is an example from a recent project. What stood out as most important was usability of the end result. This particular project was for internal use so the client was happy to dictate which browser to use so portability didn't matter.

Quality Factors for Project X:

Factor	Rating
Conformity	
Usability	
Efficiency	
Maintainability	
Reliability	
Portability	
Reusability	

Factor	Rating
Security	
Auditability	

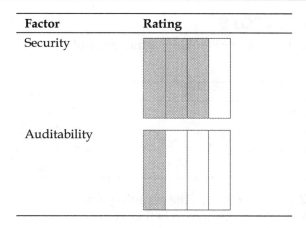

Estimation

At this point, we have an idea of what the client wants, what really matters, and what we are using to build the solution, i.e. eZ publish. What we don't know is how we are going to implement the solution within the eZ publish framework. But that won't stop the client from asking how much it is going to cost (in the case of internal projects, the question is more likely to be how long). The reality is we can only make a guess of how much it will cost, we can only make an estimate. When it comes to estimations, we need to understand the language we are using and the games people play in coming up with estimates.

Reality Check

Estimates are often wrong.

The accuracy of a particular estimate will depend on the experience of the team, the client, and the complexity of the task.

A task will take as long as it takes, regardless of what estimate is given.

We can't accurately state how long something will take unless we have done it before, under the same conditions.

The bottom line is we can't accurately estimate the project until we know exactly how we intend to implement it.

Estimation Errors

Barry Boehm did a study in 1999 looking at the range of estimation errors during a project lifecycle.

Stage	Estimation Error
Project Start	+ / - 400%
Requirements Gathering	+ / - 200%
Requirements Analysis	+ / - 150%
Specification	+ / - 50%

In the context of eZ publish projects, the planning workshop can be considered requirements analysis. What this means is that at the end of the planning workshop, any estimate you provide your client can be up to 150% more than the true cost. If you try to provide an estimate before you have requirements, you could be up to 200% out. If you have an initial meeting and the client asks at the end of the meeting, how much (which happens A LOT), you could be up to 4 times out. For high risk projects with high complexity, estimation errors can be 5 times out (Rand Corporation, Charles Perrow [1984]).

Hopefully, this will scare the pants off you every time you think about doing an estimate and you'll think long and hard about any estimate that you do provide. Of course, ideally we only provide an estimate after the specification phase but sometimes you have to give an indication of price to even get to that stage. That's a part of doing business; what you need to be aware of are the risks involved so that you can avoid the common mistakes in estimation.

Usual Situation

What usually happens is we don't have enough information when the client asks us for a price, but because we are keen to please, we take a guess at what we think it will cost and the project starts. At some point, the reality of what we are doing is established, as well as how long it will take and what it will cost. Then, we have to somehow convince the client to come up with more money. There are three outcomes, the client pays the extra money, the project is cancelled or you are forced to deliver for the initial estimate given. None of these options are particularly pleasant.

So why are our estimates so bad? The short answer is because we provide estimates when we don't have enough information and we don't ask the right questions. There are also other reasons why our estimates are wrong. It depends who you ask and what their motivation is.

The Developer's Estimate

When you are asking a developer for an estimate, what you are saying is:

"Based on your experience and understanding of the project, and based on the information I've given you, how long will it take?"

Developers are mostly honest but optimistic. They will do their best to please and provide a best-case scenario. On the other hand, some have been burnt doing this and go the other way providing a worst-case scenario to protect themselves. Either way, the quality of the estimate will be based on the quality of the information they have been given. But rarely will you get malicious or wrong estimates from developers.

The Project Manager's Estimate

Project Managers as a whole are more aware of the blowouts that occur during projects and will take a more conservative approach. By default, I will get my developer to provide me an estimate of their component that I will then build into the overall estimate. As a rule of thumb, I always add a percentage to any estimate given to me to allow for some error. The size of the percentage will vary based on the experience of the developer and the complexity of the task. E.g., if a developer continually gives me best-case scenarios, I'll protect myself by adding 40% to the estimate to allow for that. On the other hand, with a more conservative developer who I have worked with before and can trust, I don't have to worry about adding additional margin.

Low Bid

The low bid is a dangerous but sometimes necessary approach. It's about sales, not reality. If you go in with what you think the project will really cost, chances are you may not win the project. Alternatively, if you go in with a low bid, i.e. the minimum cost for the features and leaving out elements such as content population and training, you stand a better chance of getting the project. However, that doesn't mean the price quoted is the final cost. You'll have to manage the budget issue at some point, through scope creep, variations, whatever term you like to get the budget to equal the true cost. This is a somewhat underhanded way to get there but sometimes it's the only pragmatic way. Once the project starts, you stand a better chance of getting more money than you do upfront. People don't like to cancel projects and you'll have more leverage. Ethically, it's questionable, but it can work.

The Sales Manager's Estimate

When sales people are involved, the only thing you can be sure of is they are more concerned about getting the sale than making sure the estimate is accurate. Some sales people will promise the world and let the developers worry about how to deliver for the price given. It's a recipe for disaster and puts the project team under a lot of pressure. There is good reason to be wary of sales people; however, without someone to make the sale, we wouldn't have any projects to work on, so they have a role to play.

Management/Client Directive

Basically, this is when the client says, I want it for $30,000, or for internal projects, management states, it's to be delivered by 30th Oct. Either way, the terms of the job have been set for you. Your choices are:

1. Accept — start the project, get to a point when it's clear that it can't be done for the set time/cost and try to negotiate for more time/money.

2. Reject — say it can't be done, then risk losing your job or the project.

Neither outcome is particularly pleasant. Although harder, rejecting the directive is actually the better outcome, even if it means losing the project or your job. By losing the project, you can take the time to find a project that will be profitable. By losing your job, hopefully you can find one where you get treated better. If these outcomes aren't realistic, then at least you know what you are facing and can work on ways to deal with it.

Common Language

What is handy is to have a common language when it comes to estimations. There are three types of pricing.

Guess

A guess is an uninformed predication; that's when you ask your developer how long it will take to integrate eZ publish with an external database and they come back with the helpful statement, as long as a piece of string. Fortunately, we all know the length of a piece of string is twice as long as the distance from one end to the middle. Not very useful. A guess is simply that, a guess that we can place no guarantees on; guesses are to be avoided like the plague. Fortunately, my lead developer Bruce has an inbuilt guess avoidance feature. If I ask him to make a guess, his answer is more than 3 hours, less than 3 months. And he's usually right. The short answer is, don't make guesses!

Estimate

An estimate is an informed/expert opinion based on an informal and incomplete documentation and process. Basically, we have discussed what it is that we intend to implement, done some basic documentation, and a bit of research and have a reasonable idea of what we are doing but there is still a lot more work to be done to provide a true estimate. Estimtes are what we provide once we've got the requirements and have completed the planning workshop. We have a pretty good idea but the devil is in the details and that's why it's only a guesstimate. If you provide an estimate to a client, be careful to explain that it **WILL** change and has a reasonable margin of error. You may choose to increase the estimate to protect yourself but it may also backfire as you may lose the job if you are too conservative (trust me, I've been there!).

Fixed Price Quote

A fixed price quote is what we are after. It's an informed opinion based on formal, agreed documentation. In our case, it's the specification. Until you have a complete specification that the client has signed off, you are dealing with estimates. Based on a specification you can give a fixed price quote estimate and be confident that you can deliver for that price.

 Note: Even then, there can be room for error as Boehm's study on estimation errors has indicated. However, given we are working with an established framework, the margin of error is reduced and an variances will be caused by the project team's experience level and the quality of the content/data provided by the client.

The Ideal Situation

Don't give a fixed price quote unless you have enough information or call it an estimate so the client knows it's not final. Otherwise, get time to do enough investigation to get the information you need—a simple solution but not always easy to pull off!

Summary

The goal of defining a project is to make sure both the project manager and the client (internal or external) have a clear and common understanding of what the final outcome will be. This is not an easy process as there are many ways to capture information that can be misinterpreted and lead to expectations and assumptions. By being aware of the inherent risks in gathering requirements and through the use of practices such as success sliders in a planning workshop, you stand a much better chance of defining the project in a pragmatic manner. The more realistic your plans are, the greater your chances of success.

How to Write a Specification

Writing the specification for a project is one of the hardest parts. If done well, it will mean the implementation should be trouble free and have few complications. It's very much like creating the blueprint for a house. You should be able to hand the specification to the developer, and it should have all the information they need. Of course, it's hard to get it completely perfect, so some refinement may be required during the implementation phase, not to mention changes requested by the client. But, for all intents and purposes, the specification is the bible for the project.

However, there is no such thing as a specification template. Each specification will be unique, as each project is unique. The amount of detail you need to capture for your project will depend on the nature of that project. Not all of the elements defined here are necessary for every project. Simply use the ones you need for your project. The elements outlined here cover projects that deal with content, extensions, and workflow. In time, there may be more possibilities that eZ publish provides, so this chapter should be considered a guide only. The following list contains elements drawn from a number of specifications to create as full a list as possible.

- Object Relationship Model
- Database schema
- Users and Groups
- Features
- Site map
- Content Types, Rules & Views
- Custom Templates
- Screen & Performance Standards

There are also other ways to capture the same information; if you have a better way, that's fine, use it. The goal is the same: capture all the details necessary so that development can commence.

From a commercial perspective, you have a few choices. Do the specification on a time and materials basis, provide a fixed price cost for the specification only, or include the cost of the specification as a cost of the entire project (which you can only establish once the specification is complete — see *Estimation* in Chapter 4).

In terms of elapsed time for writing a specification, it will depend on the size of the project and the availability of the client. In practice, it will range from a few weeks to several months.

In this chapter, we will look at each of the different elements that a specification can contain with examples from real projects.

First we'll define all the elements, and then go over the process of writing a full specification.

Content Model

The purpose of the content model is to define the main content classes in the system and how they relate to each other. It is a high-level view of the system; details of each of the content classes will be defined later in the specification. This model becomes the foundation for the solution. The approach used here is based on object role modeling, which maps the traditional concept of an object model with relational database schemas (for more information, see http://www.orm.net). It is not the only way to capture this information but one that works well in this environment. You can replace this with your own form of modeling — the key is to understand the objects and the relationships within the business environment.

The Studies in Australia Model

The following diagram outlines the main content classes, and relationships between them. The example used here is from the Studies In Australia website (http://www.studiesinaustralia), which provides detailed information on all tertiary-level courses offered by educational institutions in Australia, as well as a comprehensive inquiry system. The idea is to search for a course and then submit an inquiry, which is then forwarded to all the institutions that offer that course.

There was an existing database that contained details regarding courses and institutions (i.e. Providers). We were able to work from there and establish the following rules.

- A provider is an institution that provides courses to the public.
- A provider has one or more sites (e.g. physical locations).
- A site belongs to one provider.

- A site is located in a state (note, a site can't be in two states).
- A course is owned by a provider.
- A course is provided at a site.
- A course is associated with a field of study.

From these facts, we are able to derive the following model:

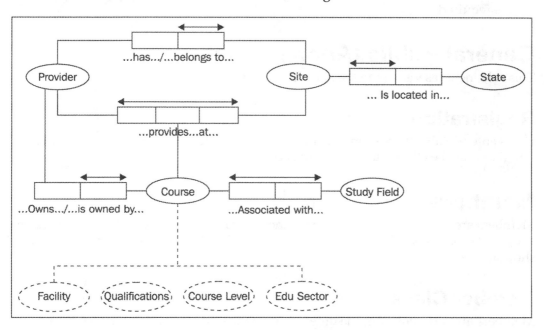

This model then informed what content classes we could create, and how to set the rules for associations between the classes.

Users and Groups

In users and groups, we need to define the users who will interact with the solution and how they are to be grouped.

 This should be from the business perspective, as apposed to how we might see users within a standard eZ publish installation.

It's also important to use the same language or terminology as the client. Although a standard user in eZ publish is an editor, the client may use the term author or publisher, in which case, we should use that name to avoid confusion. This allows us to design the system to meet these goals.

The following is an example of users and roles for an e-commerce portal. Firstly, we list and define the specific roles, then for each role we define any further details required.

General Public (Anonymous)

This role includes visitors to the site that do not log in.

Registration

Users enter details, then a confirmation email is sent to their email address with a link that must be clicked to activate the account.

Members

Members are users that have registered their details in the system. These users have a login and password. Users must have registered, and be logged in to process their shopping cart.

Member Class

Members are different from the other users in the systems (which are based on the inbuilt user class) and therefore any additional details need to be captured.

Attribute	Type	Notes
Given Name	Text Line	
Surname	Text Line	
User Account	User account	Includes • login • password • email address
Date of Birth	Date	Note: Standard eZ publish date datatype only stores dates from 1/1/1970 — you may need to create custom data type to handle this.
Delivery Street	Text Block	
Delivery Suburb	Text Block	

Attribute	Type	Notes
Delivery Town	Text Block	
Delivery Country	Text Block	
Delivery Postcode	Numeric	
Custom Delivery Notes	Text block	
Billing Street	Text Block	
Billing Suburb	Text Block	
Billing Town	Text Block	
Billing Country	Text Block	
Billing Postcode	Numeric	
Home Phone	Text line	
Work Phone	Text Line	
Mobile	Text Line	

Member Functions

In this example, we need to add more details about what functionality is available to members. Some of these are already standard features of eZ publish, but it's better to be explicit so that the client is aware of the exact functionality that they are getting—it's easy to fall into the trap of saying that it's standard functionality, but sometimes clients aren't aware of what eZ publish provides by default.

Login

Users enter login/email address and password.

Forgot Password

Users enter their email address and are sent an email with a link. Clicking on this link generates a new password, which is emailed to their address. The user can login with the new password and change it to something they choose.

Change Password

When a logged-in user clicks on this link they are presented with a form with three fields:

1. Old password
2. New password
3. Confirm new password

Successfully entering these values will update the password.

Manage Details

Ability to edit personal details (name, address, email, etc.).

Editors

Editors will have the ability to:

- Add / Edit / Delete all content from all shops
- Generate reports

 You can be more specific about the exact permissions defining what content, and where the editor can create it.

Administrators

Will have the same abilities as an Editor as well as:

- Add / edit / delete member & editors
- Add / delete shops

Features

For sites with custom functionality, the flow of functionality needs to be defined. This can involve a number of diagrams covering front-end display, interaction design, and administration wireframes. The features defined will follow the object relationship model already defined. In the Good Company example, the main objects are Wish, Volunteer, Community Group, and Staff—for each of these objects, there will be a set of features that will define how the objects will interact in the system.

Good Company Feature Overview

Having an overview is a good start to defining how the features work within the context of the site. Then for each feature, we can drill down into the details and specific workflows.

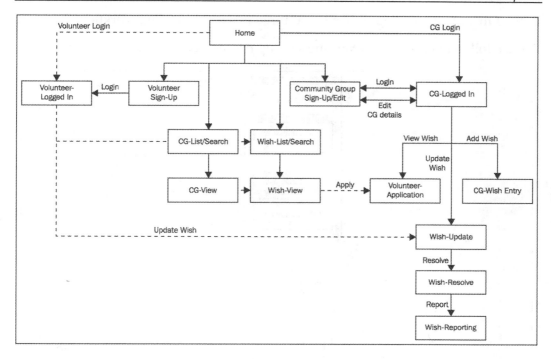

In this diagram, we have an overview of each of the workflows available for volunteers and community groups. Each of the features are then captured in more detail with an interaction design, e.g. a flowchart.

There are three main features available from the homepage:

- Volunteer signup and login
- Wish search and application
- Community group signup and management

Once a volunteer has logged in, they can access the wish search feature and view wishes. They can also apply for a wish that then becomes a wish application.

On the community group side, they have the following options:

- Login
- Edit their details
- Submit a wish
- View a volunteer application
- Change the status of a wish e.g. update, resolve, report on

Each of these features would then be captured in a more detailed workflow diagram.

E.g. the following diagram details the sign-up process for a community group:

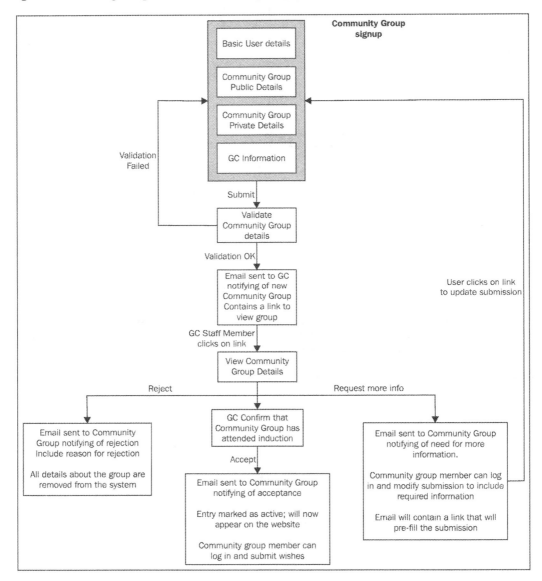

In this diagram, we can see that there are a number of steps to signing up a community group. They need to fill out their details, which triggers an email to be sent to Good Company management. Good Company management then has three options, reject, accept, or request more information.

Community Group Registration and Administration

The following diagram shows how the community group sign-up feature would be presented on the screen using a wireframe diagram.

Community Group Registration Wireframe

This wireframe shows the first part of the sign up process, i.e. the community group's basic details. If this information is not entered, they can't move to the next screen. What's important about this screen is the fields chosen. In particular, legal status and ABN. If the wrong legal status is entered or there is no ABN (Australian business number) then the sign up can't continue to the next page.

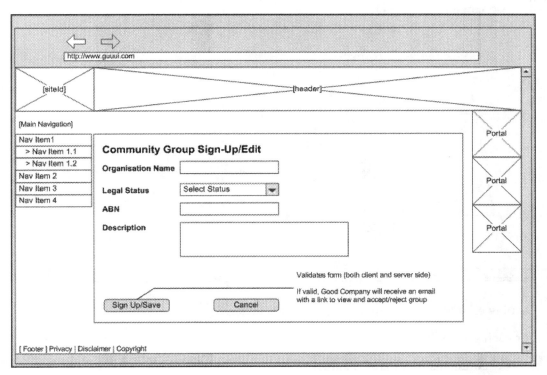

Community Group Administration Wireframes

As a part of this feature, there is also custom functionality in the administration area that needs to be defined.

Community Group Listing

This wireframe shows a basic administration screen that lists all of the community groups with content, category, state, and a link to the group's wishes.

It's easy to forget about administration screens or not put as much effort into them as the public facing screens, but they are also important and need to be properly defined so the client understands how they are going to interact with the solution, and your developers know what to build.

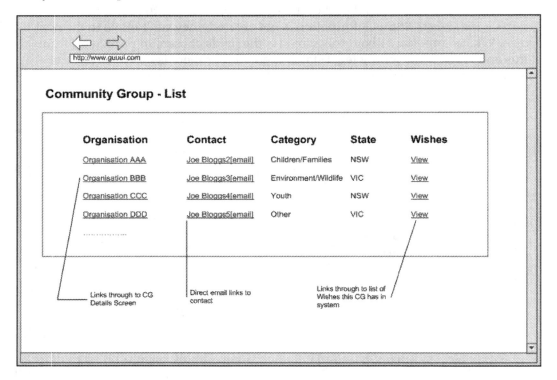

Display all matching groups in alphabetical order.

For each group display:

- Name (as link to full details)
- Contact (as link to full contact details)
- Category
- State
- Wishes (as link to full list of wishes)

Community Acceptance Wireframe

This wireframe shows the details of what is displayed to a Good Company manager when they are deciding on whether or not to accept the sign up of a new community group. We can see the three options (from the workflow seen earlier in the chapter) represented on this screen as buttons on the bottom of the page.

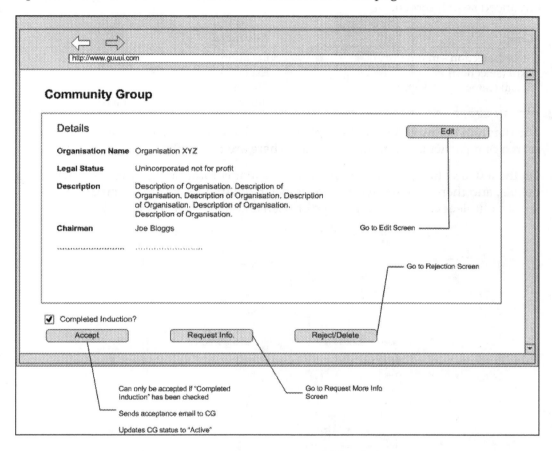

For a community group, show all attributes associated with community group content classes.

Functions

Accept (only displayed if not already accepted)

Request Info—goes to request info screen

Reject / Delete—removes entry

Edit—goes to edit screen

Wish Searching

This shows how the search feature works on the same site.

It will be possible to search for wishes using a variety of criteria. The table below defines the core criteria. The additional criteria will be available as a part of an advanced search screen.

Core	Advanced
State (selection - mandatory)	Location
Skill (selection)	Expertise
Social Category (selection)	Time required
	Individual, team or group wish

The diagram below shows that people will be able to get to wishes via either a wish search or a particular community group. There are two paths.

On the left, a volunteer can search for a particular community group, view the group details, and then see what wishes are associated with that group. Alternately, on the left, a volunteer can search for a type of wish and then view the wish details.

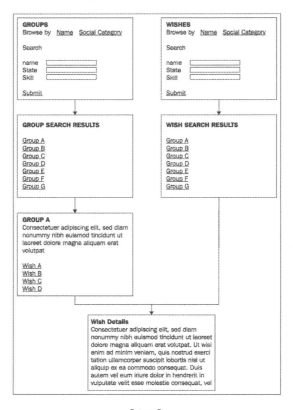

The following wireframes indicate the details for this flow.

Wish Search Results

Once a search has been conducted, we need to define how the results will be displayed on the screen as well as decide in what order they are to be displayed.

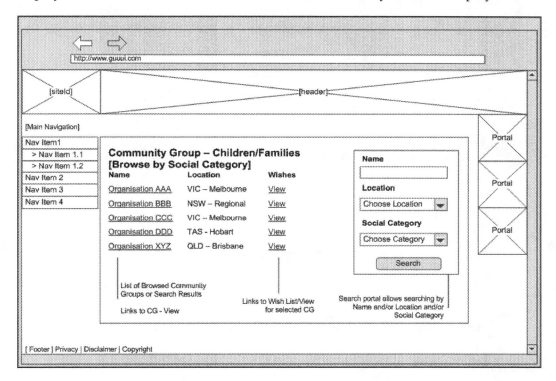

Display list of matching community groups in alphabetical order with community group search portal.

For each community group display:

- Name (as link to full details of community group)
- Location
- Wishes (as link to list of wishes for community group)

Wish Search Details

When viewing the details of a wish, we need to define what attributes we are going to display and what features are available.

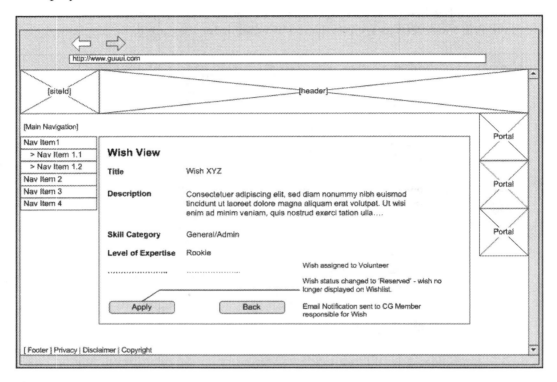

Display the following attributes for the wish:

- Title
- Description
- Skill Category
- Level of Expertise
- Estimated Time required
- Location
- Timeframe

Also display the name of the related community group.

In this diagram, we don't actually display all of the fields. We took a short cut expecting the wireframe to be an indication only, and that the client would read the details underneath. They didn't, and asked for more fields to be displayed. We learned from our mistake and made sure from then on that a wireframe should display every attribute. It is also helpful for designers to make sure they are able to accommodate for everything that is to be displayed.

Site Map

A site map is something web developers will be familiar with, and can also be referred to as the site structure. It's a representation of how the public view of the site will be structured. It captures the way the navigation will be defined.

The following site map is of a straightforward content-focused website. It has the main sections linked from the homepage, and pages identified beneath each section. The block to the right of the homepage shows the pages that appear on the footer of every page.

This where we derive the node tree in eZ publish. It provides the structure of content within the administration area.

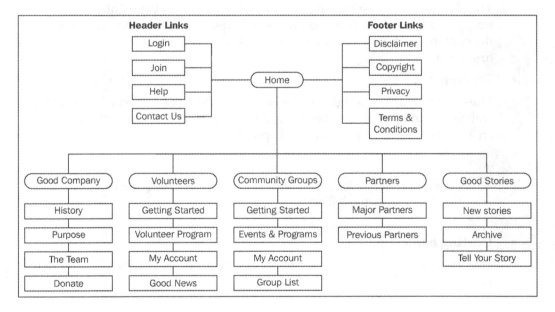

Content Classes and Rules

An eZ publish project can be treated similarly to a normal web application development project with one significant difference—the need for content. With web applications or traditional software development, there is little content; it is usually about data and that either already exists or will be entered by the users of the application. With eZ publish projects, content needs to be modeled, gathered, and entered into the system developed before it goes live. The problem is people aren't used to modeling and preparing content. Often it's left to the last minute, at which point the project has to be delayed as the content issues are not yet resolved. In a recent project, for a standard corporate website, the launch date was delayed by six months as the client worked on getting the content together. The key to success is in appropriate content modeling, and then gathering while the system is being built.

Content Analysis

There are three typical scenarios that occur in eZ publish projects, and often you will have a combination of two or three of these scenarios.

- **Existing website**

    The client has an existing site, whether it's a public website, intranet or extranet. The content only exists on the website, and there is no other source of the content except maybe some original Word docs in which the content was first written.

- **Existing database**

    The content exists in a database, which could be either a part of the existing website or an internal database, e.g. a propriety application such as an ERP, an MS Access database or an Excel spreadsheet.

 It's not uncommon for some clients to consider a spreadsheet as a form of database even though it isn't.

- **Existing hardcopy**

    The content exists as a printed catalogue, brochure, or another form of marketing collateral.

The problem with all of these scenarios is that the format of the existing content rarely matches the format required for the new system, and the transformation is not taken into consideration until the content has to be entered into the system. Automating this process is difficult. If the content is well-structured, e.g. an existing database, then it is possible to enter content, but rarely will it cover all the content that is needed for the new system. Nor will it take into account linkages between content.

There are two steps that need to be taken to ensure a successful outcome: content modeling and then content gathering. The tasks themselves are not overly complex, but as not many people have experience with content management, it can prove to be confusing. The biggest problem is the lack of discipline. Content modeling is required for the development to commence so it tends to be included in planning. Content gathering, however, can slide and won't be caught until the development is done and the system is ready for the content to be entered. At this point, unless the content has been gathered, in the right format and structure, the project will stall.

Content Modeling

As discussed in a previous chapter, content modeling as a discipline is fairly new. It has elements of database design in terms of structuring the content, and is similar to object modeling in terms of relations between content items and the site structure.

Good content modeling is a skill in its own right just as creating an object model is a skill in object-orientated programming. The skill is to get the right number of content classes and the relationships between them. As mentioned in Chapter 2, it's making sure the content model reflects the content that is being stored. Having too few content classes reduces the flexibility of the system, having too many makes it more complex to create and use. Ideally, the content model is based on existing content that has been analyzed and has a clear structure. If there is no existing content, the model will need to be tested against the content once it's been created and adjustments made.

A content model consists of content classes and their relation to the site structure.

- Content classes consist of attributes and have rules.
- An attribute is an element of a content class; it has a name and type.
- A rule defines where a content item can be added within the system.

E.g. here are two content classes:

Item	Attributes	Attribute Types
Photo Gallery	Title	Textline
	Introduction	XML text
	Images per page	Numeric

Rules:

- A photo gallery can be added to any part of the site structure below the main navigation.
- A photo gallery can contain photos.

Item	Attributes	Attribute Types
Photo	Title	Textline
	Date	Date/time
	Caption	XML text
	Photographer	Numeric

Rules:

- A photo can be added to a photo gallery.

Relation to Site Structure

Once all the content items have been defined, we need to decide how they will relate to the site structure. Some of this is obvious. If the site includes a product catalogue, then it stands to reason that you would add products only to that section. If we are displaying a list of training courses, a course content item would be used. However, when it comes to less structured content, it's not always obvious what approach to take. We are used to creating site maps but not assigning which content item we will use for that part of the site and how the page is to be structured—e.g. information design. Do we use a "section" content item? Do we need to allow for sub-navigation? If so, how many levels?

Here's an example of assigning content items to sections of the site:

About us	section content classes
Company history	info page content class
Contact Us	info page content class
Feedback	form page

This is a visual representation of the same rules.

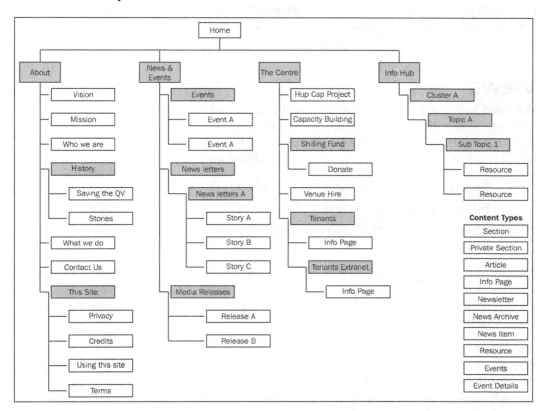

In this diagram, we capture the site structure and also which content classes are used to create the structure. It shows that certain classes can only be related to other classes. In the "Info Hub" section, we can see the rules for clusters and topics e.g.:

- A cluster can contain a topic.
- A topic can contain a sub topic.
- A sub topic can contain a resource.

Under the events section, we can see that news items can only be added to a news archive.

Things may change if there are issues in the content gathering phase or when it comes to actually entering the content. However, if this is not decided prior to the start of development, it can lead to rework; it also makes it difficult to ensure when content is being gathered that it will be in the right format for entering into the system once it's ready.

Once the model is defined, it's important to ensure there's sample content for each content type to test that the model is sound. Too often, it gets to the stage of entering content, and the structure of a content item or the rules prove to be wrong and rework is required to fix the situation.

Views

We need to know how a particular content class is to be displayed, and what the different views are. For example, a news item can be displayed in a number of ways, and each of these is represented by a view that is implemented by creating a custom template. A news item would typically have three views:

- Full view — the entire content of the class is displayed on a single page.
- Summary view — a summary of the content, e.g. title, author, date.
- Line view — the title of the news item represented as a link to the full view, e.g. as on a search results page.

The number of views required for each content class dictates the number of custom templates required and how they are to be programmed. Each view should be represented by a wireframe displaying the fields and the order in which the content is to be displayed.

The key to success starts with proper analysis of the content. This should lead to a well-defined content model, tested with sample content, and a plan for gathering content that is implemented while the system is built so that when the system is ready, the content is ready for entry. Without planning for content modeling, gathering, and population, you'll be planning for the project to be anywhere from one to six months late.

The following examples bring together the content model, rules, and views for a product catalogue for an arts supplies website. This shows the main products page, a product category page, and then the product details page. For each of these pages, we will have to create a custom template that will include other templates, e.g. on the product category page, we have summary views of each product.

Products Main Page

Contains line view of product categories as sub-navigation and in main content area.

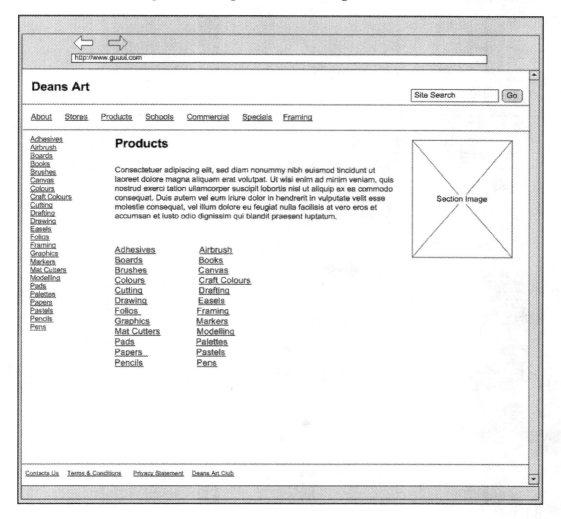

Product Category View

Lists all products for that category in alphabetical order.

For each product, display:

- Thumbnail
- Name (as link to full view)
- Price

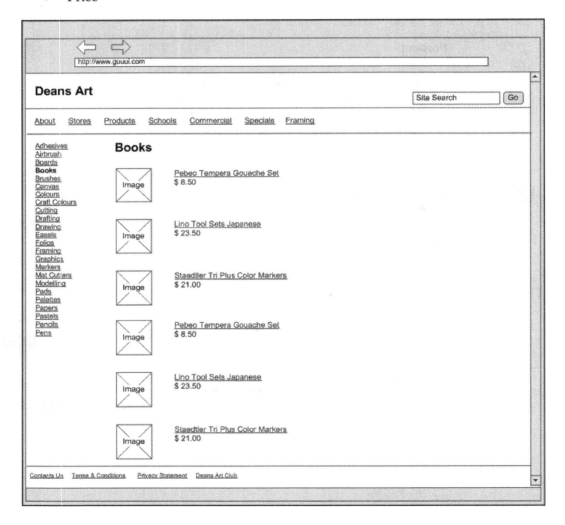

Product Details

A product consists of the following fields:

- Name
- Image
- Description
- Price (inc tax)
- Fact Sheet (PDF upload)
- Manufacturer (aka Brand) & logo — link to manufacturer website

Note: if the product is on special, the special price will also be displayed.

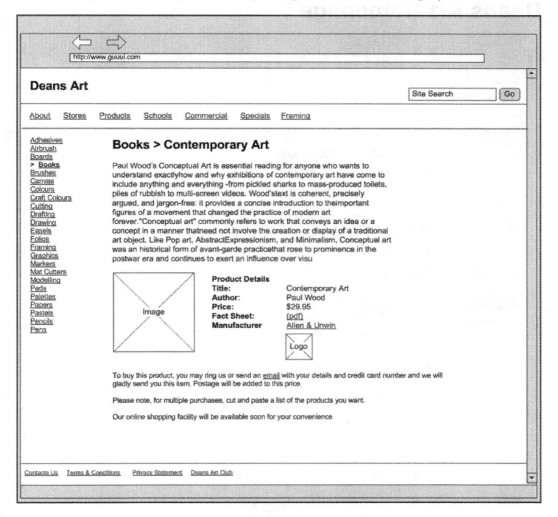

Custom Templates

We have already covered the views for specific content types. These are also custom templates but are related to a specific content type. For most sites, there will also be custom templates that will use a number of content types to create a single page. The most common examples of this are the homepage and section pages.

The specification should contain a wireframe for each template as well as note the views for each content type and any rules for those views. The following wireframe shows a homepage for the arts supplies site referred to in content types and rules previously.

Deans Art Homepage

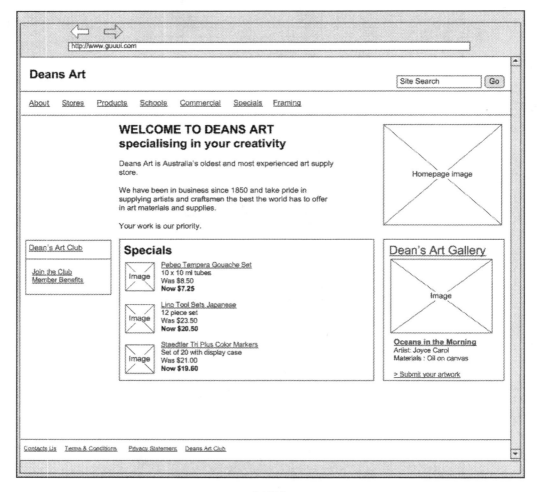

The homepage will contain introductory copy with the following elements:

- Logo
- Homepage image (editable in CMS)
- Specials — (custom content type) as selected
- Gallery — displaying featured work
- Deans Art Club portlet — links to Club pages

Queen Victoria Women's Centre Homepage

This is another example of a homepage that will require a custom template:

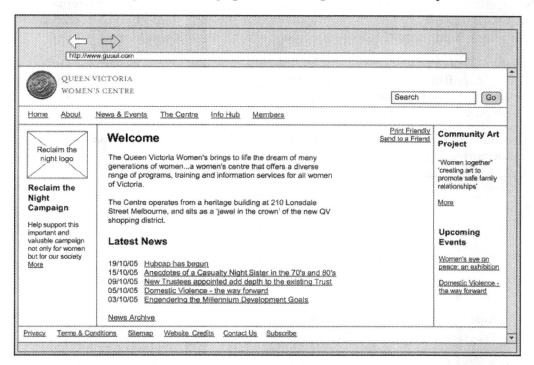

In this case, we define the source of the information displayed on this page.

Welcome: Sourced from homepage folder description

Info Hub: Sourced from info hub section description

Upcoming events: Most recent 5 events listing in events section

Latest News: Node list — most recent 5 news articles

Screen and Performance Standards

We have already defined what is going to appear on each screen by using wireframes. However, we also need to consider issues such as accessibility, browser compatibility, screen resolution, and performance of the system as a whole.

Browser Compatibility

Browsers are always changing; what was standard two years ago is different to now. However, what's important here is what browsers your client will require you to support now, and in the future. Simply accommodating the most popular browsers now will mean that when the newest browser becomes the most popular, there's a good chance rework will be required, e.g. when IE7 first came out, the adoption rate was slow, but soon it became far more popular. Creating a solution that catered for IE6 only would mean that in a short space of time rework would be inevitable.

As there is no true standard set of browsers with which to be compatible, you'll need to firstly confirm any specific requirements set by the client (e.g. governments tend to support older browsers) and then make any recommendations you might have, based on your own experience.

The final result is a table of what browsers (with operating systems) will be supported.

Browser	OS	Versions
IE	Windows 2000 Windows XP Vista	IE 6.0 and IE 7.0
Firefox	Windows 2000 Windows XP OS X Vista	1.5 to 2.0
Netscape	Windows 2000 Windows XP Vista	7.0
Safari	OS X	1.32 and 2.0

 Note: the reason we also include operating systems in browser compatibility is simply because the same browser version can behave differently on different operating systems.

Screen Resolution

As with browser compatibility, screen resolution is constantly changing. The default used to be 800 x 600, but that's on the way out and soon even 1024 x 768 will be a resolution of a bygone era. What we need to capture is the minimum resolution for the site to operate in; and what is meant by "operate"?

"The major functions of the site should be visible in 1024 x 768 without scrolling."

This statement would then need to be further qualified with what are considered the major functions — e.g. primary navigation, site search, help, etc.

There is also the question of whether the design is fluid or fixed, i.e. does it expand with the browser size? Once again, the rule needs to be captured so the designer and developer can build to whatever the specification is.

Accessibility

For some sites, accessibility is not an issue, for others, there are minimum standards that need to be met. It will depend on each project. What needs to be captured is what level of accessibility is required for the solution. These standards are set by the W3C consortium and are described in detail at the following URL:

`http://www.w3.org/TR/WAI-WEBCONTENT/`

The purpose of the guidelines is to help make web content accessible to people with disabilities. Many governments are now legislating that certain websites should have a basic level of accessibility. It's important to know what standards your website has to adhere to, otherwise you could be exposing your client (or business) to legal action.

Performance

This is something that is easy to forget; on larger sites, however, the performance of the site is very important and needs to be defined to ensure that the site delivers.

There are a number of key performance indicators:

- Page load time
- Page requests per minute
- Page requests per day
- Sessions per day

All of these are different indicators and need to be defined separately. Consideration should be given as to the expected connectivity, e.g. page load on a 56k modem.

Any peaks need to be noted separately, e.g. a site might have to cater for a particular event during which the load on the server is much higher.

The best way to deal with this is to state the average and then any peaks that are to be expected and what performance is expected during both.

Specification Process

Trying to identify all the functionality is an overwhelming task, and is not possible in a single go; so rather than trying to get everything, we start with a workshop that enables us to capture a high-level view of the domain. This is about understanding the business of the client and how they operate so that we understand the context within which the end solution has to work.

High-Level Specification Workshop

We start with a workshop to capture the following in a high level specification:

1. Domain overview
2. Users of the system
3. Object model
4. Key relationships between objects
5. Relationship diagram
6. Feature overview
7. Site map

Domain Walkthrough

The client and domain experts walk us through the entire project. Even though we may have a requirements document, drafted the project brief, and been through the planning workshop, it's still important to get the client to take us through the domain. When they talk about the domain, we glean information that we may not already have in particular, we can establish which requirements are the most important. We can also question if any requirements are not necessary or if the client is open to different ways of solving problems. If we rely on the documentation alone, there's a good chance we'll miss aspects of the project that haven't been captured in writing. Not all requirements may make it into the specification, and on the other hand, new features may be identified that should be captured.

Users and Roles of the System

The goal is to identify the main users of the system.

We should have an understanding of how these groupings are viewed by the business and the marketing approach towards each from the domain walkthrough already conducted. This allows us to design the system to meet these goals.

Object Model

The goal of this part of the specification is to get an overview of the key objects within the model. For the e-commerce portal example, the key objects would be:

- Member
- Store
- Product

These will be fleshed out later, but in the initial stages, it's enough to identify them. The detail will be added later.

Key Relationships between Objects

This is about establishing the main relationships between the objects. It's not an exhaustive process, just the high-level relationships. The details will be fleshed out later.

Here are some examples of key relationships:

1. A Location is in a State (e.g. Brisbane is in Queensland, Gold Coast is in Queensland, etc.).
2. A Business is located in a Location—can Businesses have multiple locations?

Object Role Diagram

This is a combination of the previous steps captured in a single relationship diagram. This consists, at its most basic, of a sketch of circles with object names attached and arrows indicating the relationships.

Features

Basically, what features there are in the system and who has access to these features.

For each Object listed, identify what functionality is associated with it. This is top-level stuff, but should consider the life-cycle of an object in the system from creation, modification, to deletion e.g.:

- Business User signs up and creates a Business Profile.
- Business Profile is approved by Bride Online Admin and published to site.
- Business User purchases package to add Products to Business Profile.

Site Map

Create a site map for the site, covering both the front and back end.

At this point, we have a strong high-level overview of the project and can provide a fairly accurate estimate of what the project will cost and how long it will take.

Detailed Specification

After creating the high-level specification, we review it with the client to ensure we have an accurate understanding of the domain, and the core features required. Then, we go through the process of filling out all the details of the project, e.g. wireframes, interaction design, business rules, performance, and browser specifications.

After each revision, we review the specification, with the client in person, to ensure the details are correct. This process can be repeated anywhere from three to nine times. You should be able to capture all the details within ten revisions, although depending on the nature of your client, you may find that details emerge in content analysis or business rules that change the shape of the project. This process is one of discovery and you can never be sure what you'll find. The goal is to make sure there are no surprises when development commences, so if changes are required during specification, that's fine; this is the time to find out all the details.

Creative Brief

The creative brief extends the initial project brief in which the high-level details of target market, audience, and project purpose were captured. For the designer to come up with a visual treatment, answers to the following questions are extremely helpful.

Note: Not all questions are appropriate for all projects, so it's just a matter of asking the ones that do apply. Like the functional specification, the creative brief should provide the designer with all the information they need to create the visual design.

The following is an example of a questionnaire with answers for a seed wholesaler.

The Product or Communication Task

What is the product that this client is selling?

Seed — positioning Seedtech as the No 1 wholesaler of seed

What information is the client communicating or receiving?

Stock availability

Variety availability   > any trial information

The Type of Product

What type of product does our client produce?

Seeds for primary industry

Target Market & Audience

Who is the client's market?

3 major corporate agricultural companies

Wesfarmers, Elders, CRT (Combined Rural Traders)

Each ag co has hundreds of outlets

Who buys their product?

The outlets of the corporations

80% of these companies — 20% individuals

Who are they interacting/communicating with?

Generally dealing with nominated seed buyer in each retails store, & a person in each head office. Head office — State Managers — National Purchasing Officers — Regional Sales guys and Farmers.

Which segment of the Target Market is this execution aimed at?

Retail outlets

Farmers

Seedtech deal with farmers directly but they go to the retail outlets (approx 400-500) to actually purchase the seed.

Which segment of the Target Market is going to be using this site the most?

Currently farmers get info from brochures or call the Seedtech office…it is hoped farmers will use, but the people using the site will mostly be the retail outlets.

Is there a Primary Audience and a Secondary Audience?

Retail outlets are the primary audience and Farmers are the Secondary although the farmers make the choice as to what to buy — Retailers are there to provide info & pass this on to farmers.

Demographic Profile

What is their age?
20-70

Where do they live?
Rural areas only

How much money do they earn?
They are always budget oriented

What is their level of schooling?
50/50 Secondary level — tertiary

Would they access the site from home or from work?

Work – (and in farmers' case home is work)

What is their bandwidth?

Small to tiny

Are they "net-savvy'?

Retailers are used to it.

Farmers are getting used to it—Internet familiarity is becoming widespread.

Psychographic Profile

How do they feel towards our client's brand?

The brand is fairly new and knowledge is limited.

What is their perception of our client's brand?

Seedtech hasn't performed as well as it would like.

It's a new brand Seedtech—used to be called Premier Seed Co

Do they spend money on a whim?

No, never, very budget conscious.

Who makes the decision when it comes to online purchases of our client's product category?

Really anyone who looks at the site—because mostly it will be the farmer.

Farmers need to be impressed with the product range—the detailed information is the key to how they make their decision. These need to be available straight away.

Farmers are the end user and make the decision on what to buy.

Has to be very simple and printable, with simple header containing company logo.

Marketing Objective

What is our client's main business/communication objective in going online?

To get to the market because of not having employees on the ground.

To save time by putting information online.

To get bulk information out quickly.

Creative Strategy

What are we going to try to achieve creatively, with our client's product or service?

Make the site become their man on the ground.

Fantastic quality of information and links.

Competition

Who else is selling/doing the same thing our client is?

1. Plantech — for sales
2. Pacific Seeds
3. Pioneer

Competitor sites

www.pioneer.com — internationally largest co.

www.pacseeds.com.au — regarded highly, domestic only

www.seedco.com.au — good website, domestic & international

What are they doing?

Pac Seeds has credibility

Pioneers is International (but 2nd or 3rd in Aust)

Other Points

Getting access to technical information is key factor to success.

Technical info is in different formats—either PDF or Word docs.

Sometimes field days are used to inform people of products but there are only 12 reps for the whole country.

Want to be known for fantastic seed quality—customer may not know SeedTech but will know the local retailer.

Much of range is created by orgs such as CSIRO who will also have information on the product.

Existing Branding

Do you have an existing Logo?

Yes

Is there an existing branding style guide?

No, only the work done on the annual report and brochures to date.

If no, then do you require branding and logo creation?

N/A

Is there a company slogan or tagline?

No

Summary

In this chapter, we have covered how to specify the functionality of a website that is to be implemented in eZ Publish. We started with the overall content model that identified the key classes and their relationships to each other. From there, we looked at the users and groups and what permissions each of these would have. The next part of the specification is detailing each of the features to be created and how they would operate. Finally, we looked at the way the features were to be displayed through content classes and views of that content.

What is important in creating a functional specification is to define how the requirements are to be delivered. The features are a manifestation of the requirements in concrete details and therefore it's important to get the specification as accurate as possible. This is the hardest part of the project and, if done well, will make the implementation go smoothly. A lack of detail in the specification inevitably leads to problems during development as questions arise and need to be answered, sometimes leading to discoveries that require changes to work already done.

A major part of a successful project is getting the specifications right.

6

Content Modeling

Organizing content in a meaningful way is nothing new. We have been doing it for centuries in our libraries—the Dewey decimal system being a perfect example. So, why can't we take known approaches and apply them to the Web? The main reason is that a web page has more than two dimensions. A page on a book might have footnotes or refer to other pages, but the content only appears in one place. On a web page, content can directly link to other content and even show a summary of it. It goes way beyond just the content that appears on the page—links, related content, reviews, ratings, etc. All of this brings extra dimensions to the core content of the page and how it is displayed. This is why it's so important to ensure your content model is sound. However, there is no such thing as the "right" content model. Each content model can only be judged on how well it achieves the goals of the website now and in the future.

The Purpose of a Content Model

The idea of a content model is new, but it has similarities to both a database design and an object model. The purpose of both of these is to provide a foundation for the logic of the operation. With a database design, we want to structure the data in a meaningful way to make storage and retrieval effective. With an object model, we define the objects and how they relate to each other so that accessing and managing objects is efficient and effective. The same applies to a content model. It's about structuring the content and the relationships between the classes to allow the content to be accessed and displayed easily.

The following diagram is a simple content model that shows the key content classes and how they relate to each other. In this diagram, we see that resources belong to a collection which in turn belongs to a context. Also, a particular resource can belong to more than one collection.

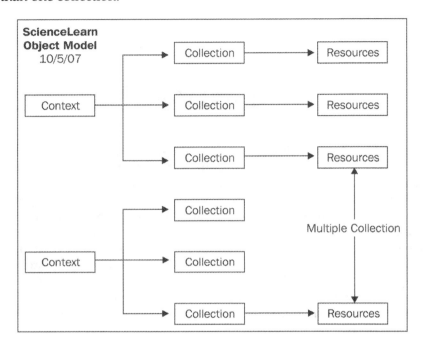

As stated before, there is no such thing as the "right" model. What we are trying to achieve is the most "effective" model for the project at hand. This means coming up with a model that will provide the most effective way of organizing content so that it can be easily displayed in the manner defined in the functional specification. The way a content model is defined will have an impact on how easy it is to code templates, how quickly the code will run, how easy it is for the editors to input content, and also how easy it is to change down the track. From experience, rarely is a project completed and then never touched again. Usually, there are changes, modifications, updates, etc. down the track. If the model is well structured, these changes will be easy, if not, they can require a significant amount of work to implement. In some cases, the project has to be rebuilt entirely and content re-entered to achieve the goals of the client. This is why the model is so important. If done well, it means the client pays less and has a better-running solution. A poor model will take longer to implement and changes will be more difficult to implement.

What Makes a Good Model?

It's not easy to define exactly what makes a good model. Like any form of design, simplicity is the key. The more the elements, the more complex it gets. Ideally, a model should be technology independent, but there are certain ways in which eZ publish operates that can influence how we structure the content model.

Do we always need a content model? No, it depends on the scale of the project. Smaller projects don't really need a formal model. It's only when there are specific relationships between content classes that we need to go to the effort of creating a model. For example, a basic website that has a number of sections, e.g., About Us, Services, Articles, Contact, etc., doesn't need a model. There's no need for an underlying structure. It's just content added to sections. The in-built content classes in eZ publish will be enough to cater for that type of site. It's when the content itself has specific relationships e.g., a book belongs to a category or a product belongs to a product group, which belongs to a division of the business — this is when you need to create a model to capture the objects and the relationships between them.

To start with, we need to understand the content we are dealing with. The broad categories are existing/known content and new content. If we know the structure of the content we are dealing with and it already exists, this can help to shape the model. If we are dealing with content that doesn't exist yet (i.e. is to be written or created for this project) it's harder to know if we are on the right track. For example, when dealing with products, generally the product data will already exist in a database or ERP system. This gives us a basis from which to work. We can establish the structure of the content and the relationships from the existing data. That doesn't mean that we simply copy what's there, but it can guide us in the right direction. Sometimes the structure of the data isn't effective for the way it's to be displayed on the Web or it's missing elements. (As a typical example, in a recent project, the product data was stored in three places — the core details were in the Point of Sale system, product details and categorisation were in a spreadsheet, and the images were stored on a file system.)

So, the first step is to get an understanding of all the content we are dealing with. If the content doesn't exist as yet, at least get some examples of what it is likely to be. Without knowing what you are dealing with, you can't be sure your model will accommodate everything.

This means you'll need to allow for modifications down the track. Of course we want to minimize this but it's not always possible. Clients change their minds so the best we can do is hope that our model will accommodate what we think are the likely changes. This really can only be done through experience. There are patterns in content as well as how it's displayed. Through these patterns e.g., a related-content box on each page, we can try to foresee the way things might alter and build room for this into the model. A good example was that on a recent project, for each object, there was the main content but there were also a number of related objects (widgets) that were to be displayed in the right-hand column of the page. Initially, the content class defined the specific widgets to be associated with the object.

The table below contains the details of a particular resource (as shown in the previous content model). It captures the details of the "research report" resource content class.

Research Report Resource

Attribute	Type	Notes
Title	Text line	
Short Title	Text Line	If present, will be used in menus and URLs
Flash	Flash	Navigator object
Hero Image	Image	(displays if no flash)
Caption	Rich text	
Body*	Rich Text	
Free Form Widgets	Related Objects	Select one or more
Multimedia Widget	Related Object	Select one

This would mean that when the editor added content, they would pick the free-form widgets and then the multimedia widget to be associated with the research report. Displaying the content would be straightforward as from the parent object we would have the object IDs for each widget.

The idea is sound but lacks flexibility. It would mean that the order in which the object was added would dictate the order in which it was displayed. It also means that if the editor wants to choose to add a different type of widget, they couldn't unless the model was changed, i.e., another attribute was added to the content class.

We updated the content class as follows:

Attribute	Type	Notes
Title*	Text line	
Short Title	Text Line	If present will be used in menus and URLs
Flash	Flash	Navigator object
Hero Image	Image	(displays if no flash)
Caption	Rich text	
Body*	Rich Text	
Widgets	Related Objects	Select one or more

This approach is less strict and provides more flexibility. The editor can choose any widget and also select the order. In terms of programming the template, there's the same amount of work. But, if we decide to add another widget type down the track, there's no need to update the content class to accommodate it.

Does this mean that anytime we have a related object we should use the latter approach? No, the reason we did it in this situation is that the content was still being written as we were creating the model, and there was a good chance that once the content was entered and we saw the end result, the client was going to say something like "can we add widget x" to the right-hand column of a context object? In a different project, in which a particular widget should only be related to a particular content class, it's better to enforce the rule by only allowing that widget to be associated with that content class.

Defining a Content Model

The process of creating a content model requires a number of steps. It's not just a matter of analyzing the content; the modeler also needs to take into consideration the domain, users, groups, and the relationships between different classes within the model. To do this, we start with a walkthrough of the domain.

Step 1: Domain Walkthrough

The client and domain experts walk us through the entire project. This is a vital part of the process. We need to get an understanding of the entire system, not just the part that is captured in the final solution. The model that we end up creating may need to interact with other systems and knowing what they are and how they work will inform the shape of the model. A good example is with e-commerce systems, any information captured on a sale will eventually need to be entered into the existing financial system (whether is it automated or manual).

Without an understanding of the bigger picture, we lack the understanding of how the solution we are creating will fit in with what the business does. That's when there is an existing business process. Sometimes there is no business process and the client is making things up as they go along, e.g. they have decided to do online shopping but they have never dealt with overseas orders so don't know how that will work and have no idea how they would deal with shipping costs.

One of the typical problems that will surface during the domain walkthrough is that the client will try to tell you how they want the solution to work. By doing this, they are actually defining the model and interactions. This is something to be wary of. It is unlikely that they would be aware of how best to structure a solution; what you want to be asking is what they currently do, what's their current business process.

You want to deal with facts that are in existence so that you can decide how best to model the solution. To get the client back on track ask questions like:

- How do you currently do "it" (i.e. the business process)?
- What information to you currently capture?
- How do you capture that information?
- What format is that information in?
- How often is the information updated?
- Who updates it?

This gives you a picture of what is currently happening. Then you can start to shape the model to ensure that you are dealing with the real world, not what the client thinks they want. Sometimes they won't be able to answer the question and you'll have to get the right person from the business involved to get the answers you want. Sometimes you discover that what the client thought was happening is not really what happens.

Another benefit of this process is gaining a common understanding. If both you and the client are in the room when the process for calculating shipping costs is being explained by the Shipping Manager, you'll both appreciate how complex the process is. If the client thinks it's easy, they won't expect it to cost much. If they are in the room when the shipping manager explains there are five different shipping methods and each has its own way of calculating the costs for a shipment based on their own set of international zones, you know modeling that part of the system is not going to be straightforward unlike what the client initially thought.

What this means is that the domain walkthrough gives you a sense of what's real, not what people think the situation is. It's the most important part of the process. Assumptions that "shipping costs" are straightforward, so you don't need to worry about that, can be a disaster later down the track when you find out it's not the case.

Also, don't necessarily rely on requirements documents (unless you have written them yourself). A statement in a requirements document may not reflect what really happens; that's why you want to make sure you go through everything to confirm that you have all the facts. Sometimes, a particular requirement can be stated in the document but when you go through it in more detail, ask a few questions, pose a few scenarios, the client changes their mind on what it is that they really want as they realize what they thought they wanted is going to be difficult or expensive to implement. Or, you put an alternative approach to them and they are happy to achieve the same result in a different manner that is easier to implement. This is a valuable way to work out what's real and what really matters.

Step 2: Identify Users of the System

Hold a workshop in which you identify the main users of the system e.g.:

- Admin
- Business User
- Subscribed users
- Non-subscribed users

We should have an understanding of how these groupings are viewed by the business and the marketing approach towards each from the domain walkthrough in Step 1. This allows us to design the system to meet these goals.

Once again, we are dealing with the true roles within the business. It might be that these roles are carried out by one person in the business or mixed, but when defining the model we need to be clear on the differences so we can appropriately define the permissions.

Step 3: Identify the Key Classes

Define the key classes within the model:

- Business Profile
- Location
- State
- Product/Service
- Category

These are fleshed out with attributes in the functional specification but for preliminary work it should be enough just to identify them. We aren't trying to identify EVERY object in the system; that will come later. There will be key objects that provide the core of the system. We can add other objects at a later date that may have nothing to do with the model and are just for additional content, more to do with sales and marketing than the business process we are automating.

When defining these objects it's important to use the same language as the client. For example, if the client groups products by "variety" then use the term variety rather than product group. If you try to use your own terms then there's the possibility for confusion at a later date when you're talking about details to do with product groups and the client has forgotten that you mean "variety" and doesn't realize that a permission or relationship is wrong because they don't fully understand what we mean by a product group.

Once again, if we are dealing with a known business system, chances are the objects we are talking about will already have known terms. If we are dealing with a new system that is being created as a part of the solution being built, then it's a bit more tricky. Names are very important—although Shakespeare wrote "What's in a name? That which we call a rose, by any other name would smell as sweet;" in a content model, the name given to the object is important. It has intrinsic meaning and if you use an arbitrary or misleading name, it can create confusion not only for the client but developers also, and ultimately the user. When choosing names, there are a couple of simple rules: be clear, keep them short.

Clarity comes from the name reflecting the nature of the object e.g., customer, member, supplier, product, property, etc. Name length is important when it comes to programming and displays. Long names take longer to type, a simple thing, but you don't want to have to be typing "science_ideas_and_concepts_worksheet" each time you want to access that particular object. Even though eZ publish will allow the identifier to be different from the name, it's a good idea to make them the same to avoid confusion.

Long names are also a pain when it comes to displaying the class. Often, the class name will be displayed as a part of the navigation, e.g. in a breadcrumb or as an identifier in a search result. This is where long names can cause problems. Once you've set the name, it's understood by the client and developers, templates have been coded and content entered, changing that name will be a lot of work. This is somewhat pendantic but names have instrinsic meanings. Great care needs to be taken in selecting names. What seems like a simple thing upfront can have ramifications down the track if care is not taken.

Step 4: Identify Relationships between the Classes

Capture the relationships between the classes which are stated as rules:

- A Location is in a State (e.g. Brisbane is in Queensland, Gold Coast is in Queensland)
- A Business is located in a Location

These relationships create rules, set patterns, permissions, and define how the content will be entered, managed, and related. They set what belongs to what. They're fundamental. If a product can only belong to one variety, then this is set as a rule. Changing it later becomes problematic as changes are required on a number of levels, especially if content has already been entered. For instance, if you decide that a product can only belong to one variety then it's straightforward, you never have to worry about displaying the product in different locations and deal with the different display rules that could be associated with it. You don't have to worry about it coming up in a search for products listed by variety, etc.

These rules also inform the way that content is entered into the system. We need to take into consideration the people that will be entering and maintaining the content. They will not necessarily understand the model and it's not always apparent from the way things are structured in the administration interface. So making sure we capture the rules properly will help on this level. It will stop mistakes such as an editor trying to add an object to a part of the node tree where it doesn't belong and that has no custom template to display it. A simple example is that of nesting. Let's say we are dealing with a news item. It's a common object in a CMS. One rule could be:

- News items can be added to folders

Another rule could be

- News items can only be added to news listings

There doesn't seem to be much difference to these rules. Object can be added to parent object. When it comes to using the system, it can make a big difference. The "folder" object is a standard object within eZ publish. It can contain many different types of objects and there are standard displays associated with it. If you don't want to do anything special with the news item, this will work fine. But you are at the mercy of the editors to decide which is the appropriate content type to use when they are adding content.

The second rule is more specific. It means that a news item can only ever belong to a news listing. It means that the display of the news listing and news item are set in a particular fashion. It means that the "news item" object has a particular meaning because the rule won't let the object be used for different purposes. It will force the editor to consider the nature of the content being added.

From a programming perspective, it's also easier to manage as you don't have to consider the display of the item in different contexts. For example, if the rules allow different objects to be displayed in the same parent object, we have to think about the navigation in greater depth. Let's say the folder object can contain articles and news items. A typical approach to navigation is to have all the objects within a folder listed as links down the left-hand side of the page as links to the full view of that object. How will the user know which object is a news item and which object is an article? Do we have to write extra code to differentiate between the two? Does it matter what order they are displayed in? If the news item has a date, then do we need to order them differently from the articles, which are to be displayed in an alphabetical order by name? All of these questions arise if the rules aren't clear and precise.

If the rules are clear and accurate, then development and use of the end solution will be more straightforward with less possibilities arising. The more vague and open the rules, the more the problems that arise when content is entered and you discover there's a situation that hasn't been accounted for. And also, it doesn't make sense to the end user. Then, you have to superimpose rules, which could mean re-entering of content.

However, making the rules too strict can limit the flexibility that ez publish provides. Finding a happy balance is the key. The content itself will suggest the rules and then you need to confirm them with the client by considering the edge cases and posing questions such as:

- Can a product ever belong to more than one variety?
- What happens if a variety has no products?

Step 5: Create a Relationship Diagram

This is a combination of the information from Steps 2 through 4 captured in a single relationship diagram. It consists, at it's most basic, of a sketch of circles with object names attached and arrows indicating the relationships.

A relationship diagram is similar to an object role diagram.

The model is where the objects and relationships come together in a single diagram. It captures the foundation of all work to follow. If there are mistakes in the model, there will be problems down the track. However, if you get your client to sign off on the model, then if something changes, you have concrete justification to change the budget and timeline (although the client is rarely happy about this!). It helps to protect again the evils of scope creep.

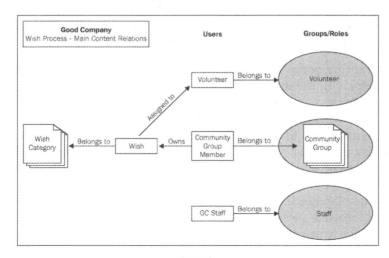

The example displayed is based on the concept of an object role model and is an effective way to capture and define an object model (for more information see `http://www.orm.net/`). An object role model is "a fact-oriented approach used to conceptually model information systems" (`http://www.objectrolemodeling.com/AboutORM/tabid/34/Default.aspx`). Given what we are doing with a content management system is modeling content (or information if you wish), the ORM approach works well. But, it's not the only way to capture a model, it's just one way to do it. If you have your own approach to modeling, that's fine as long as you capture the information in a way that you, the client, and the developer can understand. That's the key here, to get a common understanding of how things relate to each other.

Step 6: Create a Glossary

A part of the modeling process uncovers a series of terms that have a particular meaning within the system. It's important to capture the meaning and make sure there's agreement on the definitions of each term. The plain English definition of a word like "group" can have a specific meaning within a business context. The catch is that sometimes the client will use the same term to mean different things depending on the context. In one project, we had the following definitions:

Graduate Destination Survey (GDS)

The graduate destination survey is made up of two parts:

- Graduate Questions
- Course Experience Questions

However, often the "Graduate Questions" part was referred to as the GDS; as it is where the actual details of the destination of the graduate was captured. So, when talking about the "GDS", it could refer to either the entire survey or just the first part of the survey. Even though we had the definition in the glossary and the client agreed to the definition, they still used the same term to mean different things depending on the context. This is an easy trap to fall into and requires diligence to check with the client when they use a term what they are referring to. It can muddy the waters greatly when trying to create a model that is accurate and reflects the actual business system being defined.

Summary

The purpose of a content model is to capture a high-level view of the system to be created. Getting this right allows you to then go into more depth into each of the classes. It's similar in nature to a class diagram, which captures the names, attributes, and methods for all classes and the relationships between them. Everything then flows from the model: the content classes to be created, the permissions that need to be established, and the views of each content class. It's the foundation of the functional specification. Getting the model right is fundamental; if the model doesn't accurately reflect the business domain, then chances are, when the system has been built, there will be problems that will be difficult and expense to fix.

7
Planning and Pricing

With a complete specification, which the client understands and has signed off, you can now plan development and work out a fixed-price cost for the rest of the project, assuming it's an external project. For internal projects, pricing is less relevant although it still can be useful to indicate the commercial value of the project.

Project Planning

At this point, we can split the project into three distinct parts: development, content population, and testing. However, that doesn't mean that it will necessary follow that these parts will be done in succession. For smaller, less complex projects, you can complete each part after the other. In larger projects, it's not always practical or advisable to take that approach. Chances are you'll have to release some features to the client for review or provide a snapshot of the development to the client for content population. Of course, taking a staging approach with a number of releases has its advantages and disadvantages.

Standard Approach

In the case of smaller projects or projects without extensions, you can create a straightforward project plan. Those of you familiar with Microsoft Project can present a formal project plan in the form of a Gantt chart. Alternatively, a Word document will also suffice. The tool is not that important; the key is to communicate what tasks will be completed when, dependencies, and milestones.

The following table shows a plan for a standard eZ publish site without any extensions or workflow:

Task	Duration	Person Responsible	Due By
Create custom content classes	1 day	Developer	Mon 1st Oct
Implement site structure	1 day	Developer	Tues 2nd Oct
Supply sample content	-	Client	Tues 2nd Oct
Enter sample content	1 day	Developer	Wed 3rd Oct
Create custom templates	5 days	Developer	Wed 10th Oct
Apply styling	3 days	Designer	Mon 15th Oct
Testing (functionality & cross browser)	2 days	Developer & Design	Wed 17th Oct
Release to Staging	1 day	Developer	Thurs 18th Oct
Content Population	5 days	Client	Fri 26th Oct
Repeat testing & apply updates if required	2 day	Developer & Designer	Wed 31st Oct
Deploy to Production	1 day	Developer	Thurs 1st Nov

There are a few things to note about the above plan:

1. It assumes that infrastructure is in place and that eZ publish has already been installed and is ready to go.

2. The time allowed for each task is **elapsed** time, not the actual time it takes. I always allow some room for movement with each task, assuming that someone entirely dedicated to a task can lead to problems. All you need is one hiccup to put your plan out of whack.

3. The milestones are highlighted. If these milestones are not met, the project will be delayed (this is easy to show in Microsoft Project).

4. We only care about the due date, not the commencement date of each task (assuming the project starts on time). Whether the task starts early or late, it doesn't matter as long as it's delivered by the due date.

5. Stating the person responsible makes it clear who gets in trouble if things go wrong. This is mostly a protection exercise for clients who are notorious when it comes to supplying content. You can almost be sure the client will delay the project either with the lack of sample content or in the content population phase.

A key point to remember is that when you create your project plan, it's based on certain assumptions, i.e. that things will go according to plan. They rarely do and you can't plan for all possible contingencies, e.g. developers getting sick, content being late, problems arising, the client canging their mind, etc. This is just a part of life. The project plan is a reflection of how we hope the project will work but we shouldn't expect that it will always work out that way. We need to be flexible and accommodate change when it happens. Of course, when we make a change, sometimes it won't have an impact on the overall deadline but sometimes it will. This usually happens when a deliverable is late. Sometimes, it means we can't proceed and that means the deadline has to change. This is when relationships can be strained, especially when it's the client that has delivered content late and they still expect the project to be on time. The project manager has to be strong and say that unless something else changes, e.g. scope or budget, the project will be late. Of course, there are lots of ways to deal with this situation. Basically, there are three factors:

- Deadline
- No. of features
- Budget

If any one of these factors changes, it affects the other two. If the client is late on a deliverable, then unless they are willing to pay more or reduce the number of features delivered, the project will be late. It's a matter of negotiating with the client what it is that is most important to them. Some clients are happier to reduce the number of features than shift a deadline or pay more, but that will depend on the particular project or client. As a rule of thumb, if any of these factors change by more than 10%, the project is in trouble. So, you can accommodate some delays, additions, or changes but once it gets beyond 10%, the project will be in trouble. That's when you need to start negotiating to adjust the project plan.

Staged Approach

When the specification is complete, and it's clear how large the project really is, there are a number of ways to tackle it, which will depend on budget and resources. For larger projects, it's normal to break the project down into different stages; often it will be due to the client wanting to stay within a certain budget and not wanting to extend the deadline. That's when you work out what is needed for the first stage and move other features to later stages.

However, a staged approach can be more complex as you have to prevent any issues occurring with ongoing development and content population. There are a number of reasons you may choose to take a staged approach; the most common is to allow content population to occur while development is underway. For larger projects, it's also a good technique to keep the client happy and get feedback along the way rather than waiting until the end of the project, releasing everything, and waiting for all the bugs to surface and then fixing them. Another advantage is that it will help to focus your development efforts by breaking down the overall project in to "chunks" of work.

The key to the staged approach is to make sure that dependencies are managed properly. From your specification, you should be able to identify parts of the project that can be released without impacting on the rest of the project. For instance, a set of content classes and templates that relate to a particular section of the site only. That's a good stand-alone part of the site that you can release for the client to review while you move onto the next part of development.

Ideally, you should aim to have releases at set intervals (e.g. once a fortnight or once a month for larger projects). This helps to keep both you and your client focused. If you can have smaller releases, every two weeks, without significant overhead, that's even better.

The downside with a staged approach is when content population happens before the site is finished. This means you have content in a system that is still being worked on. If a change is necessary, it can affect the content already entered and mean that content has to be re-entered. Ideally, content population should be done on a staging server AFTER the content classes and users and groups have been defined.

The following project plan is an example of a staged approach taken on a recent project that included an external data feed.

Normally, all data and specification is done prior to the project. We had structured the project plan around this. Then when it came to the project starting, the client had internal difficulties delivering the data; therefore, the features that required the data could not be started and the project plan had to be adjusted. Given that we had a number of feature sets, we moved forward the ones that didn't rely on the data. We then set a date for the delivery of the data and made it extremely clear that every day the data was late, the project would be late. We put the responsibility back on the client for that part of the project.

Regarding content population, we planned to deliver a set number of features prior to allowing content population to commence. We also had to ensure the data feed was in place and working. This was deliberately structured to minimize the risk of starting content population before the data feed was ready, as that data had to be associated with custom classes we had created. The later features did not affect the content classes already released, so there was little risk of problems surfacing.

All dependencies were considered before allowing content population to commence even though the client wanted it to start much earlier. The way to manage clients that are keen to start content population early is to simply explain that if content population is started too early, it may lead to content having to be re-entered.

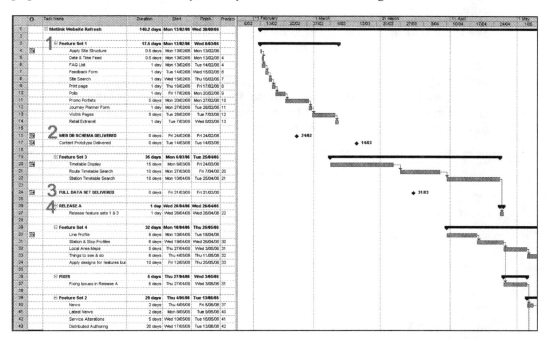

Notes:

1. We broke the project into nine feature sets, each with a set of similar features. This way we could focus on a part of the site at a time, and also have work happening on different feature sets in parallel. In this case, we initially had all the feature sets to be done in order but due to the delayed delivery of sample data, we adjusted the order and dependencies. We started with the easiest features first because we were waiting on data.

2. As a part of the project, we were building an extension to handle data that would be imported from an external system. In the original project plan, we were supposed to have the schema and data before the project commenced but the client was late in delivering this. Therefore, we weren't able to complete the schema for the extension until after we had started development, and the project plan had to be adjusted to accommodate this. Otherwise the start of the project would have been delayed by over a month.

3. In reality, the data set was late but the project deadline couldn't be moved. In this situation, the only choices available are to get more resources on the project or to reduce scope. In the end, it was clear some of the features specified were not going to be needed for the initial launch, so the scope was adjusted accordingly.

4. We planned for three separate releases during the project to allow for a staggered review of features and testing. The plan was to release a set of features, have the client review it, and then get feedback. Time was allowed during production to implement fixes. This would then mean that not all testing would be left to the last minute. It also had the advantage of the client being able to see something tangible early on in the project rather than having to wait several months before seeing anything.

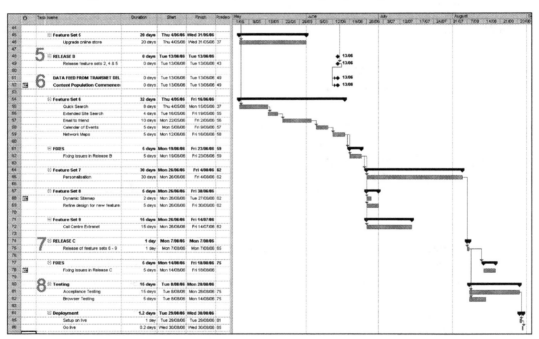

5. This shows what features were to be supplied in the second release for the client to review. As we adjusted the order of development, the features we released weren't in the same order as when the features were initially defined. The point to note here is that what was initially planned isn't the way things necessarily happen during production. The key is to identify all the features and group them in a meaningful way, normally types of functionality. Then, if you need to adjust the order, it's clear if there will be any ramifications. It might be that one set of features is dependent on another and therefore can't be moved. It might be some features are easier to get done and ready for review. This will depend on each project. As a rule of thumb, getting the most difficult features done first is a good idea to manage risk and provide enough time for review.

6. In this project, we were getting an external data feed that would be managed by the extension we had built. Even though the data feed was not our deliverable, we noted it on the project plan as it would affect content population, which in turn affected the timing of the project. In this case, content population was set to start approximately two months before the end of the project to allow for plenty of time for review. From previous experience, we knew this part of the project to have the greatest potential for blow-out as the client discovers that content either needs to be created or needs extensive review — despite the content planning done.

7. Once again, a release of a set of features. These features were specifically chosen as minimal content population would be required for these. Only one actually required the client to enter content, the rest were features that used content from the data feed.

8. Functional testing was done after each release therefore at the end of the project, all that was required was acceptance testing and browser testing. Acceptance testing covered the end-to-end testing of all features. Browser testing was making sure the site worked properly in all the specified browser/OS combinations. What actually happened during the testing phase was a combination of functionality and acceptance testing. There was also scope for updates required, which we expected would be necessary once all the features were available together in the one site.

In all, there were about eight versions of the project plan over the course of the project. As each problem arose, we had to adjust the project plan to ensure the project was delivered on time. The main problems were with the supply of data and the data feed. These delays had a significant impact on the project. The main outcome was a reduction in scope. Features that related to administration of the site were sacrificed for user functionality and were either dropped altogether or scheduled to be implemented after the site went live. The other adjustment was that the time allowed for content population was extended as some key staff left the project a month before the original go-live date. Overall, the project was delivered three weeks late, to allow for content population with a reduced set of features. Within a month after that, all remaining features had been delivered.

Pricing Your Project

There are two ways you can approach when pricing your project. The traditional method is time-based, the alternative is value-based.

This assumes:

a) you are working on an external project or

b) for internal projects there's an internal charge

If you are working on an internal project and there's no need to price the project, you can skip this part of the chapter; however, I think it's always good to have an understanding of the value of a project.

Time-Based Pricing

This is what most people use. It's based on how long it will take to complete the project multiplied by the hourly rate.

E.g.

Task	Time	Rate	Cost
eZ Installation	2 hrs	120	240
Design concepts	8 hrs	100	800
Create custom content classes	4 hrs	120	480
Implement site structure	4 hrs	120	480
Enter sample content	4 hrs	120	480
Create custom templates	35 hrs	120	4200
Apply styling	20 hrs	100	2000
Testing (functionality & cross browser)	14 hrs	100	1400
Repeat testing & apply updates if required	14 hrs	100	1400
Deploy to Production	4 hrs	120	480
Project Management	15 hrs	120	1800
	TOTAL		$15,760

For project management, I take a rule of thumb of 15% of total production time (development and design), also, when I present the budget, I remove the hours and rates and only provide the cost—unless they ask for a break down.

The advantage of time-based quoting is that if you have a clear specification, it should be accurate. Where it falls down is when it comes to who actually performs the task. If the same person always performed the same task, it would be fine because we'd know how long they take to get things done but different people work at different rates. What one developer can achieve in a day will take another developer a week. It comes down to a combination of intelligence and experience. Some developers are better than others, and the same goes with designers.

The final caveat with time-based quoting is that some clients are easy to deal with, some are difficult; you can't tell until you work with them and the impact is most likely to be on the amount of project management time required to resolve any issues that arise.

Value Pricing

Value pricing is when you apply a price to the project based on what you believe the value of the project is to the client. It's a subjective measure and is based on what you believe you can charge as opposed to what the project will cost to deliver.

 Value pricing is only relevant for external projects. If you have an internal project with internal charging, it doesn't make sense to use "value" pricing.

The benefit of this approach is that you can get a higher profit margin while still keeping the client happy. It's a win-win if what you supply to the client is equal to the value you are charging. Of course, the trick is to know what the value of the project is to the client so that you price it appropriately.

Tasks	Cost
eZ Installation	1500
Design	1500
Styling	2500
Shopping Cart	5000
Calendar	2500
Survey tool	7500
Total	$20,500

In this case, the project management and testing is included in each of the features rather than being broken out into separate tasks.

The catch is that you can over-value work and if the client questions how you came up with the price it can be hard to justify. It's also difficult when the client has comparative quotes and the figures are way out. The final risk is consistency, for example, if one client finds out how much you charged another client for the same feature, you can find yourself in an embarrassing situation. But, if you get it right, you can make a good margin with value pricing.

Summary

In planning a project there are many factors to consider. What's most important is what's the priority of your client, what their expectations are, and managing the project to that expectation. E.g. if they are flexible on timing, you can take a more relaxed approach to deadlines; however, if you have a fixed deadline, every day late will affect the project and you have to be far more diligent. The key here is to understand what is the driver of the project, which will be based on the client's expectations that you have established as a part of the project planning workshop.

What's important to realize is that whatever you plan upfront is more than likely to change, so you need to be able to adapt and change your plan if and when the need arises. There's no such thing as the perfect project plan. Each project requires its own plan and the only thing you can be sure of is that it's unlikely to work out exactly as you'd planned it.

With pricing a project, for internal projects it's a function of the amount of time the project will take. For external projects, you can take the same approach, or if you have a good understanding of the client, you can take the value-pricing approach and charge what you believe the client is willing to pay: a more profitable but more risky approach.

8
Risk Management

We are all intuitively aware of the risks that we face in projects. We know them only too well as often we are the ones who deal with them when they come to light.

As developers, we want to duck for cover when a new feature gets added as a great new idea and "we'll work out the details later".

As project managers, we get suspicious when a developer says "if we just upgrade to version x" it will be all fine.

As the project team, we want to run and hide when the Sales Manager tells the client "sure we can have it done in six weeks".

We talk about what we know is going to be a problem after the meeting, over coffee, at drinks after work. We know when a project is going to be problematic, when the timeframes are unreasonable, when the feature doesn't make sense.

We know this in our hearts. But what do we do about it? Most often, the answer is not enough. And that's not because we don't care or don't want to, it's because there's rarely a formal approach that we can use to raise awareness of risks and get something done.

Risk management has been a problem in traditional software management for a long time and it's no different in an eZ publish project. In some respects, it's even harder; as often we are dealing with content that doesn't exist. But it's not that hard; there are only two goals we are trying to achieve with risk management:

- Take action to minimize risk
- Raise awareness so that if things do go wrong, we avoid the blame game

The rest of this chapter covers, in detail, what's involved in risk management and how to apply it to eZ publish projects. Much of the material is based on the Risk Toolset created by Rob Thomsett of Thomsett International.

Key Steps in Risk Management

The first thing to understand in risk management is that it's an on-going activity. It's not about identifying risks upfront and then forging ahead regardless. It's too easy to forget the risks once the project is started, and fail to recognize and raise new risks when the project is underway.

The key steps to risk management are summarized below:

- Risk Assessment
- Risk Reduction / Minimization / Containment
- Risk Monitoring
- Risk Reporting
- Risk Evaluation

A key part to project management is a common language. The diagram below shows the key steps of risk management in the overall context of analysis and control. As outlined in the introduction, there are two key outcomes for risk management, action and awareness. Through risk control, we manage action; through risk analysis, we manage awareness.

The diagram below shows the breakdown of risk management. On the left, we have risk analysis, which comprises reviewing risks, evaluating risks, and reducing risks. This is the "action" side of risk management. On the right, we have risk control, which comprises risk monitoring and reporting. This is the awareness and prevention side of risk reporting.

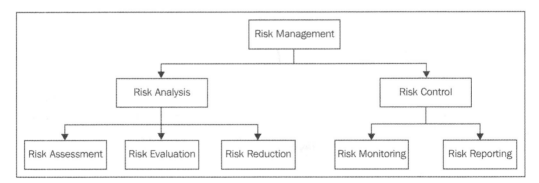

Case Note

On a recent project, I was given a perfect opportunity to raise any risks that I thought would affect the project before we started production. The specification had been completed so we knew what we had to deliver as well as the timeline. I dutifully followed the process outlined in the rest of this chapter. I put together a document that contained the six key risks that the project was facing. For each key risk, I presented a risk memo that outlined the risk, the impact on the project, the potential cost of non-containment, a solution and contingency plan. It was a bit more than the client was expecting. I thought that the client would be happy to know the risks upfront and be able to take action.

After the initial shock of seeing all the things that could go wrong, we had awareness. Half the battle won. In the other half, action didn't quite happen. Although the actions for each risk were detailed, very few of them were followed up (the majority of the actions were the responsibility of the client). When the risks started to impact on the project, then the client wasn't happy. They had accepted the risk, but hoped it would not surface and did not take any action to prevent it occurring. Unfortunately, when the risk did arise, it took more work to repair the damage done than if preventive measures had been put in place. As the project manager, although I had raised awareness, I hadn't continued to report on the risks. So, the client was in a false state of security assuming that the risk was no longer there.

Risk Assessment

The goal of risk assessment is to identify the risk factors that are a part of the activity being undertaken. Basically, it's about working out what could go wrong.

For example, the task could be attending a client meeting. The possible risk factors would include:

- Distance from office to client's premises
- Number of people who have to attend the meeting
- What materials are required for meeting (e.g. Laptop, projector, etc.)
- Availability of cabs
- Availability of public transport
- Time of meeting, e.g. Mid-day, peak hour

The more risk factors there are with a given task, the more the chances that the task can go wrong.

Risk Evaluation

Once you have identified the risk factors, then you have to work out what impact they can have on the task.

Following the previous example, what would be the impact of arriving at the meeting late?

- Would you lose the account?
- Would you get fired by your boss?
- Would it have an impact on your next review?
- Nothing, the client won't mind

If the impact is low, the risk doesn't require much attention

Risk Reduction

Risk reduction can also be termed risk containment or risk minimization. What term you use doesn't matter as long as you are consistent. There are two parts to risk reduction:

- Plans or actions that can be taken to reduce the risk
- Introduction of strategies that will minimize the impact of the risk

For getting to our client meeting on time, we could take the following actions:

- Leave earlier (allow more travel time)
- Shift the meeting to non-peak travel time
- Call the client to let them know we are running late

The idea is to avoid the risk altogether, but if that's not possible, have plans in place that can minimize the impact.

Risk Monitoring

Risk monitoring has two dimensions. Firstly it's about keeping an eye on the risks that you've already identified to see if anything has changed, if the impact has increased or decreased, which could require action. And secondly, to see if there are any new risks that have arisen during the project.

For example, while we're on our way to the client meeting, we could be keeping an eye on the time while listening to traffic reports for any potential traffic delays.

The most important thing to remember is that just because we have identified risks upfront, that doesn't mean new ones won't emerge.

Risk Reporting

Risk reporting is about ongoing awareness and the effectiveness of any actions or strategies taken to contain or reduce risk. For example, calling your colleagues about traffic delays or train cancellations.

The goal of risk reporting is to keep an eye on the existing risks to help tackle any new arising ones.

Types of Risks

Now that we've covered the key tasks of risk management, we need to understand that there are different types of risks, which have different impacts and therefore need to be treated differently. The following list covers pretty much every risk you can think of; fortunately, they don't always apply. For example, if you have been working with the same team in the same office for many years — the team environment risks won't apply. But it's good to be aware of all of the types of risks as it helps to understand all the things that can go wrong. It might seem a bit overwhelming to consider things from such a negative point of view, but that's what risk management is about. It is trying to work out what all the problems are, so that you can avoid them or manage them effectively. A lack of risk management is what leads to the high failure rates in projects.

It's important to understand that risks aren't just confined to the project, they also apply to the business, the suppliers, the people working on the project, as well as the system and people that have to support and use the project. There are a lot of angles to consider, some of which won't matter, some of which will be significant and need action. These can all be captured under the following five categories:

- Project Risk
- Business Risk
- Production System Risk
- Benefits Realization Risk
- Personal Risk

Project Risk

Put simply, project risks are factors that could cause the project to fail. They are the most significant of the risk types and have a number of sub-types that need to be considered. These are:

- System or product complexity
- Client or target environment
- Team environment
- Business project risk

System Complexity

This is about how big and complex the project is. E.g.:

- The number of features
- The volume of content
- The levels of workflow required
- The levels of permissions required
- The clarity of the requirements
- The expected volume of traffic
- The expected number of users
- The expected response times

Each of these factors can impact on the project, and what type of risks it is subject to. For example, a site with no workflow but a large volume of content and high traffic would need to consider performance as a major element, whereas a smaller site that has an e-commerce component would have security as a high risk factor.

Target Environment

This is about where the end solution will be used and the nature of the users. E.g.:

- The level of internet access
- The knowledge level of the users
- Public or internal system
- The required level of interaction with the system

- The quality of the equipment being used, screen resolution/ plugins required, etc.
- The degree of project sponsor buy-in and support
- The impact of the solution on the people using it

These days, internet applications are being used more and more, both internally and externally, therefore can have a significant impact on the business if they fail.

Team Environment

This would have to be one of the most important risk types. The team makes a huge difference to the success of a project. If you have a well functioning experienced team, it's a huge advantage. This risk type needs careful consideration. It can make or break a project.

The main factors to consider are:

- Is the timeline fixed or flexible?
- Has the team worked together before?
- Is the team experienced using eZ publish?
- Will the team stay consistent throughout the project?
- Will outside contractors be required?
- Is the team working together?
- Is it a positive work environment?
- Does the team have the equipment?

A new team without experience is a recipe for disaster. Anyone new to eZ publish will have a learning curve that will increase the length of the project and impact on the quality of the outcome.

Business Project Risk

Along with the overall system complexity, there's also the business project risk, which is similar but not the same. It is about the business aspect of the project, not the end result. If the project is moving into a new area that hasn't been tried or tested, the risk is greater as there's no indication of how it's going to be accepted or if it will achieve the goals it's supposed to. There's a big difference in replacing a static website with one built in eZ publish, as opposed to a web application to be used to provide online quotes for insurance products.

The factors to look for in business project risks are:

- The intrinsic complexity of the business product
- The level of innovation
- The stability of requirements
- The required level of quality
- The level of compliance to processes or legislation

For a business, a complex project has a higher chance of failing, because change within businesses can be difficult to introduce. If the level of innovation is high, there is also a risk as we are dealing with something new and unknown that might not work as expected. If we have to compile with certain legal criteria, we expose the business to legal action if it's not done properly.

Business Risk

We've looked at the types of risks that can cause the project to fail, but there's another level to consider. What happens to the business if the project fails? In some cases, e.g. re-building an intranet, the impact won't be significant if the current intranet keeps working. But if the project is the sole interface the business has to its clients, the impact could cause the business to go under. What you want to look for in this type of risk is what exposure the business will face if the project fails.

From the financial perspective, the business can lose money on the project if the benefits aren't delivered. Strategically, if the project fails, it can mean the business misses an opportunity to be first to market with a new service offering. If the site fails to compile with legal requirements, the business could be exposed to legal action. If the site isn't secure enough, it can expose the business to financial loss. If the site fails to perform and keeps going offline, the image and reputation of the business can be affected.

Production System Risk

The business case for projects often fails to consider the ongoing cost of the solution.

A simple example is the need for server monitoring and security patches. A better example is the risk faced by not upgrading to the latest version of eZ publish, once the version you're using is no longer supported. But the best example is the training and support required for people using the system and any changes that might be needed.

From the client's perspective, I've found that there's excitement and enthusiasm to get the solution up and running, but when it comes to maintenance, it doesn't seem quite as important. Once it's up and running, people move on to other projects and soon forget about the solution they just delivered. Just like a car, a web application needs regular servicing and tuning. Ignoring this can lead to performance issues if the site is not monitored and maintained.

The things to look for are:

- The provision for support and maintenance
- The experience of the production support team members
- The age of the production system and versions of software
- The level of supporting documentation and training

The higher the risk of the production system, the more likely it is that the system will fail and take longer (or more effort hours) to fix. For some web applications, outages literally cost the business money so if attention isn't paid, the client will end up paying one way or another.

Benefits Realization Risk

Although it's often forgotten once a project is underway or has been delivered, there is always a reason for the project in the first place. The reason a business undertakes a project is to realize benefits in one way or another, whether it be increase in sales or improving efficiency. It's all too easy to get caught up in the details of the project and forget the bigger picture, especially when you're struggling to get content and deliver the project on time.

What needs to be considered is how realistic it is that the business will get the benefits they hope to achieve—the factors to consider include:

- The number of different stakeholders, clients, and external partners involved
- The need for culture changes / training / acceptance of the new solution
- The degree of management buy-in
- The time-frame for benefits realization
- The size of the benefits to be realized

The more stakeholders there are, the larger the number of people who will have input and need to be consulted on decisions, hence slowing the process down. If there is a need for changes to the way the business runs, there's a chance people will reject the new process in favor of the tried and trusted method. If there isn't enough time to realize the benefits of the solution, it might be considered a failure. If the expectations are that the solution will solve lots of problems, there will be greater pressure to get things right.

Personal Risk

This is also often forgotten, especially by management (unless you are management!). What is it going to mean to you or your team if this project fails? No doubt, this is something that is going to be in the back of your mind, and it's important to bring this to the surface so that management or your client is aware of the situation. And this is a serious type of risk. People can get hurt, financially by losing a job, or their health can suffer due to stress, not to mention potential legal exposure. The pressures of work can have an impact on physical and mental health not to mention professional and personal relationships. Some people under too much pressure will literally break down. Is any project worth that?

This risk is not just on the Project Manager, although they are the most likely target for stress. It can affect everyone on the project. If the Project Manager is unable to negotiate with the client (be in an internal or external project) and the deadline can't be moved, then the pressure moves to the development team who are asked to work longer and longer hours to get the project done. This can lead to burn out, and people resigning, which of course impacts on the project and on both businesses involved (if its an external project). There's the factor of morale as well; when morale is down, people don't perform as well, and it can be harder to get things done.

Specifically, the factors, for the Project Manager, that need to be considered if the project fails are:

- The impact on your personal life
- The impact on your professional life
- How much your skills will be stretched
- The physical and emotional impact
- Potential exposure to legal action

Risk Management in Practice

The chapter started with an overview of the steps required for effective risk management, and then covered the different types of risks that we are likely to face. Next, we need to put this understanding into practice. That is, raise awareness and get action. There are a few techniques that can be used. Talking about it is the key, but it also helps to have a framework or structure to give substance to any discussions and create documentation that can be reviewed and referred to, down the track.

Depending on the nature of your projects, you may be able to sit down directly with whoever is in charge and spell out the major risks. That's not always the case; in larger organizations with a formal organizational structure, it's not so easy. Or, the management don't want to listen, there's no buy in. Even when you know it's a major problem, management doesn't want to hear it. If this is the case, doing a short risk assessment with the key people involved is a great way of getting buy-in and getting the attention of the decision makers.

Risk Assessment Overview

The basic premise is you get the key people in the project together and get them to fill out the following form. Each person MUST fill it out on their own so they are not biased or prejudiced by other people's view or influence. Then get everyone to share their results.

 Note: This is just an overview so doesn't cover every risk that has been outlined. It's a summary to get an idea of the overall risk of the project.

System Risks			
Overall System	☐ Simple	☐ Average	☐ Complex
Volume of existing content	☐ Small	☐ Medium	☐ Large
Volume of new content	☐ Small	☐ Medium	☐ Large
Integration with other systems	☐ Simple	☐ Average	☐ Complex
Functions / process	☐ Simple	☐ Average	☐ Complex
New business processes	☐ None	☐ Some	☐ Extensive
Stability of requirements	☐ Stable	☐ Average	☐ Unstable
Performance requirements	☐ Low	☐ Medium	☐ High
Level of innovation	☐ None	☐ Some	☐ Extensive
Environment Risks			
Client experience with CMS	☐ High	☐ Medium	☐ Low
Stakeholder support	☐ High	☐ Medium	☐ Low
Impact on client (e.g. new business process?)	☐ Low	☐ Medium	☐ High
Availability of domain expert	☐ Full time	☐ Part time	☐ Casual
Number of stakeholders	☐ 1 to 3	☐ 4 to 10	☐ Over 10

Team Risks			
Team skills with eZ publish	☐ Simple	☐ Average	☐ Complex
User skills with eZ publish	☐ Small	☐ Medium	☐ Large
Project Manager experience	☐ Small	☐ Medium	☐ Large
Size of team	☐ Simple	☐ Average	☐ Complex
Use of contractors	☐ Simple	☐ Average	☐ Complex
Project length	☐ None	☐ Some	☐ Extensive
Deadline	☐ Stable	☐ Average	☐ Unstable
Physical Environment	☐ Low	☐ Medium	☐ High
Total			

Once you get each person to fill this out, you count up the number of ticks in each column to get the total. The column with the highest number gives you a high-level indication of the risk profile of the project.

 The more ticks there are in the left column, the lower the risk. The more ticks in the right column, the higher the risk.

So, in the span of about 15 minutes, you can get a pretty good idea of the risk profile of your project. The benefit of getting the stakeholders involved is that you're creating instant awareness. You haven't had to say anything, they can see it in front of them! Hopefully, that means you can get straight down to focusing on what to do about the major risks. If there are too many risks, then now's the time to stop the project.

In particular, there are two things that you are looking for:

- What people agree on
- What people strongly disagree on

For the elements that people agree on, whether it's that the project has little risk or there is an aspect that is high risk, at least the key people are of the same mindset, and any arguments will only be over what to do about the situation. You've achieved what you wanted, raised awareness; and hopefully, got agreement that action is to be taken (what action, depends on the project and the risk itself).

For the elements that people strongly disagree on, e.g. Person A says it's not a risk and Person B thinks it is a big risk, then you've identified yet another risk, the ability to get consensus.

For a project manager, this is powerful insight into the potential issues you may face down the track when decisions need to be made. Projects rarely run smoothly and changes are inevitable. If you have stakeholders or decision makers that can't agree, it's going to be hard to get direction on what to do, and you don't want to be stuck in the middle. This is a perfect example of a personal risk factor. Of course, this approach doesn't resolve the issue, but it makes you as the project manager aware of it, and you can then decide how you're going to manage it, e.g. take the risk or walk away (assuming that's an option!).

Of all the risks identified, the most important ones are the team risks. If you have an experienced team that has worked together, you can counter many of the risks. But if your team is inexperienced, even medium-level risks can become problems. At the end of the day, the success of a project is going to depend on the team.

Risk Memos

An alternative approach is for you as an individual, or each member of your team, to identify, analyze, and evaluate all the potential risks. Then, it's just a matter of working out what can be done to prevent them from happening, or contain and control the impact they will have on the project.

Now, all projects will have risks, there's always something that can go wrong and identifying every risk is counter productive, it's only the high risk factors that need to be brought to the attention of management to get action or create awareness. Trying to cover off every risk is not possible or productive. That's why this chapter is titled "Risk Management", because at the end of the day, that's all you're doing, managing the risk. The small or remote risks are going to be there anyway; what you need to do is make sure the major risks are dealt with.

A simple way to do this is using a risk memo, which states the risk, the impact on the project, the potential cost, reduction strategies, and a contingency plan. It may seem like a lot of work but it's pretty straightforward using the following template.

Risk Memo

Risk Factor	Legacy database structure is not optimized for website needs.
Impact (if not resolved)	Site will perform slowly.
	Development will be complex.
Cost of non-containment	Estimate additional 1 month development & testing work required.
	Cost: $25 – 30k
Minimization Strategy	Design database structure for website and migrate external data into the web database.
Contingency Plan	Purchase more hardware to manage increased load.

The above example is from a real project. It took approximately ten months to complete, from the start of the specification, to go live. After the specification was completed, I identified the major risks. There were seven in total. All seven risks had the potential to put the project over time by anywhere from one to four months. Anything that was going to cause a delay of less than a week, I didn't bother to document, because those sorts of problems could be dealt with during production. The key was to make sure to identify any problems that would cause a serious overrun in terms of budget or timeline.

Shooting the Messenger

If you take the risk memo approach and then present it to management or the stakeholder, beware of the "Shoot the Messenger" syndrome. In the project from which the above risk memo example comes, I was considered a messenger with bad news and it wasn't taken well. Rather than focusing on the risk at hand, management looked at me as the problem for highlighting the risk. In hindsight, I would have been much better off taking the short assessment approach because then I wouldn't have ended up at a meeting table with a barrage of angry faces and shouts of "why didn't you tell me this earlier!". Trust me, it's not much fun!

The reality is no-one likes bad news. Knowing this, I started the meeting with a quote from the most recent Standish Report on Project Success; it said that over 70% of software projects fail—not something management likes to hear. My rationale for saying this was to prepare the stakeholders for bad news, that chances were, their project would fail. Of course, I felt safe in the knowledge that I had the answer and if they followed the minimization strategies outlined in the risk memos, everything would be fine.

To some degree this approach worked, but mostly it just got a lot of people worried and upset, including me. From my experience, you can't just tell people bad news and expect them to accept it and act immediately. In my case, I got some action and then the rest of the risks were ignored and dealt with later. A better approach is to get people to come to there own conclusions; this is why starting off with the short assessment form is an easier way to deal with risk management.

Risk management itself is a risky activity, but an important one. It's a bit like insurance; you can get away without it until something goes wrong at which point you wished you had done something earlier.

Who is Responsible?

If you've gotten to this point in one piece, you're doing well! Hopefully, you've got awareness of the risks and agreed on action. Now, it's a matter of making sure the action is taken by the right people and that depends on the nature of the risk.

For business risk, it's the project sponsor and stakeholders that are ultimately responsible.

For project risk, the project manager is in charge, hopefully with support from stakeholders.

For production / system risk, it's usually the IT team.

For benefits realization risks, it's back to the stakeholders as they are the ones who stand to lose if this is not addressed.

Finally, personal risk, and that's up to you!

Risk Reporting

Once the project is underway, it doesn't end there. As mentioned at the start of the chapter, risk management is an **on-going** activity.

The following risk report is an example of what needs to be updated on a weekly basis to:

- Monitor progress on minimizing known risk
- Identify any new risks

All that is required is a list of all high-risk factors, in order of priority, with the number of weeks the risk has been on the list. For each risk, there should also be a risk memo that has more details that can be referred to, if needed. This is a summary that can be used to maintain awareness and make sure action is taken.

Risk Report

This Week	Weeks in Total	Risk Factor	Minimization Strategy
1	4	External schema not optimized for web	Create, define new data structure and script transformation for data feed
2	4	Interactive Planner integration needs, uncertain	Get technical documentation for interactive planner
3	1	Sample data not available	Create sample data set for initial testing
4	5	Performance requirements not confirmed	Define performance requirements for normal & peak load times – concurrent requests per second
5	5	Unclear roles & responsibilities	Draft roles & responsibilities and assign to team members

There are a few points to note in the above example:

The third row shows a new risk. In this project, there was a milestone for the client to provide sample data for the developers to use in constructing a particular feature. The deadline passed and even though emails had been sent noting this—it wasn't acted upon. Being able to add this to the risk report raised the profile and helped to make the stakeholder aware that something needed to be done and pressure was placed on the department that was supposed to supply the data.

The fourth row shows a risk to do with performance. It's placed lower in the list as it won't impact on the project until the later stages, but it was important to have it on the list so that it could be dealt with in due course.

The fifth row shows a risk that was noted upfront but not dealt with. The project was moving forward without too much issue, but there was still some confusion as to who was responsible for some parts of the project; however, it wasn't having too significant an impact on the project. In time, some risks prove to be less serious that initially expected, so can come off the list.

Key Risks in eZ publish Projects

The majority of the information in this chapter could apply to most projects. For eZ publish projects, there are two main risks to be aware of:

Experience

The most important is the experience level of the production team. Despite the level of documentation and the ease of installation, eZ publish is a sophisticated application and not something that can be installed and configured in a week. It takes time to get a full understanding of the application and how it operates, to then be able to effectively use it to deliver quality solutions.

If you're starting on your first project with eZ publish, and you don't have an experienced eZ publish programmer, at least double the amount of time you think it will take. The official technical training course takes 4 days. That's for a developer with PHP and MySQL skills. Then allow another 2 – 3 months of working with eZ publish for that developer to be proficient enough to be able to develop sites with any level of interactivity.

The same goes for clients; if this is the first content management based site that they are embarking on, there will be a learning curve for them to understand how eZ publish-based solutions differ from a static website. It will definitely increase the time taken to get the specification right and ensure that there's a full understanding of how the end result will be implemented and work.

Finally, the experience of the end user of the system is important to ensure it achieves the expected benefits. Part of this can be managed by training, but there is still a factor that relies on the people using the system. They have to be proficient with the Web and at the same time, have an understanding of content. Naturally, people who understand the business domain and have worked with content management systems are at an advantage but it's the understanding of content and how it works with eZ publish, differing views, different locations, etc. that really matters.

Content

Over four years and 30 projects, I've only had one client that had all the content written, in the right format, and ready to be entered into the site, when production had finished. The worst example was a site that sat for six months as the client got their content together, and that was after I offered to enter it for them for free!

When it comes to content, expect the worst! Mostly likely it will be incomplete, poorly written, or in some cases, non existent. And that's even with the best intentions! Getting the content and getting it into the system is the single largest risk for project delays. Allow plenty of time for this task; if you can, take control of this and get your team to enter the content; leaving it to the client is a huge risk and puts the schedule out of your control. Naturally, if the content doesn't exist, there's not much you can do but there are techniques (see Chapter 10) that can help to mitigate this risk.

Summary

Risk management isn't a complex task, but it is a tricky one as it's rarely good news. But, it does act to avoid unrealistic expectations and provide a clear understanding of the true nature of the project. It helps to avoid the surprises that can derail a project and cause untold grief. When it comes to risk management, it pays to be paranoid and avoid problems rather than to take the "she'll be all right" attitude as much as sometimes we'd rather ignore it and hope that it doesn't happen, because if you do, you can pretty much guarantee something will go wrong!

Open Project Management

- 19% of projects will be cancelled before they ever get completed.
- 46% of projects will cost time and budget overruns.
- 35% of projects are completed on-time and on-budget.

These are some pretty alarming statistics (from the Chaos Report 2006). Although they related to software projects, I've little doubt the numbers are similar for content management projects if not worse. Basically, this means that two-thirds of projects will get into serious trouble. And the majority of that will NOT be for technical reasons; the majority of problems on projects are people related, whether that's poor requirements gathering, poor communication, poor choice of staff, poor management, or just plain ignorance.

If you are considering your first eZ publish project, it's a new technology in the emerging field of content management where there is little to guide you. How is this likely to affect your chances for success?

Ok, so far it's not looking so great—but don't give up just yet, the question we should be asking ourselves is what can we do to avoid this happening to our projects? The good news is there's a lot that can be done. The hard part is actually doing it! It's like anything that requires discipline: getting fit, losing weight, learning a new language, etc. It's about discipline and dedication.

Motivational techniques are just a bit out of scope in this book, but what this chapter does provide is a series of management techniques that are straightforward to apply and will go a long way to keeping your project on track. These practices are not the only practices out there. There are plenty to choose from and don't feel that you have to stick to the ones described here. These are simply ones that I have found to work well in content management projects. They can apply equally to web development or even software development, with some adjustments.

The management practices described in this chapter (and other parts of the book) are drawn from a variety of sources: people I've worked with, books I've read, things I've worked out myself through trial and error. There's nothing particularly original about any of the practices and I have no pretences that they are THE way to do things. There is no one perfect way, just lots of techniques that you can rely upon to help you at different points during a project.

That being said, many of the practices here are based on the same principles, getting the job done. The principles have been captured more succinctly in the Agile Manifesto. The Agile Manifesto was written in 2001 at Snowbird in Apsen. It was a gathering of a number of highly regarded software developers and managers including the likes of Kent Beck, Jim Highsmith, Alistair Cockburn, Martin Fowler, Ron Jeffries, Ward Cunningham, Ken Schwaber, etc.

In the late 90s, this group of people had been trying different approaches to delivering software as it seemed projects going overtime and over budget were the norm. They started using what were called "light-weight" methodologies. One of these (Crystal) was invented by Alistair Cockburn and it was Alistair that brought the group together in 2001 to see if there was anything in common between these light weight methodologies even though on the surface they used different approaches. Over the course of several days, the Agile Manifesto was written.

The Agile Manifesto is not a method, simply a mindset on what matters when it comes to building software; it is equally as relevant to implementing content management systems.

Manifesto for Agile Software Development

The following is the original Agile Manifesto (http://agilemanifesto.org/):

"We are uncovering better ways of developing software by doing it and helping others do it. Through this work we have come to value:

- Individuals and interactions over processes and tools
- Working software over comprehensive documentation
- Customer collaboration over contract negotiation
- Responding to change over following a plan

That is, while there is value in the items on the right, we value the items on the left more."

It's pretty simple but very powerful if you are able to apply it. It can also be easily mistaken and used as an excuse to avoid doing any management. Let's look at each of the values.

Individuals and Interactions over Processes and Tools

It's all too easy to get caught up in the dogmatic debates over which tool should be used for capturing requirements, version control, project planning, editing, file transfer, etc. These arguments are often distractions from what matters, i.e. getting the job done. The tool you use doesn't really matter as long as it works.

Similarly, processes can get in the way. There are some people who will follow a process or procedure to the letter, without thinking, or even worse, when the result actually hinders the project. There are times when the process can get in the way, and it's more important to get to the point. That's when talking to people is the key.

Rather than going through a formal business case proposal, sometimes it's far more useful to pick up the phone and call the project sponsor and ask a question. It's quicker and to the point. That doesn't mean we forget about documentation—we definitely want to document things, but ask the question face-to-face, then write down the answer and get confirmation that you've captured it right. That's using interaction over process and will get you much better results.

Working Software over Comprehensive Documentation

On the surface, this contradicts the importance of documentation, which is often lacking in projects and can cause problems. This value isn't saying that documentation is not important, but, when it comes down to a choice between finishing a project with a working outcome and incomplete documentation or the project being overtime but with full documentation, I'm pretty sure I know what the project sponsor is going to choose.

Once again, that's not to say documentation is not important; it's a question of what to value more and given the failure rates of projects, actually delivering the project on time is an achievement in itself. Documentation, if it's really important to the client, can be completed after the project has been delivered. Mind you, most of the time, this approach means the documentation never gets finished. But, if the project has been delivered—how much does it matter? Sure, later it becomes an issue, there's no argument there, but at least you've gotten to that stage where most projects don't.

Customer Collaboration over Contract Negotiation

I've been involved in many projects where the site has gone live around the same time as the contract has been finalized. That's not to say it's the safest way to manage a project; it's not. The purpose of the contract is to ensure that responsibilities and deliverables are clear, as well as providing a framework for resolving issues should they arise. If you have a good relationship with your client and are able to resolve things amicably, a contract is more like an insurance policy should things go wrong. The idea is to not let things go wrong in the first place; that's why there's greater value on customer collaboration rather than contract negotiation. If you're spending more effort working on clauses in a contract, you're not focusing on the project and delivering a working site. The contract is a part of the process, no doubt, but it shouldn't take precedence over dealing face to face with your client to work things out.

Responding to Change over Following a Plan

One of my favorite quotes is from Dwight Eisenhower; he said "plans are useless but planning is indispensable". Being the good project manager, I used to produce detailed Gantt charts using MS Project until I realized that the project never turned out the way I planned it. Now I know that they almost never will.

Creating the initial project plan is an important process to capture all the tasks required, the ideal order in which they should be done, and most importantly, to identify dependencies. However, what's captured in the initial project plan and how things happen in reality are often quite different. As President Dwight Eisenhower stated, "Plans are useless but planning is indispensable".

The purpose of the plan is to know what you are deviating from when you have to make a change. Change is inevitable, there's no point in fighting it. The best thing to do is simply accept it and work out how best to manage it. That doesn't mean you let the client change things at the drop of a hat—every change has its ramifications. And because you've planned out your project at the start, you know what those ramifications can be, and can let your client know what the change means. If a client asks me, halfway through a project, if they can change something, the answer is always yes, as long as the client is willing to change the timeframe and budget, accordingly. That tends to keep things focused!

Open Management Practices

These practices have one thing in common, they are about keeping the project open. Information should be transparent. Everyone should know what's going on, at all levels of the project. The presentation of the information may change depending on the audience, e.g. summaries for management, detailed specifications for developers, but it should all be accessible by anyone on the project.

Team Dynamics

The first and most important part of the project is creating the team. Jeff Deluca (inventor of Feature-Driven Development) talks about building the system that will build the system. What this means is a group of people with clear roles, responsibilities, and a framework for working together to produce the end result. The team is the system that will build the site. If the team works well together, the project will go smoothly. If the team doesn't work together, the project will be difficult, regardless of what process you use.

Who's on the Team?

You'd expect a standard team to consist of a Project Manager, an experienced eZ publish developer, a designer, and perhaps a system administrator. If that's what you expect, you're missing a very important element — the project owner. That's the person who makes the calls on what can be cut, what can be moved to stage two, what extra features have to be added (with the appropriate cost and time increase, naturally). It's a mistake that is very easy to make. By excluding the client, project owner/sponsor (or whatever term you use for the person that has the final say), it sets up the potential for a negative dynamic. I call this the "Us" and "Them" syndrome. It's an easy syndrome to fall foul of; it only takes a few requests or changes of mind to get a developer's back up and suddenly the developer starts cursing every time the client comes into the room to check on what's happening.

As a Project Manager, I've also fallen for this trap and ended up avoiding meetings with the client so that I didn't have to continue to explain why any change would cost more money and take more time. All I did was avoid the inevitable and made it worse. The key is to realize that everyone is actually on the same team; it may not feel like it at times but the reality is, everyone should be trying to achieve the same thing, a successful outcome! If not, then you've got a serious problem to solve.

It's important to build trust and respect between all the people on the team. It may not be possible to achieve this 100%, and in those cases, it's a matter of finding ways to minimize the impact of any negativity. If that means changing roles or changing people on the team, then just do it. A motto I learned from Jeff Deluca about project management is simply do "whatever it takes" to get the job done (within the bounds of the law of course!).

In terms of practical steps, the most important is to make sure roles and responsibilities are clear. Simple and effective yet not that common in practice. Sure, we all know what a designer and a developer do, but on a particular project, these roles can differ depending on the nature of the people involved and the project itself. So, the goal is to have a page that outlines all the roles and responsibilities and who has been assigned each role. On smaller projects, one person may play multiple roles; on larger projects, multiple people may play the same role. What matters is everyone knows what their role is, and what they are responsible for.

The following diagram and role details are an example of the standard roles in an eZ publish project:

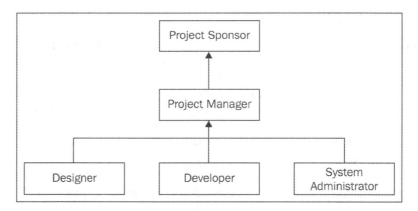

Project Sponsor/Client

Responsibilities	• Defining and approving project objectives • Reviewing and approving project deliverables • Realizing project benefits • Approving / rejecting change requests
Assigned To	----
Reports To	CEO

Project Manager

Responsibilities	Project-wide management of planning, tracking, reporting, and quality management: • Issue & risk management • Planning • Progress reporting • Scope change management
Assigned To	----
Reports to	Project Sponsor

Designer

Responsibilities	• Creating visual layout (Photoshop) • Creating web images • Building CSS • Ensuring accessibility AA rating (according to W3C standards)
Assigned To	----
Reports To	Project Manager

Developer

Responsibilities	The developer is responsible for the configuration of eZ publish and implementation of custom features: • Design features • Code features • Unit testing • Debugging • Creating templates
Assigned To	----
Reports To	Project Manager

System Administrator

Responsibilities	Ensuring systems are configured and operational for project: • Setup of dev & preview environments • Maintenance of dev & preview environments • OS configuration • Web server configuration • eZ Publish installation • Ensuring system meets performance requirements
Assigned To	----
Reports To	Project Manager

Avoiding the "Us and Them" Syndrome

If you make the mistake of thinking that the team **doesn't** include the Client, then chances are you'll fall into the "Us and Them" syndrome. This typically happens when the developer has worked hard to deliver a feature, which the Project Manager then presents to the Client. The Client then changes their mind about what they really want, now that they can see that what they asked for isn't quite right. This happens all the time and is a naturally part of projects. Despite the best intentions, sometimes when a feature is delivered, the Client realizes their initial thoughts were wrong. So, the changes are worked out and the developer informed. The first time it's OK, the second time you might hear a few grumbles from the developer, the third time, be prepared for expletives!

What happens here is the Developer starts seeing the Client as one of "Them", "they" are causing all the problems because "they" can't work out what they want and it's "their" fault that weekend work is going to be needed to finish the job.

This type of mindset can happen between anyone who provides input into the project and even within the team, and it's insidious. People start to become difficult, push back on things, deliberately slow down, cause problems, and basically undermine the project. As professionals one would like to think we would rise above this but we are also human and prone to frustrations. The key is to be aware of this so that you can do whatever it takes to avoid this syndrome. Involve the Developer in meetings with the Client, try to make sure they see each other's point of view, and if that doesn't work, get someone to facilitate or change the people on the team to keep things moving.

I was working on one project where the Client and the Lead Developer, the two most influential people in the project, would no longer talk to each other, unless it was to abuse one another. It basically brought the project to a standstill until something was worked out. In the end, we had to replace the Lead Developer in order to move things forward. He was still working on the project but another Developer acted as the go-between to ensure the project was able to proceed. This situation was far more difficult to resolve than any technical issue the project raised.

On the other hand, if you are able to build an environment where there is trust and respect between everyone, things are much easier to resolve. If an issue arises, then everyone helps to solve it even if it's not directly their responsibility. The roles are there to help keep people focused but if there's a problem stopping production, then it's handy to have a team that's flexible and will help out if they can. That goes for the Client as well, e.g. allowing changes to the timeline to accommodate unexpected illness.

It's actually quite simple, either you're working together or not. If you're not working together, it's going to be a hell of a lot harder to get things done!

Daily Meetings

The idea of a daily meeting is not new and you'll find it in most of the agile methodologies. It's a simple and effective way of keeping the project on track. It's not about micro management but rather, keeping focussed and being proactive about issues that surface on a day-to-day basis.

The meeting can't be long, if it is, people will lose attention and the meeting will lose its impact. In Scrum (a popular agile methodology—http://www.controlchaos.com), they call it a "Stand Up" meeting and literally have it standing up to make sure it doesn't go on too long!

There are only three questions that need to be asked of each person on the team:

1. What did you do yesterday?
2. What are you going to do today?
3. Is there anything impacting on you getting your work done?

There are also many other things that you will learn during this meeting that you may not normally be aware of. There are subtle things that surface. The first is often punctuality, getting people around a meeting table at the same time everyday is a challenge in itself but worth it. If people don't turn up on time, they let other team members down and usually it resolves itself. If not, the person who is continually late needs to be managed. If they refuse, then they shouldn't be on the team. Of course, it's not always that easy if they play a vital role but it's all the more reason to deal with it as soon as possible as it will only cause greater issues down the track.

By getting people to state what they have done, in front of everyone, they become accountable. If they say that they will complete task X today and the next day it's not done, for most people there's a sense of guilt. This is a good thing! Either the person underestimated the task, which provides the opportunity to adjust the plan, or they need help, which can also be addressed. Basically, by being open about these things, there's a transparency about what's happening. If one person is continually failing to do what they say they will do, it won't take long to find out, and then you can decide how to manage the situation. It's much better to find out the next day than wait a week and find out something is late, when steps could have been taken earlier.

Most of all, you'll find out all the little things that get in the way of moving forward. Like sample content, feedback on designs, refinement of features—anything that might slow down progress. Knowing this, means you'll be able to act and adjust the plan, if needed.

Daily meetings are one of the most effective ways of managing the development part of a project and are a must for any team.

Communication

For a project to work, there must be clear communication between all members of the team. Sounds simple but is hard in practice, not because of time or physical constraints, e.g. the Client being out of town or a staff member on holiday, but because communication itself is imprecise. What I write and what you read it to mean can vary greatly. And that's just with the written word.

What's important to understand is that there are different forms of communication with different levels of effectiveness. The goal is to make sure the best form of communication is used. The daily meeting is an excellent example of good communication. Emails, although convenient, are easy to misinterpret.

Forms of Communication

There are three basic forms of communication: written, verbal, and visual. A combination of all three yields the best results. However, it's not always practical so it's important to know when you need to have a face-to-face meeting and when it's fine to send details via email.

Another aspect to consider is how we absorb information. The rough breakdown is as follows:

- Visual — 65%
- Auditory — 30%
- Kinesthetic — 5%

(Data from Penn State New York Learning Centre http://www2.yk.psu.edu.)

For most projects, the default approach is written documentation. The Client produces a requirements document (perhaps written by a Business Analyst or Manager), which is given to the Lead Developer to read and understand. There are so many nuances about the project that will be missed despite the best intentions of all parties. What is really important and what really matters can be missed. A single meeting between all parties can save a hell of a lot of time and effort.

On a recent project, there was a requirement for distributed authoring. The Lead Developer was on holiday when this part of the project was being specified. What the Client was after would require three levels of authorization. An external author would submit an article, their Department Manager would then approve, before going to the Web Manger to publish. When the specification was passed to the Lead Developer to estimate how long it would take, he gave what he thought was a fair assessment of the work required. When it came to actually build the feature, we found out that there was no need for the Department Manager to approve the article as that would be done **before** it was entered into the CMS. If the Lead Developer had been in the meeting when the specification was done, and was able to ask how the business process currently worked, it would have been obvious that only a two-level approval workflow was needed and time and effort could have been saved.

Unfortunately, written documentation is one of the least effective but most commonly used forms of communication. The following diagram (source: Alistair Cockburn) shows that the most effective form of communication is a group of people, in the same room, with a white board and flipchart paper to draw on. It covers all the forms of communication and types of learning.

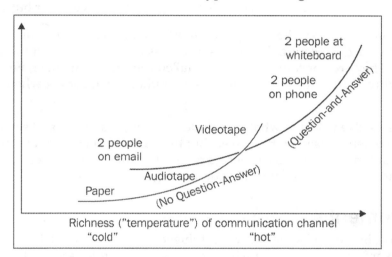

What this diagram shows is that different forms of communication have varying degrees of effectiveness. The scale across the bottom goes from cold to hot representing the least to the most effective form of communication. There are two curves on the graph. The first indicates information supplied one way—i.e., delivered to the user without any question and answer.

A paper document is the least effective, with audiotape (sound only) being better, and videotape (on film) being the best. But these are still less effective approaches than when there is interaction between the parties, i.e. the chance for question and answer. This is shown by the second curve starting with people communicating via email all the way through to two people in the same room using a whiteboard—the "richest" form of communication.

Progress Reports

Daily meetings are great to keep things moving forward during production. It's rare for the Client to be at these meetings so there needs to be a way to keep them in the loop. I've found that the best way to do this is to produce weekly progress reports. There are a number of benefits that a weekly progress report will achieve, one of the most important being a check of how things are tracking against the overall production schedule and also as a means to keep things transparent. They also can be very handy when you need to reflect on what was happening at a particular point in the project—sometimes we forget the decisions made early on and having them captured can be a lifesaver (not to mention a great way to cover your butt!).

It shouldn't take long to write a progress report. If it takes more than an hour, then you probably need a meeting; I find most progress reports take about half an hour to produce. They are not comprehensive detailed reports—remember, written communication is the least effective form—but rather a snapshot of where the project is at.

Over the years, I've adjusted what to include in a progress report and sometimes change the contents based on the project but the following headings are the core elements that I include in every progress report. For some weeks, there's nothing to say for a particular heading, which is fine, as long as it's captured.

Achievements

This is really simple—what has the team achieved in the last week. It's a straightforward question and there have been times on projects when I've actually had to stop and think about it. If there are no achievements, there better be a good reason! Sometimes there is a good reason, like lack of content or missing information (which should have already been identified in daily meetings) but given that Clients are rarely at daily meetings, this is how they find out. However, be careful about overstating achievements, it needs to be real, you don't want to lead the client into a false state of security by stating something has been done when it hasn't; avoid exaggeration or optimism, this should reflect the true state of the project, be it good or bad.

It's also a good thing to be able to clearly state what's been achieved; it's a positive sign. Sure, sometimes the achievement may not mean a lot to the Client as they may not fully understand what was done, but at least they can see that something is being done!

Basically, it forces a big picture review of the project and helps to raise issues and avoid slippage.

Dependencies

During a project, there is almost always a point in time when one member of the team is waiting for something from another member of the team. In eZ publish projects, the most common dependency is either content or a decision from the Client. Explicitly stating the dependency will hopefully make the Client aware of this. Sometimes it's not the Client directly who is supplying the material, it can be one of their staff and the Client might not be aware that it hasn't been delivered. This puts the pressure back on the Client to fulfil their role on the team.

What this part of the report should state is:

- Are we waiting on anything?
- If so, what?
- Who's responsible for delivery? E.g., waiting on design approval, sample content, etc.

Assumptions

Assumptions are the cause of many problems. Not stating and testing assumptions can lead to wasted time, effort, and money. It's also a good way to raise issues in a non-confrontational way.

It's much better to be safe than sorry and state any assumptions as soon as they arise. And it's surprising how many assumptions are made during a project. It comes back to the imprecision of communication. When there is a gap in understanding, sometimes we make an assumption rather than asking for confirmation. Do this enough times and the gap between what the Client expects and what the Developer builds can be enormous.

So, state any assumptions and get the Client to confirm if they are true or not. E.g. we assume that the content will be entered by hand, not imported from the existing database.

Issues and Risks

In Chapter 8, we discussed risks. This is the perfect place to report on existing risks and raise any new ones. It's also the place to raise any issues that have arisen during the project that need to be addressed.

It doesn't have to be comprehensive, a summary is enough. If the issue is significant, a meeting should be held to resolve it. By putting it in the progress report, you capture when the issue was first raised.

In this section, you need to include the following:

- Any problems that have occurred
- Any new risks that have surfaced
- An update on any existing risks or issues

Resolutions

The purpose of this section is to capture decisions made to resolve any issues or risks that have arisen. Once again, the full details may be captured elsewhere, e.g. in meeting notes or an email, but by including it in the progress report, it's easy to go back and see when the decision was made. It also acts as a reminder to the Client that the issue has been addressed and what the solution was.

In this section, all you need to include is a summary of what issues have been resolved and how the solution will be implemented. Sometimes, it might simply be a statement that it was decided that it wasn't a problem, and no changes are needed after all.

Sample Progress Report

Achievements

- Addition of GC-specific Admin interface
- Community Group Approval process
- Homepage design applied
- Wish lifecycle complete
- Wish reporting complete

Assumptions

- Don't need to support IE 5.0

Dependencies

- Design sign-off required by 15th Oct to meet 31st Oct release date

Issues and Risks

- **Design Concepts**
  Further revision required

- **Community Signup**
  As a part of initial registration, we need to ensure that we collect:
  confirmation of DGR status, organization name, location (NSW & Vic only).

Resolutions

- **Resolve Wish**
  No need for the text field "reason for wish being resolved" — this will come
  out of the reports each party has to fill out.

Project Extranet

Even though written documentation is a poor form of communication, it's one of
the few ways we have of capturing information. On every project, there will a series
of documents and materials that will be required by different members of the team
over the entire lifecycle. Before I decide to create Project Extranets for every project,
the amount of time I spent searching for documents and emailing copies to different
people was beyond the pale. People kept losing copies and worse, some documents
would get lost altogether. Having a single repository for all assets for the project,
from designs to progress reports, is an invaluable asset for every project.

Creating and maintaining a project extranet doesn't have to be an onerous task,
especially if you use eZ publish to create the project extranet. Although it may seem
like overkill at the start of a project, it always proves to be more than worth it in the
long run.

The key elements of a project extranet include:

- Meeting notes
- Documentation
- Progress Reports
- Tasks
- People

Meeting Notes

It doesn't matter if the meeting notes are captured in a Word doc and put on the extranet or actually entered by hand, what matters is that the meeting notes are captured and everyone on the team can seem them. It's a basic principle of open management that everyone has access to all the information. Sure, the Designer might not care about what happened in the meeting where the Developer discussed data integration, but if they want to find out, they can, and they won't feel left out (even if they might want to, at times!).

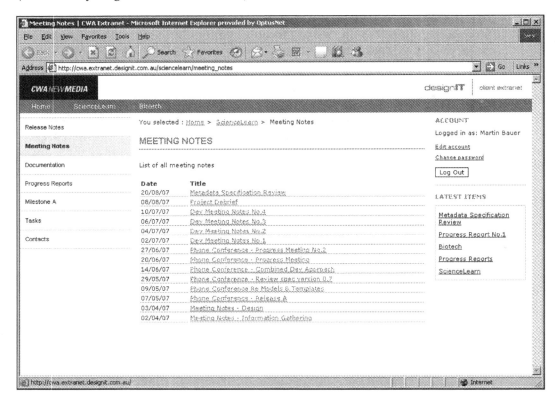

Progress Reports

Once the progress report is done, post it on the extranet for everyone to see. You should also email everyone once it's been posted.

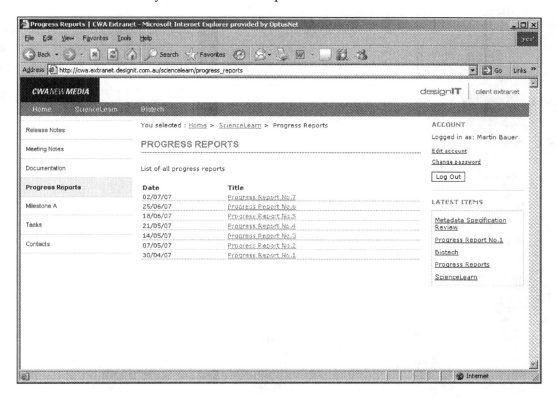

Documentation

This is a great way to make sure no one can make the excuse "I haven't got a copy!" It covers any document that has been created for the project, design concepts, specifications, project plans, budgets, reports, etc.

Tasks

I color code tasks to make it easy to see what's been done (green), what's in progess (blue), and what's late (red). As this is public information, it's pretty obvious where the fault lies if the project is running late. Especially if the task is a deliverable from the Client!

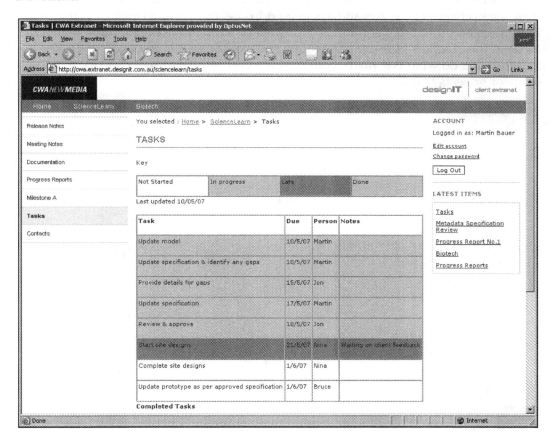

Summary

Managing projects is actually about managing people. The practices described in this chapter are people-focused. They are about getting people to work together for a common goal. By being open about every element of the project, there's less chance of surprises down the track. By considering everyone as a part of the team, there's less chance of the "Us and Them" syndrome. By meeting every day, there's individual accountability and by reporting every week, there's team responsibility. None of the practices here are complex or time consuming. It just takes discipline and focusing on what is actually going to help you avoid ending up as one of the 60+% of projects that fail.

10
Implementation

Now that we know what we are building, how it is to be built, how much it is going to cost, and what the end result will look like, it's time to actually make it happen. Looking over previous projects, the actual implementation is about a third of the entire project, the first third being in defining the project and specification, the final third being in content population and testing. The reason that implementation is not larger is because we are building on top of an existing framework, i.e. the eZ Publish Content Management Framework where much of the work has already been done, and we are only configuring and customizing as per the client's needs.

Infrastructure

Before you start configuring eZ publish based on your specification, you need to make sure you have the appropriate environments in place. For any decently sized project, you should have three environments: development, staging, and production. All three environments need to be identical in terms of configuration. The same versions of all software need to be on all servers. This is vital; a minor difference in versions of any part of the environment can lead to problems. Having a different point release of MySQL may cause problems when you move from one environment to the next.

In terms of hardware, they can be different; the development server need not be as powerful as those for staging or production. But it must have a reasonable performance or it will slow down the progress of development. If you try to cut corners and only set up a single environment, you will inevitably run into problems later in the project when content population starts and especially when there's a need for maintenance. It's best to start with the proper setup to ensure you can run the project effectively.

Development

The development environment is where the bulk of the work gets done. This is for the developers and designers to configure, code, and style the site. Clients do not need nor should have access to the development environment. This is for work in-progress only. If the development server is brought down by a bug or performance issue it doesn't matter.

Staging

This is where completed work is deployed for review by the client and for content population, review, and testing.

 Note: Do not allow content population to happen on the development environment. It's not a stable environment and chances are content can be lost. That's why any content population should happen in the staging environment, which should be a stable release of the code base and configuration. This can cause some issues when releasing new features to staging and potentially some rework, but it's a more controlled way of managing releases than having clients enter content into the development environment.

Production

This is the live server. For some projects, it's OK for the staging environment to become the production environment negating the need for a stand-alone production environment. However, this will make any future work difficult as there will no longer be a staging environment for previewing new features. That's why it's safer to have all three environments from start to finish.

Version Control

When there is only one developer working on a project, it's tempting to forget about version control and just do the work, after all, it's not like a single developer is going to have a conflict with himself! But, there are good reasons to implement version control even for projects with a single developer, and many more when there are multiple developers involved.

The main reason for version control is to protect against the fact that we are human and can make mistakes. For example, we have to extend some existing code to allow for additional functionality. In the process of extending the code, we break the original function. It happens, even developers are human! Without version control, we would have to start all over again instead of simply rolling back to the previous version. When there are multiple developers involved, there are times when you'll add code that causes something to break in another part of the system; having version control means you can roll back and return the system to a working state.

In a simplistic way, version control is like a big "undo". It helps to prevent loss of code and time, and is an essential tool in any development project.

As for which system to use, there are plenty to choose from and it will depend on your environment and how much you are willing to invest. You can pay a lot of money for a professional system or you can utilize open-source solutions such as CVS or Sub Version. Each system has its pros and cons that you'll need to investigate yourself. From experience, Sub Version has proved to be an effective solution but it doesn't matter so much which system you use as long as you are using one!

Setup

The next step in the project is to install and set up eZ publish on all three environments. This step requires commitment to a particular version of eZ publish. As the framework is constantly being worked on, you need to choose which version you are going to commit to.

This is not a straightforward decision. It may seem obvious to go for the latest release but that might not be the wisest decision. You need to look at the status of the more recent versions and pick the most stable to go with, whether it be latest or not.

For instance, it's probably not a good idea to base a project on a release candidate that hasn't been thoroughly tested. The release candidate might have more features but if they are buggy, they can cause problems during development. It's safer to go for a more stable release that may not have every feature, but is less likely to have bugs during development.

The only reason you would pick the very latest release is if it had a feature that was absolutely necessary for your project, and then you would need to keep an eye on the status of that release so that you could apply any patches during the project if they were released by eZ systems. As all code is publicly available, you can always find a stable version.

Configuration and Development

Once you have your environments set up and eZ publish installed and configured, you're ready to start configuring the system as per the specification. As a rule of thumb, the steps are as defined overleaf:

Note: This is a guideline only, and depends on the nature of your particular project. In complex projects, sometimes tackling the extensions first is a good idea, getting the hardest work out of the way. Also, it depends on how many developers are on the project. If you have a number of developers, you can have some of these tasks working in parallel.

Content Classes

The first step is to create all the content classes that have been defined in the specification. This should be a straightforward task that shouldn't take more than a few hours. It's just a matter of applying what's already been defined.

Site Structure

With the content classes in place, you can now go about creating the site structure as per the site map in the specification using the appropriate content classes. At the end of this stage, you have a complete site, albeit it is empty and with no styling, but you should be able to navigate through the site and have it match the site map exactly.

Sample Content

Now that the site framework is in place, you can add sample content to fill out the site. This can be a laborious process as you will need several copies of each content type for the site to have depth, and to see how the site holds together. Also, if your client hasn't provided content as yet, you'll have to make it up so that there's at least something in place for development to move forward.

Custom Templates

For each custom content type there will be a need to create at least one custom template, if not several e.g. full, summary, and lines views.

eZ publish has default templates but you should never touch them; instead create overrides for your custom content types. Having the site structure in place and sample content will make this process much easier. If you create the templates before you have sample content in place, sometimes you can miss finer details of the display. This is also a point where issues can arise: where the layout defined in the wireframe doesn't work well with real content, e.g. when there's significantly more or less content than expected.

Users and Groups

So far, the only user dealing with the system has been the administrator. Now, you can apply the users and groups and set the rules about what content can be added to which parts of the site and which content classes belong to which content class containers. By default, editors can pretty much add any content class to any part of the site. It may seem to make sense but, in practice, it proves to be too wide. It's better to restrict access based on the rules defined in the specification. There are two key reasons for this:

Firstly, it's about security, making sure users have the appropriate permissions and can't do things they aren't supposed to (e.g. change ini settings).

Secondly, it's to prevent people adding content to places that it doesn't belong. A good example is photo galleries. You want to make sure only images can be added to a gallery; if you allow folders to be added, it breaks consistency. It's a form of making sure the site works as it's supposed to.

Extensions and Workflow

Not all sites will need extensions or workflows but in some cases, templates will be required for extensions so you will find that further template coding is required once the extension has been built. The only way around this is to build the extension before coding the templates. This is a personal preference and will depend on the nature of the project. This is where having multiple developers can help. Have one developer working on the extensions while the other developer is dealing with content classes and custom templates. Of course, you'll need to consider dependencies in this case, which will be clear from the specification.

Styling

There are many ways in which you can choose to apply styling. You can have a single stylesheet for everything, a range of stylesheets to handle structure, content, sections, etc. There is no one correct way. The following is an approach we have agreed on after trying different approaches over a number of years. It's not the only way but it's a good start. It's based on the same mindset as the template approach in eZ systems, starting with default styling with overrides where needed.

core.css

This is where you define the overall structure of your page. Most sites follow the standard three column layout with a header and footer. This is where you define how this is to be rendered. It includes the overall structure and navigation. This stylesheet is then included in all pages. It's the default stylesheet.

style.css

You should have a web style guide that you then apply in `style.css`. This covers the content styling, e.g. headings, fonts, etc. This stylesheet will also be included on all pages.

Now that the default styles have been defined — like the default templates, we then need to define custom styles to override the default styles.

homestyle.css

Typically, a homepage is different from the rest of the site; it may even have its own custom template. This stylesheet allows you to apply the styles that are unique to the homepage. It will also include the default `style.css` so you have a starting point and then make the changes as you need them.

section_name.css

Often there will be sections that require individual styles. In this case, for each section, create a stylesheet that contains the specific styles for that section. Remember, the section will also include `style.css` and `core.css`, so you only have to define styles that are different or new from the default stylesheets.

print.css

Most sites will need a print version of the page that is formatted to fit on a standard page e.g. A4 or letter. Using a print stylesheet avoids the need to build a separate print template and is a good practice. If your client insists on a "print page" link, then you can simply make the same template render using only the print stylesheet.

Moving Code between Environments

At some point in the project, we have to move code from the development environment to the staging and ultimately the production environment. There are a number of ways of doing this.

Firstly, you need to identify what it is that you are moving across. Given that eZ publish should already be installed on the staging and production environments, you only need to upload the elements that you have changed.

This approach works fine until content population commences. Ideally, all development would happen before content population commences but sometimes, due to time constraints, content population starts before development is completed. This can work if handled carefully. What you need to do is ensure that all the content classes have been defined and permissions relating to users and groups are complete. At this point, you should be able to release this to staging for content to be entered. You can then continue developing features that will then use that content. It's a good idea to sync the staging database back to the development database at some point so that you are working with real data.

Note: If you take this approach, when deploying to staging, you would have to make sure you didn't break any of the configurations that might have altered on staging. E.g. if toolbars are added on staging, they will be captured in the `toolbars.ini` configuration file and if you pull that down to development and changes are made on the staging server, and you overwrite the staging `toolbars.ini` file with the development version, you can undo work already done on the staging environment. This is why it's much safer to complete development before you start content population. Regardless, it's likely that once the content has been entered, changes will be required that will force you into the situation of making sure the sites are in sync.

Content Gathering

This is where most projects fall down. Defining how the content is to be structured and where it is to go is simply a matter of making decisions and capturing these decisions in the form of a content model that the developers then implement within the CMS. It's not that difficult a task. The problem is when the content has to be gathered to then enter into the site. What happens in most projects is that once the model is defined, the development starts and finishes before any content is gathered. In the case of an existing database, it will be possible to transform the existing content, but often the content model will have additional content that nobody bothers to actually prepare.

This problem usually surfaces when a developer asks for sample content in order to do testing on the system. That's when things grind to a halt as someone has to take the responsibility of actually gathering the content in the right format for entry into the system.

For example, on a recent project, we were building a public website to display the full product catalogue of a car parts manufacturer. There was an existing site with a database. We were provided with a hardcopy of the product catalogue and a copy of the existing database. Based on this we created a content model and then implemented the system based on that model. We then assumed we could import the existing database. The client had been in the process of updating the content but had only done it in print format for the next printed catalogue, so the database was out of date and no longer valid. However, the data did exist in the internal database and we had to organize for an export from that database, redefine the content model as the data structure was different to what we were previously given, and then write scripts to do the transformation. This process delayed the project over a month while the details were sorted out.

The only way to avoid this problem is to make content gathering a part of the overall project plan, and assign the responsibility to someone on the project team with a deadline for having all the content ready. For smaller projects, this takes the form of a combination of Word docs and Excel spreadsheets. For larger projects, it can be worthwhile to build a small application for people to use to store the content that will then be entered into the system at a later date.

Content Population

Assuming the content model is well defined and the content has been gathered, populating the site with content should be a straightforward task. The problem that normally occurs at this point is two-fold:

- No-one is assigned to actually enter the content into the system; assumptions are made that the developer will enter content while the developer assumes the client will enter the content.

- When content is entered, the gaps in the content model become obvious and either more content must be written or adjustments need to be made to the model.

The most common outcome is that content simply doesn't exist. Even though the model was defined upfront, and someone was assigned to gather the content in the right format, there just wasn't enough content or when the content was gathered, the structure wasn't consistent, e.g., it was assumed that for all distributors there would be a head office and multiple warehouse locations, but when the content was gathered, for some distributors, the head office and warehouse were the same and the system didn't allow for it. This shows the content wasn't analyzed well enough during the modeling phase.

There are basically two types of content population, manual and automated:

Manual Content Population

Manual content population is obvious; one or more people are assigned the task of entering the content into the system. This should only be done on the staging server, which is a stable environment. This means that development, e.g. extensions, can continue while content is being entered into the system. As all the content classes and permissions have been defined, there should be no changes to the database required (other than for extensions and new content classes) and it's safe to commence content population.

Automated Content Population

This is where great care needs to be taken. Importing content is a tricky task. It should only be done for large volumes of repeatable data that have a defined structure that can be mapped to a particular content class. It becomes very difficult if the imported content has to be split across different classes. In drafting the specification, any large volumes of content should have been identified, and a sample spreadsheet provided to the client to populate with content. The spreadsheet contains named columns with examples of the content expected. Then that spreadsheet is imported into the system using a custom written script. At this point, there is no straightforward way to import content so you'll have to write your own script.

 Note: Often the content will not be correct so your script will have to validate the content first.

Things to be mindful of when importing content are that it's almost never clean or complete. Even if you supply a sample spreadsheet to the client that is structured correctly, it doesn't mean what you get back will have the same structure. Even if strict instructions are provided, sometimes the spreadsheet is returned and the structure has been slightly altered or the format of the content is different to what was expected. As a rule of thumb, the data should be reviewed and validated before the import happens.

Initial imports should be done on the development server to test that it works, then if successful, repeated on the staging server. It might seem like extra work but it's nothing compared to what can happen if you do the import on staging and it corrupts the database or causes problems with existing content. It's one of those things that you're much better to be safe than sorry about.

Another thing to be mindful of is that chances are, once you've successfully completed the import, the client will supply you with a new updated version of the content, even if they have told you the initial version was complete. So, it's good to be prepared for this contingency so that if it happens you're ready to do the import all over again. And yes, that probably means cleaning the content, importing on dev and then on staging.

Summary

Make sure you have a dedicated development and staging environments with version control and backups as this is essential. Although this seems like an obvious statement, it's easy to fall into the trap of setting up a site on a single server and working on that installation without considering what will happen once content is entered and changes need to be made. The most common problems and delays on eZ publish projects are related to gathering and entering the content; so it's important to consider that as an important part of the implementation plan. It's not just about building the content classes and developing the features, it's getting the content into the system to make sure it's working as expected.

11
Testing

The goal of this chapter is to understand the different types of testing required for eZ publish projects. This covers all levels of the end solution, not just what appears on the surface. It includes the following:

a) Load Testing
b) Testing, Monitoring, and Reporting Tools
c) Browser and User Acceptance Testing
d) Accessibility Testing

In a good project plan, plenty of time is allowed for testing and the test plan should be done after the specification, well before the solution is ready to be tested. In reality, testing time is often sacrificed to meet deadlines; this leads to the release of solutions that contain bugs that need to be fixed once the solution is in a live environment. Although it is rare for a solution to go live without some bugs, it's important to make sure obvious errors are fixed before going live. It's far more expensive and time consuming to fix problems when a solution is in production due to the additional re-testing and re-deployment involved.

Based on the nature of your solution, you may not need to perform all of the testing outlined in this chapter. Smaller, content-only solutions won't need the same level of load and user testing, but some effort should be made to ensure the solution meets the objectives of the project.

Load Testing

The first thing you need to work out is what load the solution needs to be able to support. There are a number of elements to this including standard load, peak load, and expected traffic. If you are replacing an existing solution, the best place to start is the traffic of the existing solution. In particular, what you want to look for are the peak loads. For example, the F1 website that we worked on had a particular pattern for traffic. For 11 months of the year, there was a medium load, during the two weeks leading up to the event and during the event, the peak increased by a factor of 20. So, any testing done had to work for the peak load. If that was covered, then the rest of the year, the performance of the solution would be more than enough to cope with the traffic.

The specific factors that need to be considered are set out below.

Page Views

- Average no of page view per day:
  This tells you what you'll need to deal with on a day-to-day basis, the regular performance of the site.

- Maximum number of page views in last 12 months in a single day:
  This tells you if you have to deal with any peak loads. Peak loads can happen for all sorts of reasons. E.g. for an events site, the days leading up to and including the event, holiday periods, release of a new product, an incident like an accident or tragedy, etc.

Sessions

A session is a unique set of requests from a single browser instance, the closest measurable thing to a single person visiting the website.

- Average number of sessions per day

- Maximum number of sessions in last 12 months in a single day

Web Server Connections

This is connections to the web server. A page view can create many connections to the web server depending on what the page contains.

1. Average number of connections:
   This indicates what you need to allow for on average.

2. Maximum number of connections per second:
   This gives you an indication of the peak load that the solution needs to be able to accommodate.

3. Duration of maximum number of connections per second:
    You need to know if a peak load is likely to last only a few seconds or is
    sustained over a longer period of time, e.g. minutes or hours. This is an
    important factor as solutions can recover much more easily from a spike than
    a sustained high load, where the number of incoming connections becomes
    so high that the server falls over. You also need to consider the possibility of
    memory leakage over sustained high loads. So, doing a peak load test for five
    minutes may show the solution can sustain that load — but the same test over
    a two hour period may show different results.

Database Connections

A single page view can create multiple connections to the database. Depending
on the nature of your configuration, you'll need to look at how many connections
should be in the pool and how long they should be kept alive before being released
to the pool. This is particularly important for solutions that have personalization or
accounts where caching can't be employed.

Running Load Tests

You can create and execute your own test plan using test applications such as Siege
(`http://www.joedog.org/JoeDog/Siege`).

Siege is a useful tool, it's a HTTP regression-testing and benchmarking utility. It
was built to measure the performance of a website under duress and to evaluate
how well it is likely to stand up under load once the site goes live. It allows the user
to hit a web server with a configurable number of concurrent simulated users. By
constructing standard scenarios of which pages and sections of the site you believe
are likely to be under load, you can simulate what is likely to happen in a production
environment. Based on the results, you can then look at optimization of areas that
don't meet the performance requirements.

For larger solutions, it's better to outsource the testing to a professional organization
that has the appropriate testing tools to provide you with detailed analysis
and a report.

Later in this chapter, we look at a real test plan conducted on the Metlink Melbourne
website. Initial internal testing was conducted using Seige. Once the development
team was ready for larger scale testing, an outsourced company ran further tests
using the Mercury suite of testing tools (`http://www.mercury.com/us/products/
quality-center/testdirector/`).

Note: You will need to brief the testing organization appropriately; eZ publish solutions aren't simple websites. In particular, make sure you test the solution while content is being edited. Depending on how caching has been enabled, this can have a significant impact on the performance of the solution. For example, clearing the cache while under load can cause problems that a testing organization may not consider if they are not experienced with eZ publish.

Testing, Monitoring, and Reporting Tools

It's important to understand how your solution is performing on all levels i.e. Hardware, web server, database server, and eZ publish itself. Without detailed monitoring of performance on all these, it's very difficult to troubleshoot performance issues as they can arise on one or more levels of your solution. Here, we look at what tools eZ publish has built in as well as other useful open-source tools.

eZ Debug

The first step in testing the performance of an eZ publish solution is to look at the built-in debug feature, which you can access under the **Quick settings** heading in the right-hand column of the administration section.

Once you have enabled debug on the front end, you are provided with a wealth of useful information that you can use to assess how the system is performing on a number of levels.

Note: For more detailed information on eZ Debug, see the
following article:

```
http://ez.no/community/articles/ez_publish_
performance_optimization_part_2_of_3_identifying_
trouble_spots_by_debugging
```

Debug Output

When you enable this, the debug output is included at the end of the page when
it is rendered. Note that you may need to clear the cache for it to be visible on the
front-end.

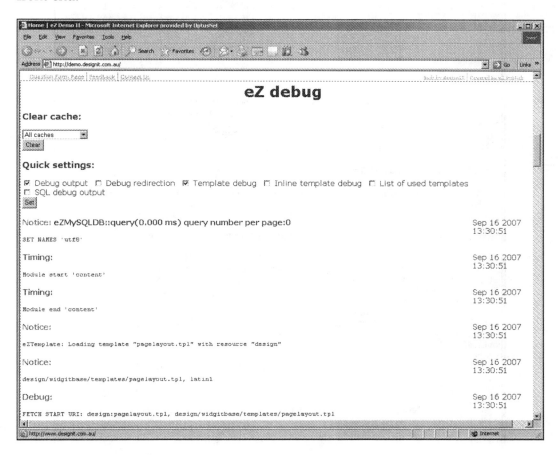

Template Debug

Template debug shows how the page is being rendered, which templates are being loaded, in which order, if there are any problems, e.g. missing variables, what design resources are being used, etc.

It also provides valuable information in terms of how long each part of the template rendering takes. The following screenshot shows the time for the module to run, and then the timing points of all of the tasks performed.

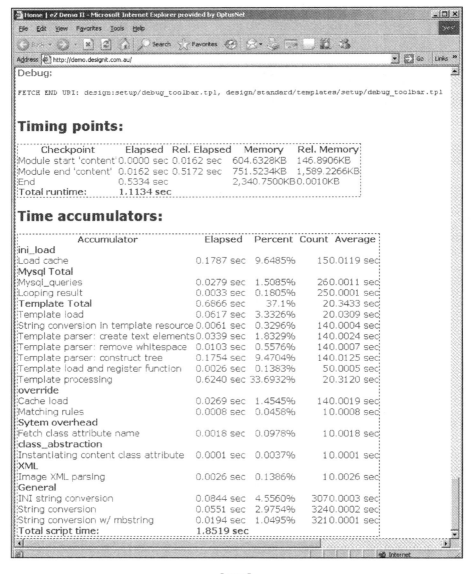

When looking at this information, what you are trying to assess is if there is a particular aspect that is taking a long time and if so, what's the problem that is occurring. For instance, a particular fetch statement could be generating numerous errors that then cause the page to take a long time to load. In the following screenshot, we can see that the template `top_navigation.tpl` is generating a number of errors in trying to access non existent variables for an array. Fixing this error would mean the page would run quicker.

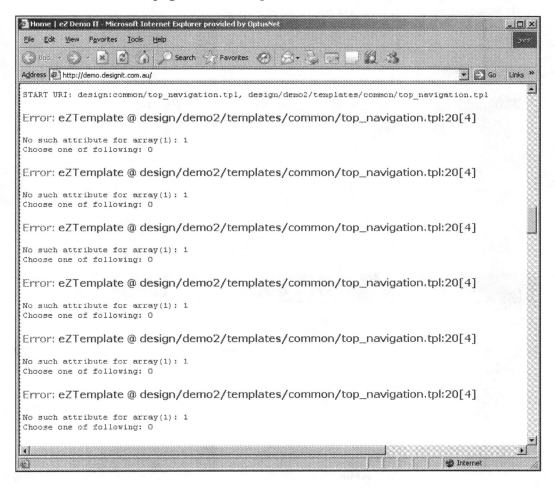

Inline Template Debug

At times you need to know which template is being used at a particular point in the rendering of the page. Inline template debug shows you the order in which templates are being used in the page by outputting the start and finish of the template, both in the source code and on the page. In the following diagram, we can see that the following templates are being used in the order displayed.

1. `design/widgitbase/templates/pagelayout.tpl`

2. `design/widgitbase/templates/common/utilities.tpl`

3. `design/demo2/templates/common/top_navigation.tpl`

4. `design/widgitbase/override/templates/full/folder.tpl`

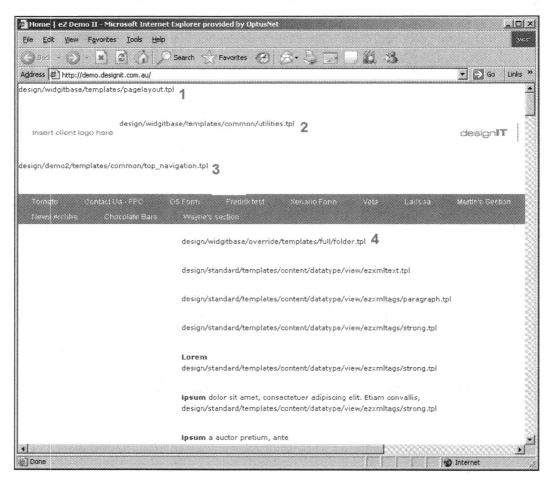

List of Used Templates

Sometimes all we want is a list of templates being used and where the template is being sourced from, e.g. is it a standard template or a custom template that is being displayed as an override? In the following diagram, we can see that the templates being used to render the page are from a variety of different designs i.e. widgitbase, demo2, and standard.

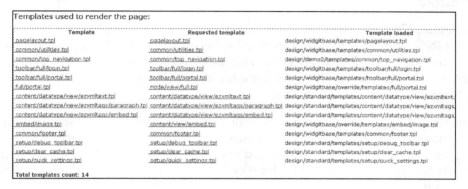

SQL Debug Output

This helps you to see what is happening during the load of the page, the specific queries being run, how many, in what order, and how long they take. When examining the SQL output, the obvious things to look for are queries that are taking a long time to run. You can then go back to your template code and see if you can adjust it to improve the performance of the page.

Nagios

`http://www.nagios.org`

Nagios is an open-source host and service monitor that is designed to inform you of performance issues before they hit a critical stage. It is often used in hosting environments to provide administrators with warnings that the system is having performance issues.

In particular, Nagios provides monitoring of network services (SMTP, POP3, HTTP, NNTP, PING, etc.). This is very important to help you know what the server is doing all the time. For instance, the HTTP service monitors if the server is responding to HTTP requests based on a particular time frame; if the server doesn't respond within time, Nagios will provide a warning.

Nagios also provides monitoring of network resources such as processor load, disk and memory usage. This is particularly useful when monitoring what happens during testing of particular features. You may find that a particular feature causes the server to have a particularly high processor load or you may find the server is running out of memory.

Having a tool such as Nagios is extremely helpful in understanding the overall performance of your site.

Cacti

`http://www.cacti.net`

While Nagios is an effective monitoring tool, it's also important to create reports to analyze the performance of your site over a period of time, to assess how it performs in different circumstances.

Cacti enables you to store information on website performance and the generate graphs of performance based on the information stored.

Typical graphs that you would generate include:

- CPU usage
- Load average
- Average no. of sessions
- No. of pages served

Mytop

`http://jeremy.zawodny.com/mysql/mytop/`

Mytop is a useful tool to monitor the performance of the database during testing. It monitors the threads and overall performances of MySQL databases. It's similar in look to the standard UNIX "top" application. It gives you the ability to monitor in real time many aspects of your database including the number of queries per second as well as the efficiency of particular queries.

Ideally, the goal is to write good SQL queries from the start, e.g. when writing extensions for eZ publish, but sometimes it's not obvious on the surface how the system will perform. Using Mytop, developers can see what is happening when their SQL queries are being run and can then look at ways to improve the queries or fine-tune the performance of MySQL. For instance, if Mytop shows that the number of inserts is much greater than the number of selects, it's unlikely that query caching will help and other solutions will need to be considered.

For more information on how to use Mytop visit:
`http://www.opensourcetutorials.com/tutorials/Server-Side-Coding/Administration/mytop/`.

Sample Test Plan

A test plan should contain details of what is to be tested, to what level and over what duration.

The following is a sample test plan for a large public website that had an extension that imported timetable data from an external database.

1.0. Executive Summary

This document is designed for the planning and execution of load testing to test the web application that is deployed to the Linux servers at GeoCentral's data center for Metweb.

1.1. Background

The proposed load tests will run a number of scenarios to test how the application performs under varying levels of usage. The tests will use a combination of up to 20 different website addresses to test the behavior of the MetWeb, VicWeb, Metstore websites, and the CMS under load. These scenarios will target three different currency levels to test the performance of the application when it is:

1. Under standard load: 200 Users and Below

2. At peak load; – as per MetWeb's documentation not to exceed 1500 Virtual Users

3. Above the peak load; maximum over 30000 user sessions

These tests will be conducted using a maximum of 30000 sessions (currently agreed level of licensing for virtual users), each virtual users simulates a number of sessions to apply the designated load during the tests. In this case, the Mercury Test suite was used to create and monitor the tests.

1.2. Scope

The tests will emulate the top 20 exit points of MetWeb's new website, based on the results for the current website that were gathered in between May and July, 2006. It will run the different scenarios by:

a) performing a controlled ramp-up to reach the level of load for a scenario, and

b) running a soak test for a period of time to identify bottlenecks and any ill effects

c) It is also designed to test the performance of the CMS when web editors are uploading content to the website during peak load periods

A preliminary report will be produced with analysis of the results. A second run will be conducted after tuning is performed. A final test report will be produced as the deliverables for the load testing. It will provide insight of the performance of the servers under various loads.

2.0. Test Design

It is important to understand that load testing is a process of approximating actual usage of a system as closely as possible, while expending as little testing effort as possible. It is not possible to exactly predict what a given group of users will do, and so approximations are required. It is also often too costly to emulate every possible usage scenario.

2.1. Test Strategy

The primary objective of the load test is to identify how the application performs under various levels of load, designed to emulate users' experience that will utilize the infrastructure at different levels, by:

a) identifying the response time of chosen queries;

b) identifying the bottleneck(s) in the application;

c) collecting the servers' performance statistics for CPU, memory, and I/O

For each and every test scenario that will be outlined in this document:

2.2. Assumptions

a) Load test will emulate the average daily load, derived from data for website hits for May-July period

b) Distribution of timetables for various types of transport will be 100% timetables for trains, using URLs provided by MetWeb

c) Each virtual user can open multiple sessions in order to generate designated loads in various load levels;

d) For each test, ramp-up time will be set to 60 seconds, and a soak run of 15 minutes taking place, providing a comfortable window for the CMS testing to be run.

e) Three different load levels will be tested:

   ° 10,000 sessions (test of under standard load) — with 20 concurrent users;

   ° 25,000 sessions (test of peak load, emulating the peak during the Commonwealth Games) with 200 concurrent users;

   ° 30,000 sessions (stress load test, if the peak load test is successful) — with 900 concurrent users;

All tests will run the same scripts that include the same test scenarios.

2.3. Test Steps

This is a description of the steps that will be taken to run the testing of the solution.

2.3.1. Setup

Installing testing tools and software on a dedicated PC that will be used to apply loads during testing.

2.3.2. Recording and Scripting

Run the steps required to complete the business process, and generate test scripts to be replayed during load testing. This will include the determination of dynamic variables for web servers, such as range of cookies for scripts to use, range of application data for queries, etc.

2.3.3. Data Population

This will ensure that the snapshot of the database is reproducible during the testing period, and allow the testing scripts to run repeatedly.

2.3.4. Test Run

The load test scripts are executed to simulate the designated load levels. The resource utilization will be monitored. Preliminary analysis of test results is performed as they become available.

2.3.5. Reporting

In depth analysis of the test results, identifying bottlenecks and malfunctions, as well as preparation of the final report.

The reports will conclude:

- How the application coped with the designated load and concurrency tests
- The usage of the server resources during the testing
- All errors experienced during testing
- If and how the tuning has improved the performance

ID	Name	Description
SC01	Train map	(place URL here)
SC02	Fare zones	
SC03	Tram map homepage	
SC04	Transport map	
SC05	Tram Quick Search	
SC06	Tram map homepage	
SC07	Timetable for Belgrave line to city	
SC08	Timetable for Frankston line to city	
SC09	Timetable for Hurstbridge to city	
SC10	Timetable for Frankston line from city	
SC11	Timetable for Hurstbridge from city	
SC12	Timetable for Belgrave line from city	
SC13	Timetable for Belgrave line to city	
SC14	MetCard store	
SC15	Timetable for Frankston to city	
SC16	Timetable for Glen Waverley to city	
SC17	Timetable for Sandringham to city	
SC18	MetWeb homepage	
SC19	Ticket Manual	
SC20	MetWeb Homepage	

2.3.6 Schedule

Task	Duration	Owner
Planning	2 days	(note owners if different parties involved)
Scripting	2 days	
Data preparation	0.5 days	
Test execution	2 days	
Analysis	(in parallel with test)	
Preliminary reporting	(in parallel with test)	
Application Dev (if required)	tba	
Final reporting	3 days	

3.0 Special Test for TransNET Update

TransNET update is a process that occurs bypassing the website application. The TransNET update, which will occur in the background and is transparent to the Web Application, will cause the cache to be out-of-date (or invalid), and the users may not get the most up-to-date information till the cache is rebuilt or updated.

The developers have introduced a process that will automatically detect any transNET update to the database, and clean up the cache that contains the TransNET information when such update is detected. Web enquiries without built cache will require more time to complete. And while the cache is being generated (triggered by a user visit to a specific web location), will also put extra load on the web servers.

In an extreme, but realistic scenario, all the cache on the web servers is cleared, and the system is under high load, or even the peak load. In this case, rebuilding the cache has been seen to crash the application, and result in Apache being restarted (i.e. an outage to the website).

The impact of such extra loads on the system was not tested in the previous tests. A particular test case has therefore been designed to perform multiple CMS update and TransNET updates while the system is under load, and manually browse the website to:

- See how the information from the updates is to be perceived by the users
- See how the application behaves and performs when the system is under load

Three tests are recommended to test the application's sustainability in handling CMS update and TransNET update together, when the system is under load:

a) A 50 Virtual User ("VU") test to emulate 50 concurrent user experience for a 15 minute run

b) A 100VU test to emulate 100 concurrent user experience for a 15 minute run

c) A 200VU test to emulate 200 concurrent user experience for a 15 minute run

Further more, two separate tests are recommended to test the application's sustainability when the entire cache is removed when the system in under load. Such tests will test the system with more reasonable peak load emulation, and include:

- A 20VU test to emulate 20 concurrent user experience for a 10 minute run
- A 50VU test to emulate 50 concurrent user experience for a 10 minute run.

3.1. General Requirements for Performing the TransNET Update and Enquiry Tasks

It is recommended that all updates of timetable information be performed for the Frankston and Belgrave lines, since these two lines are the most popular ones in the statistics, and mostly used during tests.

The following exercise applies to all tests:

Five minutes after the start of a test (for ramp-up to complete), the TransNET update, as well as the CMS update, will proceed (if necessary, take prior time in order to get the source data ready). An immediate manual enquiry on the website will be performed to retrieve the updated information, and the result, of success or failure in retrieving the updated information, will be recorded for reporting after testing.

Further TransNET and CMS updates can then be performed, and immediate manual retrievals of the information from the website are recommended, and all results to be recorded and reported.

Action plan:

Time (offset)	Action	Owner
00:00	Start baseline run for 50VU test	(define if different parties involved)
00:00	Start on screen monitoring of MySQL and servers	
00:20	Discuss test result & prepare for next test	
00:30	Start baseline run for 100VU test	
00:50	Discuss test result & prepare for next test	
01:00	Start baseline run for 200VU test	
01:20	Discuss test result & prepare for next test	
01:30	Notify George of start time for 50VU test with TransNET update	
01:35	Start the 50VU test with TransNET update	
01:40	Perform TransNET & CMS update and enquire test	
01:55	Discuss test result & prepare for next test	
02:10	Start the 100VU test with TransNET update	
02:15	Perform TransNET & CMS update and enquire test	
02:35	Discuss test result & prepare for next test	
02:50	Start the 200VU test with TransNET update	
02:55	Perform TransNET & CMS update and enquire test	
03:15	Discuss test result & prepare for next test	
03:30	Start the 20VU no cache run with TransNET & CMS update	
03:32	Perform TransNET & CMS update and enquire test	
03:45	Discuss test result & prepare for next test	
04:00	Start the 50VU no cache run with TransNET & CMS update	
04:02	Perform TransNET & CMS update and enquire test	
04:15	Discuss test result	
05:30	Copy the test results to CD-R	
05:45	Clean up on Mercury Console	

Sample Test Report

The following is an example of the reporting you would be looking for.

Test Case No. 4

Maximum Running Virtual users: 200

Started On: 25/08/2006 16:11:31

Ended On: 25/08/2006 16:27:23

Duration: Run for 000:10:00 (hhh:mm:ss)

Load Behavior: Start 2 Vusers every 00:00:02 (hh:mm:ss)

Analysis

The following graph shows hits per second for the duration of the test.

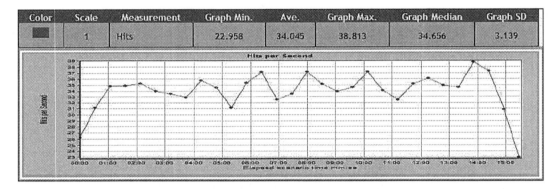

Color	Scale	Measurement	Graph Min.	Ave.	Graph Max.	Graph Median	Graph SD
	1	Hits	22.958	34.045	38.813	34.656	3.139

The following graph indicates throughput in bytes per second of the application during the test. The low points indicate that there were errors in returning data at times during the test.

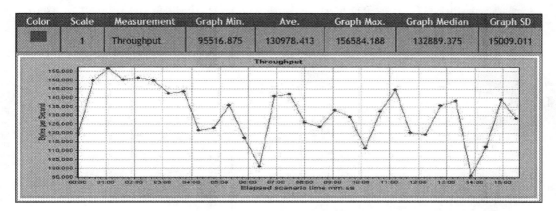

The following graph shows the response time during the test for each of the scripts run. The only one that stands out is for the Belgrave line. The Belgrave line has more stations on it and has more services than any other line in the public transport network, hence the unusually high response time in comparison with other lines.

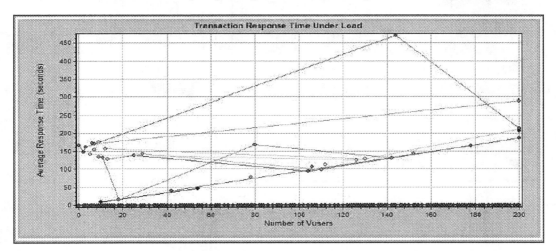

Color	Scale	Measurement	Min.	Ave.	Max.	SD
■	1	Action_Transaction	0.0	0.0	0.022	0.001
■	1	SC01_Trainmap_Transaction	39.517	102.016	164.516	62.499
■	1	SC02_Farezones_Transaction	94.046	137.055	186.096	32.899
■	1	SC03_Trammaphomepage_Transaction	127.624	165.568	211.29	34.596
■	1	SC05_TramQuickSearch_Transaction	8.601	27.392	46.183	18.791
■	1	SC06_Trammaphomepage_Transaction	98.491	123.203	143.483	18.633
■	1	SC07_TimetableforBelgraveline_Transaction	144.398	210.118	470.43	108.262
■	1	SC08_TimetableforHurstbridge_Transaction	77.465	77.465	77.465	0.001
■	1	SC10_TimetableforFrankstonline_Transaction	154.986	165.324	175.661	10.338
■	1	SC11_TimetableforHurstbridge_Transaction	124.821	133.519	142.217	8.698
■	1	SC12_TimetableforBelgraveline_Transaction	171.805	231.033	290.261	59.228
■	1	SC13_TimetableforBelgraveline_Transaction	113.279	113.279	113.279	0.001
■	1	SC14_MetCardstore_Transaction	143.092	143.092	143.092	0.001
■	1	SC15_TimetableforFrankstonline_Transaction	173.007	173.007	173.007	0.001
■	1	SC16_TimetableforGlenWaverley_Transaction	133.744	133.744	133.744	0.001
■	1	SC17_TimetableforSandringham_Transaction	106.212	106.212	106.212	0.001
■	1	SC18_Metlinkhomepage_Transaction	205.969	205.969	205.969	0.002
■	1	SC19_TicketManual_Transaction	16.114	111.907	167.358	57.155
■	1	vuser_end_Transaction	0.0	0.0	0.0	0.0
■	1	vuser_init_Transaction	0.0	0.0	0.014	0.001

a) An average of 34.045 hits /sec — an increase as expected, compared to 100 virtual users.

b) An average throughput of 130978.4413 Bytes, a decrease as compared to 100 virtual users. This is due to the high number of failed transactions that started to occur when the number of virtual users = 150 to 200.

c) Application is not accepting more enquiry while the number of virtual users = 150 to 200.

d) Transaction response time is decreasing as compared to 100 virtual users and is about 2 times higher than the time taken to record the scripts. This is due to the high number of failed transactions that started to occur when the number of virtual users = 150 to 200.

CMS test response times:

4:20 – 1.16sec

4:22 – 51sec

4:24 – 1.05sec

4.26 – 23sec

The conclusion of this test is that the application will not support more than 100 concurrent users without significant delays and errors. Given the application only needs to support a maximum of 20 concurrent users based on historical analysis, the application well exceeds the performance requirements.

Browser and User Acceptance Testing

If you have written the requirements properly, you have a list of all browser and OS combinations already defined. Then, it's simply a matter of viewing the solution using each combination to ensure the site works properly. This is a pretty straightforward test. The only thing you need to consider is that you will need to view a broad range of pages with different types of content to ensure the test is broad enough to check correct display all the content in all the browsers to be supported.

User Acceptance Testing

There are a number of ways to approach user testing. Ideally, it should be outsourced to a professional testing organization that will manage it for you and provide you with a report.

A professional testing report will provide you with details on how your expected audience interacted with the solution for a set number of tasks or scenarios. The people selected for testing should reflect the people that will be using the solution. The tasks should cover what these people are likely to use the solution for as well as the objectives of the solution. You can also include general questions such as overall impression of functionality, look and feel, etc.

For example, on a public transport site, a task would be: "Find out when the next train to Windsor station leaves Flinders street.". The testing organization will observe the person attempting to complete this task. The results will indicate the level of success, e.g.:

- Completed task easily
- Completed task with some difficulty
- Unable to complete task

Based on the results, changes to the solution can be made to fix problems that arose. Then the testing should be re-run to confirm the changes made that fixed the problems to an acceptable level.

Automated Testing with Selenium

http://www.openqa.org/selenium/

You can do the user testing and browser testing by hand or look at using an automated test tool like Selenium. Selenium is a web browser-based testing tool that allows you test if your website works correctly in different browsers on different operating systems as well as running scripts to confirm functionality works as expected. It uses a combination of JavaScript and iframes to embed test automation in a browser. It will work with most JavaScript-enabled browsers.

Accessibility Testing

Not all solutions need to meet accessibility guidelines; however, for public-facing sites, reaching at least Level 1 Accessibility is becoming a standard. For government sites, level 2 is becoming the standard.

As with user testing, this testing is often best left to experts who will provide you a full report on whether your solution meets the accessibility guidelines and also provide feedback on how to adjust your site.

You can however, do it yourself by using one of many online tools as recommended by W3C — http://www.w3.org/WAI/ER/tools/.

Summary

Unfortunately, because testing gets left to the end of the project, it's often the first thing to be cut when a project overruns. But it's important to ensure your website performs as expected. However, the key to testing is to be clear on what performance levels the website has to accommodated. Without this, it's difficult to perform meaningful testing. Like anything, without clear goals, the best path to achieving the outcomes is equally unclear.

The other thing to remember with testing is that there are a number of levels to be considered beyond just getting the client to sign off on the look and feel of the site and have it pass user acceptance testing. The lower levels such as the processor and memory usage also need to be considered, otherwise you can very quickly run into trouble if the website becomes popular.

The key is to understand what levels of performance are required so that you can put the appropriate testing in place to ensure the end solution meets those levels. Having the right tools helps but it's knowing exactly what you are testing for that's most important.

12
Training

The goal of this chapter is to outline what training is required for end users of an ez publish solution, and how to document and train users for any custom features added to their solution. The core elements are:

- Standard User Training
- Custom Training
- User Manuals
- Technical Training

Standard User Training

This training covers the basics of the system so that people can navigate the administration screens of eZ publish. It is focused on end users of the solution, not administrators of the system whose work is more technical. This training is about getting people to be able to manage content within the solution. At the conclusion of the training, trainees should be able to:

- Log in
- Add content
- Edit content
- Move content
- Delete content
- Add images/files

This training normally lasts approximately 1 hour. In practice, some people take to the system quickly and only need minimal support to be able to manage content on their own. Some people, however, find it more difficult and may require additional training or extensive phone support. It depends on each individual person. Sometimes the people being trained aren't the most appropriate for the task, in which case, the level of support required will be greater.

The best way to conduct training is through demonstration and practice. You demonstrate a particular task (e.g. using a digital projector) and then get each person in the class to perform the same task on their own machine. Simply showing people how to use the system without them interacting with it themselves will mean you'll get a lot more phone calls when the client is left to their own devices! It also helps you to work out who picks it up quickly and who's a slow learner—this is important when providing advice to your client as to who is best suited to looking after the site; it's not always the same person who has been selected for the job.

Custom Training

Once you've taken the users through the basic training, the next step is to explain to them how their site operates. Depending on your project, there could be custom content classes and custom templates that the users need to understand. For each of these elements, the user should get experience in adding, editing, and deleting them as well as seeing how their actions impact on the front end of the solution. A news story added in one section may also appear in another section, e.g. a node list on the front page; if the title is too long, it might cause formatting issues on the homepage while looking fine on the news page.

User Manual

Some clients don't need a manual, but writing one will save you a lot of time and effort down the track when you get the inevitable phone call asking something simple like "*How do I get a page out of the trash?*"

There are decent online resources for end users and recently eZ Systems have released a book to help with this—*eZ Publish Content Management Basics*. However, even if you provide a manual and a copy of the book, you should expect that you will still receive phone calls from people who aren't technically strong, and struggle even with the aid of a manual.

Even for people who have been through training, simple tasks that they don't do often will be forgotten. Some clients are smart enough to work it out for themselves but most will call you for help, that's why it's a good idea to provide them with a user manual; it's also good customer service.

There are two parts to the user manual, standard features and custom features. Standard features include everything that comes with eZ publish by default (that you have provided your client access to, e.g. administrative controls are best kept with you unless the client has technical eZ publish training). Custom features are what you have built for the client.

Standard Manual

The basics are well covered on the eZ publish website. You can create your own manual if you wish but, in doing that, you'll also have the burden of keeping it up to date with each new version of eZ publish. Given the documentation on the eZ website is quite extensive, there's little point in repeating it. However, if there are custom elements in your site, that should be documented, so the users have something to refer to later down the track. If you plan to do a number of eZ publish sites, then it's a great habit to get into, as remembering all the details of a site deployed a year ago can be a challenge!

As noted, the eZ publish instructions are good for standard tasks. They show how to add, edit, delete content; they show how to deal with versions and drafts; they explain the different areas of the administration interface; however, what they don't include is best practice, for example, when to use a folder rather than a page, when to use a link to an ezobject rather than an eznode. This "best practice" for want of a better name is what your client will expect from you. One of the strengths of eZ publish is its flexibility; that is also a weakness as there are usually many ways of achieving the same outcome, each with its own pros and cons. When it comes to managing content, the same applies. What you need to do is help your client to understand what best practice for their site is.

The basics are the same for most sites, so it's a good idea to have your own "using eZ publish" manual for your clients that extends from the basics provided by eZ Systems. Let's look at sorting content as an example; it's something that pretty much every client will want to know how to do. In the eZ publish online documentation, it's only referred to in relation to the content tab, unless you know where to look, it's easy to miss. It took me a bit of work to find it myself and I knew what I was looking for. This is just one of the tasks that need clear explanation, not just a reference at the bottom of a page if you can find it! Although constantly improving, the documentation currently provided by eZ Systems should be considered more of a reference than a user guide. The following example shows a "how to" approach as opposed to the reference guide approach that the online documentation is focused on.

Sorting Content (designIT User Manual)

You can sort items within a section alphabetically, numerically, by path, by publication date/time, and by modification date/time, by section, by priority, by name, by depth, by class identifier, and by class name.

Sorting decides in which order content will be displayed when published on your website.

The sorting controls are located underneath a section's Sub items list:

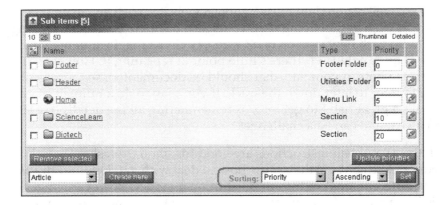

To sort content:

1. In the **Content structure tab**, navigate your way to the section you wish to edit.

2. Underneath the section's Sub items list, you will see the Sorting controls (see the previous screenshot):

3. In the **Sorting** drop down-menu, select the required option:

    *   **Name**: sort alphabetically by object name

    *   **Published**: sort by publishing date/time

    *   **Modified**: sort by modification date/time

    *   **Section**: sort by sections

    *   **Depth**: sort by item depth (in site map)

    *   **Class identifier**: sort by class identifier

    *   **Class name**: sort by class name

    *   **Priority**: sort numerically by user-defined priorities.

4. Choose either **ascending** or **descending** from the next drop-down menu.

5. Click on the **Set** button.

6. Sub items will be sorted as you requested.

[Note: you can always change the sorting at a later time, if you wish.]

Custom Manual

The custom manual should include details of how to perform the tasks that the custom features provide via custom content types or extensions. From experience, a task-orientated approach works best. Even though it helps to have an overall understanding of the architecture and object relations, clients usually aren't interested, they just want to add or change something.

When creating a custom manual, for each feature or content type, you should do the following:

- Explain the context of how the content works within the site (preferably with a screenshot)
- Provide a list of instructions
- Provide table of attributes (not absolutely necessary but a good reference)

The following is an example of a custom manual for managing maps in a public transport site.

Managing Maps Custom Feature

There are three types of maps in the MetWeb website:

- Network Maps
- Route Maps
- Local Area Maps

Each plays a different role in the site.

Network Maps

Network Maps are used to represent each mode, e.g. metropolitan trains, regional buses, etc. Network maps contain route maps (these don't appear in the sub-navigation). Network maps can also contain further network maps (e.g. city circle detail map).

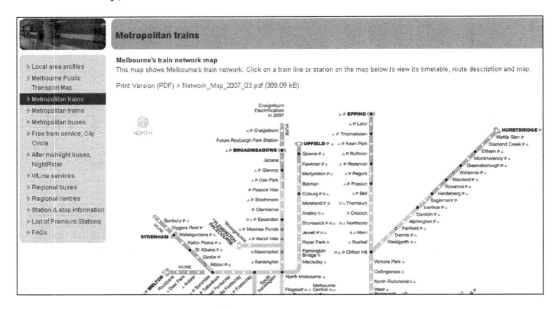

How to Add a Network Map

1. Go to **Maps Stations & Stops** in the Content Tab.
2. Select **Network Map** and click **Create Here**.
3. Enter all attributes required. Click **Send for Publishing**.

Attributes

Attribute	Type	Notes
Name	Text Line	Name of Map Displayed as page title/ head of map detail page and in menu
Map	Image	Image of map
Description	Rich Text	Displayed under map if present
PDF	Binary File	If present linked to on map detail page

Route Maps

Route maps are for each individual route, for example, the Sandringham line, the 109 Tram, etc. Route maps belong under the network map for the appropriate mode; the 109 Tram route map would live in the Metropolitan Tram Network map.

Route maps DO NOT appear in the sub-navigation and are only linked to from route profile pages, quick search results, and time table pages.

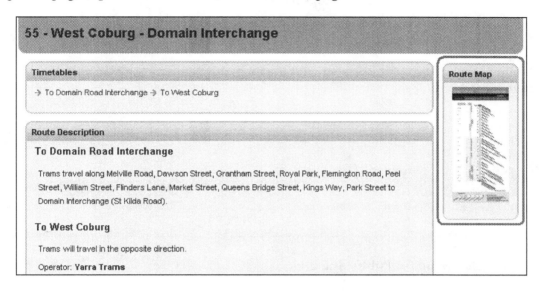

When viewing a Route Map, the associated Network Map navigation will be highlighted. E.g. when viewing the 55 Tram Route map, the "Metropolitan Tram Network Map" navigation item will be highlighted.

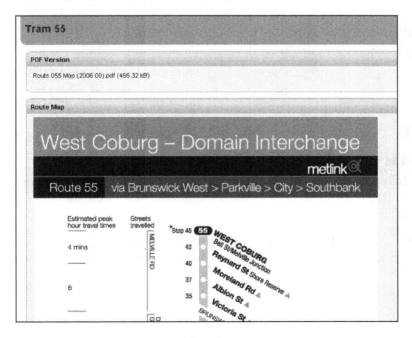

How to Add a Network Map

1. Go to **Maps Stations & Stops** in the Content Tab.

2. Go to the **Network Map** where the Route Map belongs.

3. Enter all attributes required.

You must select a route associated with the map; this connects the map with the route description from TransNET.

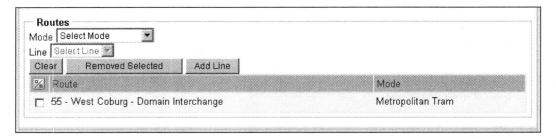

4. Click **Send for Publishing**.

Attributes

Attribute	Type	Notes
Name	Text Line	Displayed as page title/head of map detail page
Map	Image	Image of map
Description	Rich Text	
PDF	Binary File	If present linked to on map detail page
Routes	List of Routes	Routes Associated with this Map (may be multiple)

Technical Training

There are two general categories of clients, those who only want to manage the content and will outsource any technical work, and those that are willing to take on the technical management of their solution.

For the latter category, it's a matter of finding the right people within the organization and training them to become in-house eZ publish developers.

The first step is to take official eZ publish training. This will provide a base level understanding of the system and how it works as well as covering a number of useful practical tasks such as installation, configuration, and template programming.

Ideally, once basic training has been completed, the next step is to provide the in-house developer with a development environment that will enable them to practice their skills. Also, the in-house developer should be given a technical overview of the solution that they will be supporting.

I recently followed this procedure for a client. The eZ publish training went well but even with training, the in-house developer wasn't ready to start developing on what was a fairly complex solution. In reality, it takes a few months of working with eZ Publish to become proficient, and that's assuming you have good technical support along the way. eZ publish has a reasonably high learning curve and it should not be underestimated. In the case of my client, what we did was set up a process to help get the in-house developer up to speed. The process was as follows:

1. In-house developer documents change required, and defines how the change would be implemented.

2. Senior eZ publish developer reviews documentation and provides feedback, e.g. if more clarity is necessary or if a different approach would be better.

3. Once approach is finalized and approved, in-house developer implements change on development server.

4. Senior eZ publish developer reviews code and tests. Provides feedback for in-house developer if any changes are required.

5. Once approved, changes are put live.

There are good reasons for taking this approach; it gives the in-house developer the opportunity to work out answers for themselves but with the benefit of expert advice to help guide them in the right direction. It takes into account the incredible benefits that are gained from design and code reviews, which are the most effective way to reduce bugs. It also transfers a lot of eZ publish knowledge and is the most effective, I've found, to train new developers.

Once again, it take time to become proficient in eZ publish. For a single requirement, there can be many different ways to implement it; knowing what's going to be the best solution only comes with experience.

Summary

For both end users and in-house developers, the key is to provide appropriate training along with expert guidance and support afterwards. It's not enough to just run a training course; whether it's in content management or development, there needs to be an opportunity for people to work with the solution over time and be able to turn to experienced staff for support. Having trained dozens of end users, the percentage that don't require any ongoing assistance is minimal. Inevitably there are phone calls and emails requesting guidance to handle something that might not have been covered in training or the end user has forgotten. Although some people are happy to do research and actually read documentation or training manuals, the majority prefer to call or email. For in-house developers, it's even more important as the complexity of eZ publish development is much greater than content management.

In summary, the combination of training and ongoing support is the best approach to training.

13
Maintenance and Support

In traditional software development, the rule of thumb is the costs are split a third each between licensing, development, and maintenance. With eZ publish, there is no licensing cost and often clients assume that once their site is up, there will be no more costs, which is rarely the case. Additional costs can arise for many different reasons, which your client should be aware of. Just like a car, an eZ publish solution needs maintenance and servicing over time to ensure it continues to operate well. This chapter outlines the most common areas of maintenance and support.

The following information deals with projects that have a standard installation of eZ Publish with some custom code, e.g. custom templates and one or more extensions.

Patches

As eZ Systems continue to develop and release newer versions of eZ publish, there are times that a patch needs to be applied to fix a bug before the next version will be ready. There are two ways that you can handle these patches: do it yourself or pay eZ Systems to do it for you.

You can choose to purchase one of the many products that eZ Systems are now offering; they come with automatic patching and for some versions of the product, eZ Systems will also take responsibility for upgrades (more about that in the next section). The benefit of this approach is that you don't need to worry about keeping your version of eZ publish up-to-date; however, you do have to pay for this privilege.

To date, my experience with patching has been the manual approach. We apply the patches when we see them being necessary. This is usually for security patches or bug fixes that we see as necessary.

Upgrades

Upgrades have the same options as patches: you can do it yourself or pay for the eZ network solution, which includes upgrades.

As with patches, our experience has been with manual upgrades only. We aim to have each solution upgraded once a year; however, sometimes a client will choose not to upgrade their site as there is no new functionality in the latest release that they feel that they need; on the other hand, some want to upgrade or we recommend for them to upgrade as the latest release includes a feature that they can take advantage of.

When considering an upgrade, we tend to not go for the very latest release; they usually have bugs that are yet to be fixed or discovered. E.g. rather than upgrading from 3.5 to 3.6, we kept waiting until 3.6.1; this version was more stable and the inevitable bugs from a new point release had been fixed.

It's important to note that releases are cumulative. You can't pick and choose to simply jump several versions in an upgrade without considering all the changes that have been made in each version, and how that will impact on your solution. Ideally, you should keep your version of eZ publish as current as possible to avoid the issues that come with trying to upgrade after a long period of time.

However, that doesn't mean that you have to upgrade every time a new version is released. It's a matter of keeping an eye on what's in the latest release; if there's something that is useful or necessary for your solution, then upgrade.

In fact, trying to keep current with every single release can take a lot of time and not necessarily provide a great deal of value. It's when there's a major point release that you want to consider if an upgrade is necessary, e.g. from 3.6 to 3.7 or from 3.8 to 3.9.

If you do choose to upgrade, be aware of how the functionality has changed as you may need to invest time in learning how the new features work and make sure end users are trained to use the new features. For example, the change from 3.4 to 3.5 was significant as the entire user interface was updated.

In essence, you need to review the releases and pick one that you believe is stable and has features that you or your clients require before you consider upgrading.

Planning an Upgrade

Once you've decided that an upgrade is necessary, there are a number of steps that you need to take to ensure the upgrade goes smoothly.

Backup

The first thing you want to do is take a backup of the current solution. With any major change, you should make sure you have a copy that you can roll back to if thing don't go according to plan.

Setup

You need to be working with the current data. There's no use doing an upgrade with a sample set of data. Make sure you copy everything from the production server to your development server so you are dealing with the same set of content. It's a good idea to get your client to stop making changes (i.e. a content freeze) while you're doing the upgrade so you are in fact dealing with an exact copy of the production site. Most clients will understand this—if it's not possible, it's a risk you have to take and hope that none of the new content will impact on the upgrade.

Upgrade

There are instructions on the eZ publish site on performing an upgrade. It's a matter of following these to upgrade your version. This should be a straightforward task.

Testing

This is the hardest part of the process. You need to go through and check the site thoroughly to ensure it still operates as expected, especially with respect to the features that you've created or the extensions that you've added. This tends to be the most time-consuming part of the process. With changes to the way content is handled, you may find that images no longer appear because the insert object attributes have changed; you may find the display of standard content types has been adjusted, the method of caching may have changed affecting the way the cache used to operate, meaning you need to adjust this aspect of the site. The site needs to go through a comprehensive review, checking all pages, adding content to ensure things still appear as they should, etc.

We tend to allow two days of elapsed time to manage the upgrade for a medium-sized site with custom content types and an extension. The majority of this time is spent in testing.

Enhancements

Many sites are implemented with a subset of the features that the client initially wanted that have been pushed to a later stage. Also, over time, new features or changes to features are required. Doing this with a working system will require regression testing and careful management of the deployment of these features into the production system.

An enhancement should be treated like a mini project, the work clearly scoped, specified, and agreed to before development starts. For small enhancements, this can be a much quicker process that the initial scope and specification but it's still important that you follow the same steps; anything missed increases the risks of problems arising down the track.

In terms of implementation, the approach is similar to the upgrade process. Start with making sure your development environment is identical to the production environment. Depending on how long it will take to add the enhancement, you may be able to organize a content freeze; if not, you'll have to plan to sync content from production to dev once the development is done and is ready for testing.

Testing, as for the upgrade process, should cover all features to ensure that changes made haven't affected any of the existing functionality.

Once the testing is complete, release a copy of the site to a preview/staging environment for the client to review. Chances are there will be modifications to be made in which case, the updates are made, on dev and then released to preview for client review. This process is repeated until the client signs off on the enhancements and you can deploy the changes to the production environment.

Support

Whether you are supporting a client or it's an in-house solution, support can be broken down into two main categories: assistance with content management and bug fixes.

Content Management

In the majority of cases, there's a need for someone that has extensive experience with managing content in eZ publish. The flexibility of eZ publish means there are often several ways to achieve the same goal and it's only through experience that you can work out which is the most appropriate for a given situation.

Most of the time, the requests will be simple, e.g.:

- How do I add a link to an image?
- How to create a table?
- How to make the images left aligned?

This is just a matter of referring the end user to the manual or walking them through it over the phone. In extreme cases, you may need to run another training course. This often happens when a new staff member is assigned to manage the solution and has no previous experience with eZ publish.

As a rule of thumb, the number of requests for help are highest during content population and then after the solution has been put live. Then there tends to be a quiet period as things settle down. The next lot of requests are when the client has forgotten how to do something or has a request that they aren't quite sure how to implement or a new feature is required (in which case it changes from support to enhancement).

It's a good idea to allow time for support or provide a means for the end user to submit a request—for example, an online issue tracking system such as Mantis: http://www.mantisbt.org/.

For my clients, as a rule of thumb, I allow four hours of support for the first month and an hour each month after that. How you charge your client for this is your prerogative. You can bundle it into a yearly support agreement or charge on a monthly basis based on time and materials. There's no one size fits all approach as some clients will prefer a fixed support agreement and others will want to pay as they go.

Make sure you mention the need for support at the start of the project rather than at the end, so it doesn't come as a surprise to the client that there will be ongoing costs.

Bug Fixes

There are two types of bugs: those that are a part of the eZ publish core and bugs related to custom code.

The first thing to establish is a time frame for response to bugs. Whether you are supporting your client or if it's an in-house project, having an understanding of how long it will take to respond to a bug is helpful to manage expectations.

Depending on the nature of the site, how long you take to respond will vary. For simple sites, a next business day response is fine, for larger sites, you may be expected to respond within hours. This should be a part of the support agreement that you have already established with your client.

Naturally, when a bug comes in, you need to establish if it is a bug or user error; this happens a lot with inexperienced clients. Once you've worked this out, it's a matter of resolving it as quickly as you can.

Sometimes the bug is something outside of your control, i.e. it's a part of the kernel and you shouldn't be touching the kernel—that should be left to eZ Systems. In this situation, your hands are tied until eZ Systems decide to fix the problem and you apply the patch. How long this takes depends on what priority eZ Systems has given the bug. If you have purchased the eZ network solution, there are established guidelines for how quickly a bug will be patched. Alternatively, you can pay to have it fixed, in which case, eZ Systems will fix it as soon as they can.

If you don't have the eZ network solution and aren't willing to pay eZ Systems for support then it's a matter of waiting until eZ Systems get around to fixing it. This can be frustrating. Even if you choose to do the fix yourself and provide the patch to eZ Systems, there's no guarantee that it will become a part of the kernel, which then means you'll have issues with upgrades down the track. You'll need to remember what you've patched and re-patch after the upgrade, hoping the patch will still work. If you have multiple installations, this can prove to be challenging and time consuming. In this situation, it can be better to push back on the client and say you are waiting on eZ Systems to fix the bug and you'll apply the patch once it's released.

Summary

Support and maintenance is often overlooked and if attention is not paid, the quality of the solution and its use can diminish, making the solution less valuable over time. Just like a car, an application needs regular maintenance to keep it running well. Therefore it's important to consider this upfront and not wait until six months after the solution has been delivered to consider how to deal with patches or upgrades.

Overall, implementing and supporting content management solutions is not a simple task; there's a lot to think about even if you are using a well established framework such as eZ publish. The software development lifecycle (SDLC) applies equally to eZ publish-based projects as it does to custom development. There are requirements gathering, specification, infrastructure, development, testing, training, and ongoing support. It's easy to fall into the trap of thinking that because eZ publish is a well established framework you don't need to concern yourself with all the other elements of the SDLC in fact, not only do you need to be aware of all parts of the lifecycle, there's the added complexity of content modeling, gathering, and population.

However, it's important to remember what really makes the biggest difference in projects, it is, in order:

- People
- Process
- Technology

In the case of eZ Publish, the technology aspect is under control, so the focus can be on people and process. What this book covers is a range of practices that combined form a good overall process for eZ Publish projects. The one element that no book or technology can resolve is having the right people, and the right people—or wrong, will be the biggest factor in the success—or failure—of any project, eZ Publish based or not.

In essence, the key to success in eZ Publish projects is firstly getting a team of experienced people together, making sure you have a common understanding of what the outcomes are, and then following an agreed process to define and implement that solution.

Appendix A

The White Angel Foundation Functional Specification

Date: 13/02/07
Version 0.5
Author: Martin Bauer

Table of Contents

Revision Control

Date	Version	Initial	Changes
8/1/07	0.1	MB	• Initial version
18/1/07	0.2	MB	• Updated site map • Added form builder • Added membership area & login portal • Updated newsletter wireframe • Updated product content type • Added ticket product type • Added reporting
31/1/07	0.3	MB	• Confirmed features for Friends of White Angel • Updated shop content types • Added notes to checkout process • Added report details to shop
2/2/07	0.4	MB	• Removed membership • Removed membership area • Added specials • Added shipping costs
13/2/07	0.5	MB	• Added donation options • Confirmed delivery costs

1 Introduction

This document is based on an analysis of the current site and additional notes after revised estimate provided by Tony Svasek in Dec 2006.

2 Site Map

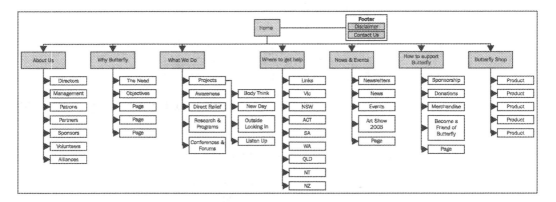

This site map is a suggestion only and can be changed.

3 Standard Features

The White Angel site will have the following standard features available for adding content to the site.

3.1   Section

This is the main building block of the site.

3.1.1   Section Attributes

- Title
- Body

3.1.2   Rules

A section may contain the following content types

- Section
- Gallery
- Article
- Info page

- News Archive
- FAQ
- Link List

3.1.3 Views

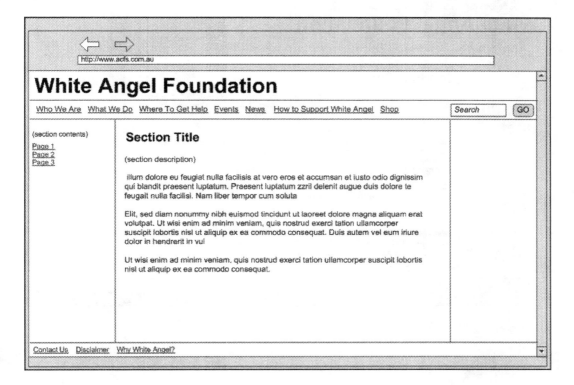

3.2 Info page

3.2.1 Attributes

- Name
- Short Name
- Summary
- Description

3.3.1 Rules

3.3.2 Views

Full View

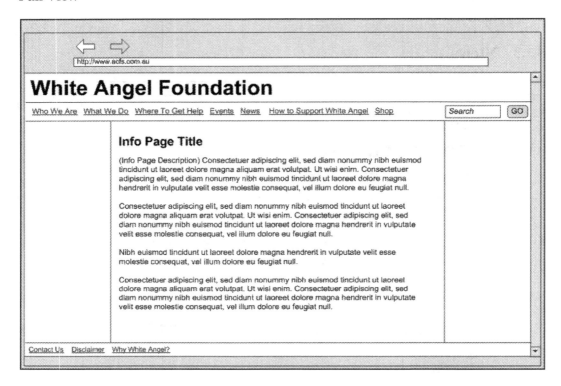

Summary View

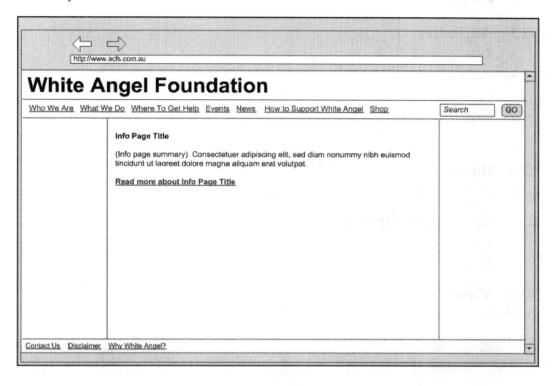

3.3   Article

3.2.1   Attributes

- Title
- Author
- Date
- Intro
- Body

3.2.2   Rules

An Article may contain an Article Sub-page Content type

3.3.3   Sub-page Attributes

- Title
- Body

3.3.4   Views

Article Full View

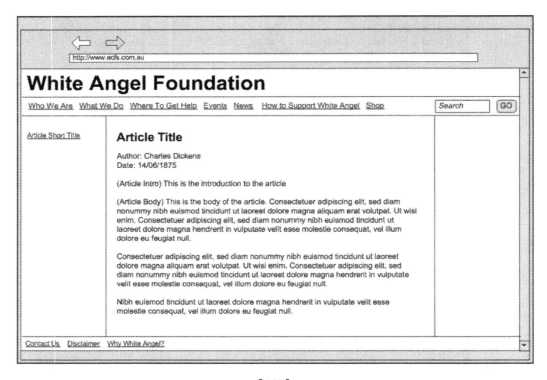

Article Full View — with Sub-Pages

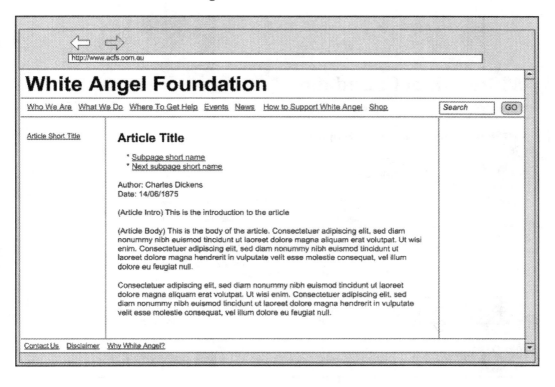

Article Sub-Page

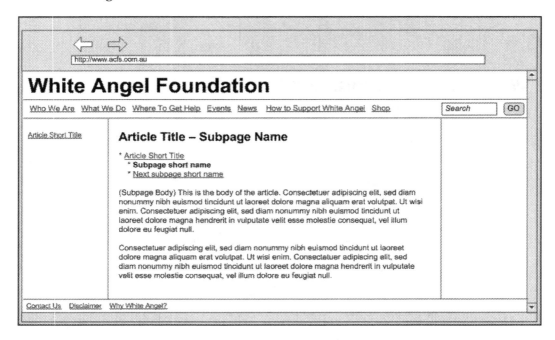

Article Summary View

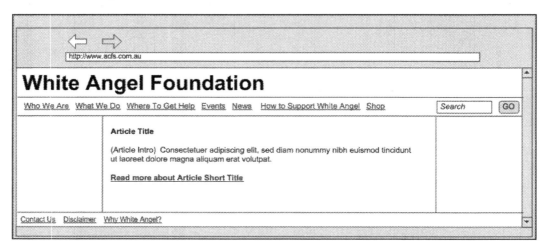

3.4 News

3.4.1 News Archive Attributes

- Name
- Short Name
- Summary
- Description
- No. of items to show

3.4.2 News Items Attributes

- Title
- Short Title
- Date
- Summary
- Body

3.4.3 Rules

The Main News Archive is a display of all news items in a descending order of their date attribute. On the main page the title, date, and intro are displayed. When the title is clicked on the full new item is displayed.

A News Archive may contain News items

3.4.4 Views

News Archive

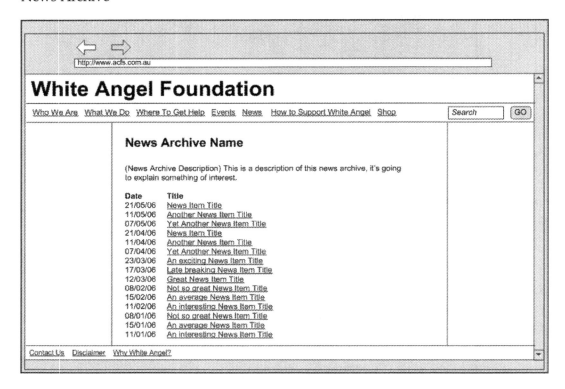

News Archive Summary

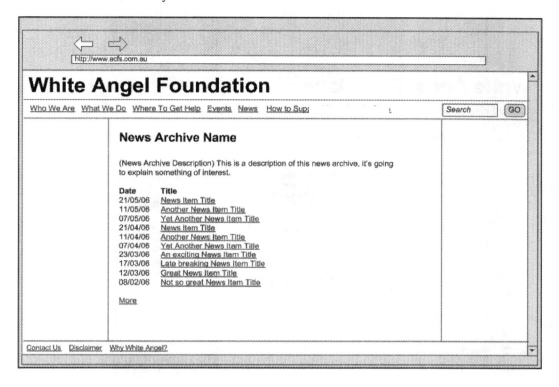

News Item

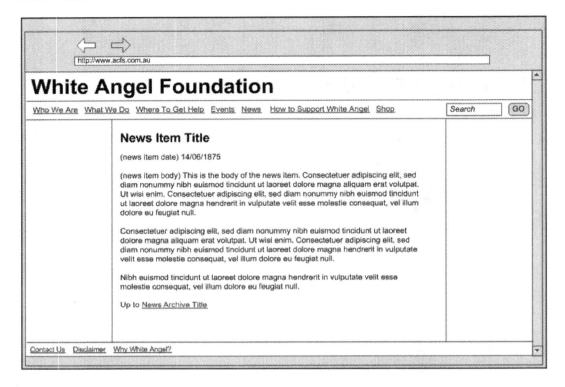

News Item Summary

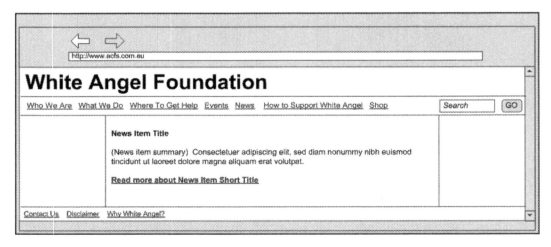

3.5 Gallery

3.5.1 Attributes

- Name
- Short Name
- Summary
- Description
- Images per page

The Images per page attribute controls the number of images that are displayed on each gallery page. If there are more than the specified number of images in a gallery Next and Previous links are displayed that allow for the gallery thumbnails to be paged through.

3.5.2 Rules

A Gallery may contain Images

3.5.3 Image Attributes

- Name
- Caption
- Image
- Alt Text

3.5.4   Views

Gallery

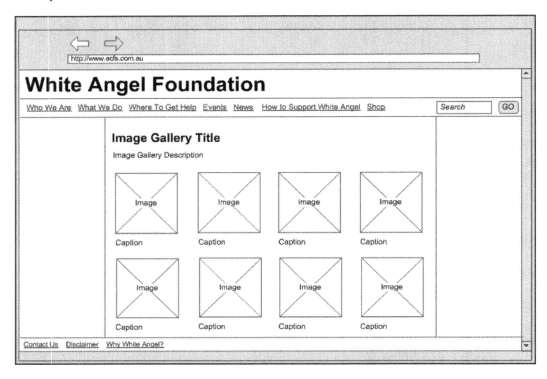

Gallery Summary

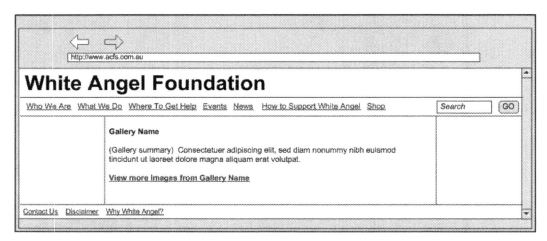

Image

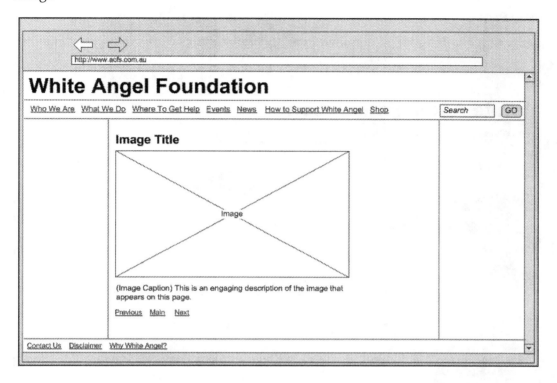

3.6 FAQ

FAQ List Attributes

- Title
- Description

An FAQ List may contain FAQ Questions

FAQ Question attributes

- Question
- Answer

3.6.1   Views

FAQ Page

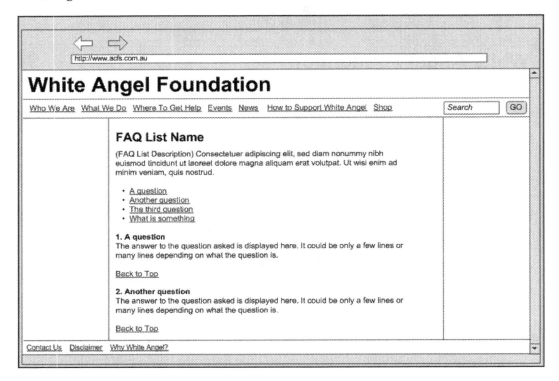

3.7   Flash

3.7.1   Attributes

- Name
- Description
- Flash File
- Height
- Width
- Quality
- Autoplay
- Loop

3.7.2 Rules

3.7.3 Views

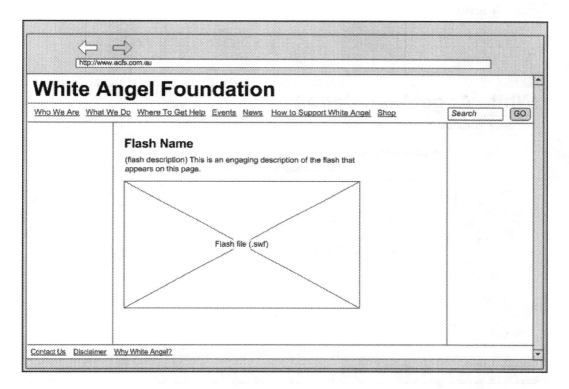

3.8 Video

3.8.1 Attributes

- Name
- Description
- Video File
- Height
- Width
- Quality
- Controller
- Loop

3.8.2 Rules

Applies for Windows media, quicktime, and realtime video files.

3.8.3 Views

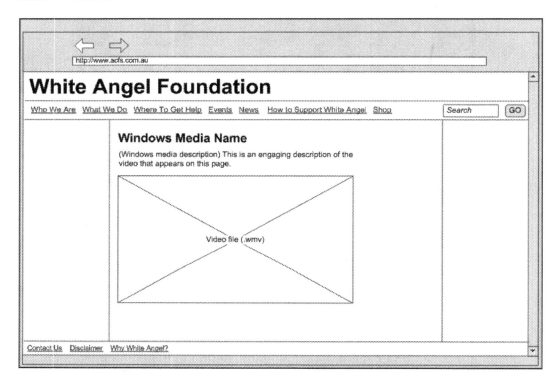

3.9 Portal

3.9.1 Attributes

- Name
- Body

3.9.2 Rules

Can only be displayed in right-hand column.

3.9.3 Views

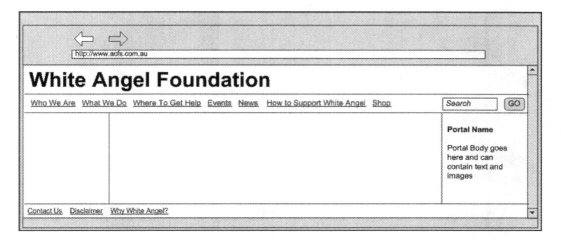

3.10 Node List

3.10.1 Attributes

- Item Source
- Title
- Show in subtree
- Number of items
- Sort on attribute
- Fetch Whole Tree

3.10.2 Rules

Can only be displayed in right-hand column.

3.10.3 Views

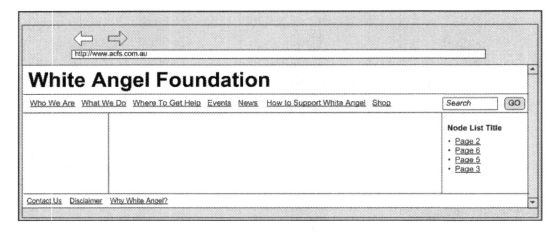

3.11 Links List

3.11.1 Links List Attributes

- Title
- Short Title
- Summary
- Description

3.11.2 Link Attributes

- Name
- Description
- URL
- Link Text

3.11.3 Rules

The main page of the Link List displays the Name and description of the link. Clicking on the name will display the link in a new window.

A Lists List can only contain Links.

3.11.4 Views

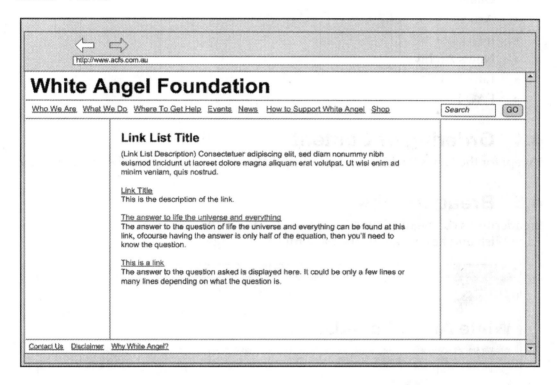

4 Page Structure

4.1 Footer

The Footer Folder may contain info pages. These will be displayed in the footer section of the page.

4.2 Site Search

Can choose which section of the site (header, footer, left, right) is displayed if at all (none).

4.3 Navigation

The content type rules determine what gets displayed in the navigation.

Currently these content types will appear in the navigation:

- Section
- Gallery
- Article
- Info Page
- News Archive
- Link List
- FAQ List

4.4 Ordering of Content

Except for the News Archive, the ordering of all content can be controlled by the editor.

4.5 Breadcrumbs

Breadcrumbs can be displayed if required. They will be automatically generated by eZ publish and appear above the page title of the page.

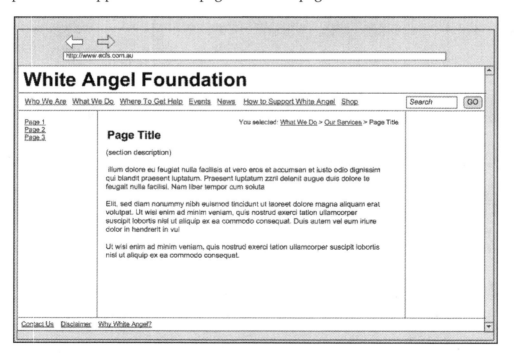

4.6 Right-Hand Column

The right-hand column can be used to place portals or node lists.

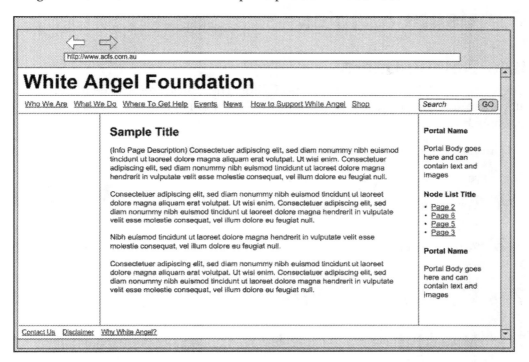

5 Media Library

There is a media library (accessed via the Media Tab in the Admin section). Images and folders can be created within this section.

The Media Section is used to store images/files that are part of other content types but are not site content in their own right. (Images in galleries that appear in the site can also be used in the rich text fields of other content types.)

The Media Library can contain the following content:

- Folders
- Files
- Images
- Video
- Flash
- Portals

Content in the media library is not accessible from the public view of the site.

6   Users & Roles

6.1   Default Users

There are two default users Admin and Editor. The editor user is used to perform all content-related actions. The Admin user should only be used by experienced eZ publish developers.

Additional editor users can be added (by the Admin) if required.

There are three user roles in the system:

1. General Public/Anonymous
2. Editors
3. Administrators

7   Custom Features

7.1   Newsletter

7.1.1   Attributes

*   Title
*   Short Title
*   Intro
*   Hidden

7.1.2   Rules

A newsletter can contain the following content types:

*   Info page
*   News Item
*   Portal

7.1.3   Views

Site View

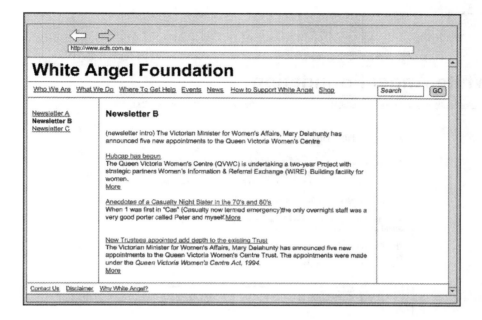

Email View

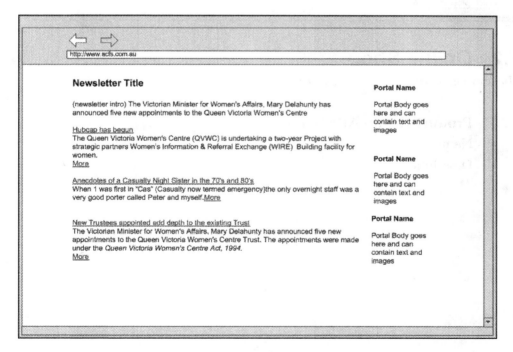

Newsletter Item

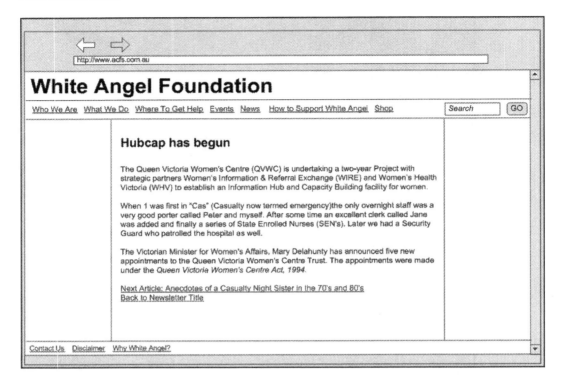

7.2 Online Shop

The shop is made up of product groups and products

7.2.1 Product Group Attributes

- Name
- Description

7.2.2 Product Attributes

- Name
- Summary
- Description
- Price
- Image

7.2.3 Event Attributes

- Name
- Summary
- Description
- Start Date / Time
- Location
- Ticket Price
- Image

7.2.4 Special Attributes

- Name
- Description
- Special price
- Related product / event

7.2.5 Rules

A product group can be added to a section.

A product group can contain products groups, products or events.

A product / event can only be added to a product group.

7.2.6 Shopping Cart

Users will be able to add, update quantity, or remove products / tickets from the shop.

7.2.7 Views

Shop

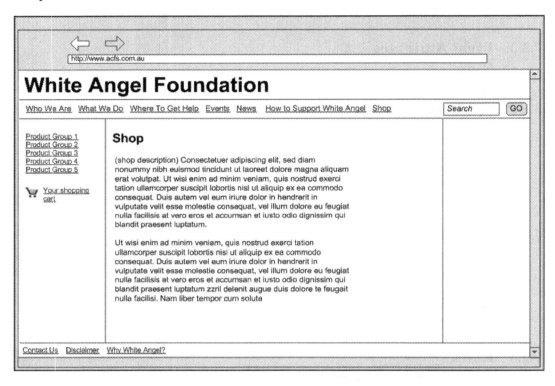

Product Group

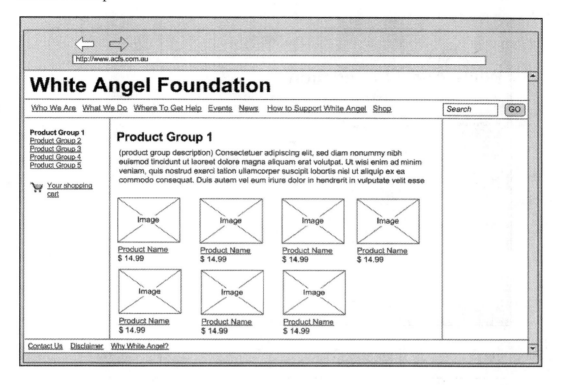

Product

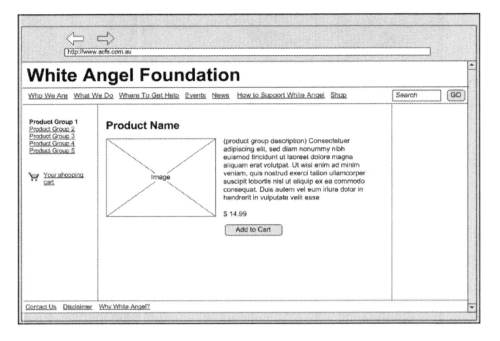

Shopping Cart

7.2.8 Checkout Procedure

The default checkout procedure is:

1. From the basket the user selects Checkout.
2. Shipping costs are calculated.
3. User fills out a personal information, billing/delivery address & comments.
4. User gets to confirm order & personal details.
5. User Clicks confirm and the order is processed.
6. User & shop administrator are sent an email copy of the order.

7.2.9 Delivery Costs

There are no delivery costs for donations or tickets.

Delivery costs for products will be based on the amount of the order.
Delivery costs are $5 per $50 of order.

Order Amount

Order Amount	Delivery Fee
$ 19.95	$ 5
$ 45.00	$ 5
$ 49.95	$ 5
$ 65.00	$ 10
$ 89.00	$ 10
$ 105.00	$ 15
$ 155.00	$ 20

7.2.10 Invoices

All orders will use a common tax invoice.
The tax invoice will include information for donations for tax purposes.
The contents are to be confirmed by White Angel.

7.2.11 Payment

Payment will be made by credit card into the current merchant account held by The White Angel Foundation.

If the payment fails, the user will be presented with the payment form so they can resubmit or change credit card details and submit.

7.2.12 Orders

- Orders will be available via the Webshop tab in the administration interface.
- Orders will be listed, most recent first.
- Viewing an order will display all details of the order (customer & products).
- Credit card details will not be stored.

7.2.13 Reports

A daily report will be emailed to a nominated email address. The email report will contain the following information.

Report title (White Angel ticket sales as midnight — 24/02/07)

- Name of event
- Tickets sold to date
- No. sold in last 24 hours

There will also be the ability to export all orders into a spreadsheet with a date range filter.

7.3 Donations

Donations can be made in two ways.

1. By purchasing a donation (added as a product to the shop with a fixed amount)
2. By the user choosing the amount of the donation
   e.g. `https://merchant.ematters.com.au/cmaonline.nsf/ MEL0147?OpenForm`

   Note: this is a once off donation; we will investigate if reoccurring donations are possible with the selected payment gateway

7.4 Form Builder

The form builder module is integrated into eZ Publish by the creation of a new "form" datatype, display functionality, a form processing module, and a form management module.

The datatype provides the link between the existing eZ publish system and the form module.

The form processing module will process a submitted form, validate the submitted data, store the data, and send any required email messages.

The form management module allows for forms to be created and edited and provides the ability to export stored data.

The types of form elements included are as follows:

- Text line
- Text field
- Options (radio/select)
- Multi-select options (checkbox/select)

When editing a content object with a form datatype the editor will be presented with a list of form names in a drop-down list.

Form List

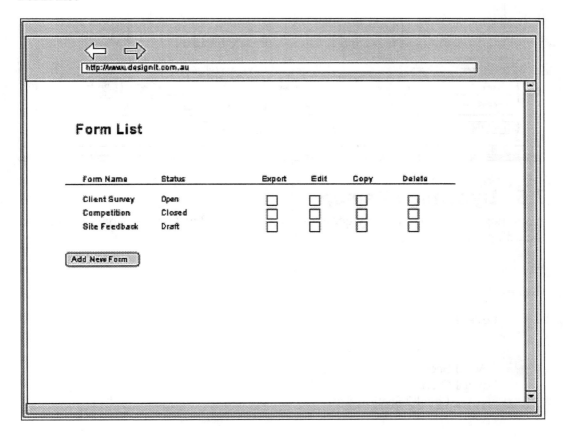

Selecting a form from that list and publishing the object will enable the display of the form in the content object.

Form Edit

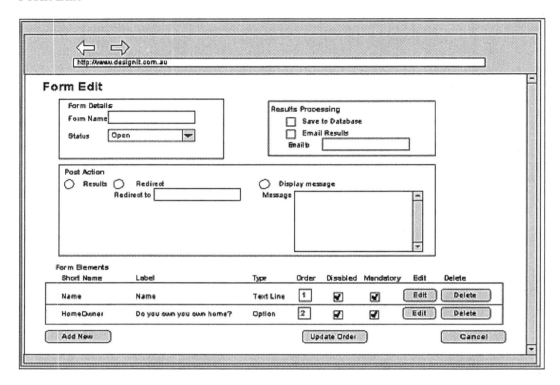

7.5 Dynamic Sitemap

A sitemap will be dynamically generated and is to display 3 levels of navigation (not including the homepage).

E.g.

Home

Level 1
    Level 2
    Level 2
Level 1 Section
Level 1 Section
    Level 2 Section

Level 3 Page
Level 3 Page
Level 3 Page
Level 2
Level 2

8   Browser Compatibility

To be designed for 1024x768 fixed width.

- Internet Explorer v6.0 for PC
- Internet Explorer v7.0 for PC
- Fire fox v2.0 for PC and Mac
- Safari v1.2 for Mac

Index

site access 65
standard, default 64
structure 64
subdirectories 64
technical design 29
visual design 14, 15, 35
directory structure 46
display blocks 48
documentation 185

E

editors 112
elements, access control
policies 68
roles 70
user groups 68
users 67
enhancements 249, 250
environment
development 204
production 204
staging 204
estimation
about 101
client directive 104
common language 104
developers estimation 103
errors 102
ideal situation 105
low bid 103
management directive 104
pricing 104
project managers estimation 103
reality check 101
sales managers estimation 104
usual situation 102
events 72
experience levels 10
extensions
about 74
creating 74

F

factors, success
about 87
budget, meeting 90

delivering on time 90, 91
example 95
project objectives, meeting 89
quality requirements, meeting 92
stakeholder satisfaction 88
team satisfaction 92
value, adding 91
features, site
community acceptance wireframe 117
community acceptance wireframe,
functions 117
community group administration
wireframe 115
community group listing 116
community group registration wireframe
115
community group sign up feature,
example 115
good company feature, example 112, 115
wish searching 118
wish searching, details 120, 121
wish searching, results 119
formats 80
functional blocks 49
functional specification 15
functions 69
functions, member
about 69
details, managing 112
forgot password 111
login 111
new password 111
password, changing 111

G

GDS 153
graduate destination survey 153

I

information architecture
about 14
overview 21
task orientated 22
information design 14, 15, 26, 27
infrastructure
development 204

out of scope 96
project understanding 11

Q

quality
about 98
factors 98
factors, example 100, 101
measuring 99

R

requirements
author 81
details, capturing 82
formats 80
interpretation 81
theory versus reality 80
vision, capturing 78
writing 78, 79
research report resource 146
risk assessment
overview 175
risk management
breakdown 166
key steps 166
putting in practise 174
risk assessment 167
risk evaluation 168
risk memos 177
risk monitoring 168
risk reduction 168
risk reporting 169
risks
benefits realisation risk 173
business risk 172
memos 177
personal risk 174
production system risk 172
project risks 170
report, example 179, 180
types 169

S

screen standard
about 132

accessibility 133
browser compatibility 132
performance 133
screen resolution 133
sections
about 54
assigning 55
managing 56
site
about 21
features 112
structuring 21
site access 65
sitemap 121
site structure 124
software, developing
Agile manifesto 184
customer collaboration over contract
negotiation 186
individuals and interactions over processes
and tools 185
responding to change over plan following
186
software working, over comprehensive
documentation 185
specification
about 134
detailed 136
domain walkthrough 134
high level specification workshop 134
key relationships between objects 135
object model 135
object role diagram 135
process 134
sitemap 136
users of system 135
stakeholders 9
static websites
about 13
content requirements 14
information architecture 14
information design 14
navigation design 14
objectives 14
versus web applications 16
visual design 14

setup 249
testing 249
users
about 67
details 68
groups 68
user account datatype 67
users and groups
about 110
administrators 112
ecommerce portal, example 110-112
editors 112
general public 110
member functions 111
members 110

V

value pricing
about 163
benefits 163
disadvantages 164
example 163
version control
about 204, 205
reasons 204
views
about 126
product details, example 129, 130
products category view, example 128
products main page, example 127
visibility
about 54
settings 54
vision, capturing
about 78
theory versus reality 80
visual design
about 15, 35
average user 39
common mistakes 37
contrast 35
design by committee 38
design by default 38
design by fiat 38
issues 37
questions 39

test, putting to 39
uniformity 37

W

web applications
about 14
functional specification 15
information design 15
interaction design 15
interface design 15
objectives 15
types 13
versus web applications 16
visual design 15
web solution
about 16
categories 16
collaborative 17
interactive 16
knowledge based 18
transactional 17
workflow based 17
wireframe
community group acceptance
wireframe 117
community group administration
wireframe 115
community group registration
wireframe 115
workflow
about 70, 72
events 72
standard events 73
standard triggers 73
starting 72
workshop
planning 86
writing, specification
custom templates 130
elements 107
features 112
rules 122
screen & performance standard 132
sitemap 121
users and groups 109
views 126

Thank you for buying

Managing eZ Publish Web Content Management Projects

Packt Open Source Project Royalties

When we sell a book written on an Open Source project, we pay a royalty directly to that project. Therefore by purchasing Managing eZ Publish Web Content Management Projects, Packt will have given some of the money received to the eZ Publish project.

In the long term, we see ourselves and you — customers and readers of our books — as part of the Open Source ecosystem, providing sustainable revenue for the projects we publish on. Our aim at Packt is to establish publishing royalties as an essential part of the service and support a business model that sustains Open Source.

If you're working with an Open Source project that you would like us to publish on, and subsequently pay royalties to, please get in touch with us.

Writing for Packt

We welcome all inquiries from people who are interested in authoring. Book proposals should be sent to authors@packtpub.com. If your book idea is still at an early stage and you would like to discuss it first before writing a formal book proposal, contact us; one of our commissioning editors will get in touch with you.

We're not just looking for published authors; if you have strong technical skills but no writing experience, our experienced editors can help you develop a writing career, or simply get some additional reward for your expertise.

About Packt Publishing

Packt, pronounced 'packed', published its first book "Mastering phpMyAdmin for Effective MySQL Management" in April 2004 and subsequently continued to specialize in publishing highly focused books on specific technologies and solutions.

Our books and publications share the experiences of your fellow IT professionals in adapting and customizing today's systems, applications, and frameworks. Our solution-based books give you the knowledge and power to customize the software and technologies you're using to get the job done. Packt books are more specific and less general than the IT books you have seen in the past. Our unique business model allows us to bring you more focused information, giving you more of what you need to know, and less of what you don't.

Packt is a modern, yet unique publishing company, which focuses on producing quality, cutting-edge books for communities of developers, administrators, and newbies alike. For more information, please visit our website: www.PacktPub.com.

Alfresco Enterprise Content Management Implementation

ISBN: 1-904811-11-6   Paperback: 350 pages

How to Install, use, and customize this powerful, free, Open Source Java-based Enterprise CMS

1. **Manage your business documents:** version control, library services, content organization, and search

2. **Workflows and business rules:** move and manipulate content automatically when events occur

3. **Maintain, extend, and customize Alfresco:** backups and other admin tasks, customizing and extending the content model, creating your own look and feel

Learning eZ publish 3: Building content management solutions

ISBN: 1-904811-01-9   Paperback: 372 pages

Leaders of the eZ publish community guide you through this complex and powerful PHP based content management system

1. Build content rich websites and applications using eZ Publish

2. Discover the secrets of the eZ Publish templating system

3. Develop the skills to create new eZ Publish extensions

Please check **www.PacktPub.com** for information on our titles

Drupal: Creating Blogs, Forums, Portals, and Community Websites

ISBN: 1-904811-80-9   Paperback: 267 pages

How to setup, configure and customise this powerful
PHP/MySQL based Open Source CMS

1. Install, configure, administer, maintain and
   extend Drupal

2. Control access with users, roles
   and permissions

3. Structure your content using Drupal's powerful
   CMS features

4. Includes coverage of release 4.7

TYPO3: Enterprise Content Management

ISBN: 1-904811-41-8   Paperback: 595 pages

The Official TYPO3 Book, written and endorsed by
the core TYPO3 Team

1. Easy-to-use introduction to TYPO3

2. Design and build content rich extranets
   and intranets

3. Learn how to manage content and administrate
   and extend TYPO3

Please check **www.PacktPub.com** for information on our titles

www.ingramcontent.com/pod-product-compliance
Lightning Source LLC
Chambersburg PA
CBHW080928060326
40690CB00042B/3220